FIGHT
or SUBMIT

FIGHT
or SUBMIT

Standing Tall in Two Worlds

GRAND CHIEF RONALD M. DERRICKSON

Published by ECW Press
665 Gerrard Street East
Toronto, Ontario, Canada M4M 1Y2
416-694-3348 / info@ecwpress.com

Cover design: Tania Craan
Front cover photograph © Gary Nylander/*Kelowna Daily Courier*
Author photograph © Suzanne Le Stage Photography

LIBRARY AND ARCHIVES CANADA CATALOGUING IN PUBLICATION

Title: Fight or submit : standing tall in two worlds / Grand Chief Ronald M. Derrickson.

Names: Derrickson, Ronald M., author.

Identifiers: Canadiana (print) 20200236261 | Canadiana (ebook) 20200236458

ISBN 978-1-77041-566-9 (hardcover)
ISBN 978-1-77305-613-5 (PDF)
ISBN 978-1-77305-612-8 (ePUB)

Subjects: LCSH: Derrickson, Ronald M. | LCSH: Businessmen—Canada—Biography. | LCGFT: Autobiographies.

Classification: LCC HC112.5.D37 A3 2020 | DDC 338.092—dc23

The publication of *Fight or Submit* has been generously supported by the Canada Council for the Arts which last year invested $153 million to bring the arts to Canadians throughout the country and is funded in part by the Government of Canada. *Nous remercions le Conseil des arts du Canada de son soutien. L'an dernier, le Conseil a investi 153 millions de dollars pour mettre de l'art dans la vie des Canadiennes et des Canadiens de tout le pays. Ce livre est financé en partie par le gouvernement du Canada.* We acknowledge the support of the Ontario Arts Council (OAC), an agency of the Government of Ontario, which last year funded 1,737 individual artists and 1,095 organizations in 223 communities across Ontario for a total of $52.1 million. We also acknowledge the contribution of the Government of Ontario through the Ontario Book Publishing Tax Credit, and through Ontario Creates for the marketing of this book.

PRINTED AND BOUND IN CANADA   PRINTING: FRIESENS   5   4   3   2   1

CONTENTS

FOREWORD

Whenever I think about Ron Derrickson, I recall the television interview in which Derril Warren, former B.C. Conservative leader, described him as "the most persecuted man in Canada." He then added: "But if he'd been white, we'd have been building statues in his honour." Those extremes aptly encapsulated the "Two Worlds." Ron was either vilified as an "uppity Indian" or lauded as a remarkable businessman and leader. The strain of those conflicting viewpoints produced a man who was invariably controversial, one forever surrounded by fervent critics or solid supporters; no commentator was ever neutral. This book, in my view, commendably explains how that came about.

It was so long ago that I cannot remember the first time that I met Ron Derrickson. But the circumstances remain vivid. It was the late 1970s, and I was working as Advisor to The Alliance of the Musqueam, Sechelt and Squamish Bands, a group directly formed by the respective leaders to pursue economic development issues.

Fred Walchli, then Director General of the B.C. Regional Office of Indian Affairs — justifiably praised in the book for his support of Native aims — had suggested to The Alliance Bands that they might want to consider inviting Westbank to become the fourth member. My rather vague impression of Ron Derrickson before the ensuing meeting was of a hard-nosed, slightly shady leader who steamrolled any opposition. Not even close! When you meet Ron, you meet a charmer, always smiling and full of humorous remarks and jokes. Yes, and a respectful listener, one who generally made a solid impression on The Alliance leaders. So Westbank joined The Alliance and, through Ron, became a forceful support for their issues. Working in that forum, Ron and I gravitated towards one another. When I was called to the Bar in 1979, both Musqueam and Sechelt retained me as Band lawyer and, not long afterwards, so did Westbank.

Working with Ron Derrickson during the seven years he remained Chief was a gift in my life. I admired his strong commitment to working hard — I shared that with him. I witnessed firsthand his dedication to his people, his love of his people, that was not readily discernible by the majority society, but that was at the root of everything he did. I used to so like going to Westbank, staying at Ron's house overnight, and then returning to Vancouver laden with files that had to be urgently dealt with. Throughout, he was a steadfast and generous friend, and we'd enjoy socializing together and having a lot of fun. However, having said all that, I must emphasize the experience that delighted me the most: it was Ron's sheer brilliance as a negotiator. One politically incorrect observer had pointed out: "Ron Derrickson was the only Indian who could negotiate with a room full of white men and leave carrying all their shirts on *his* back." Negotiating at Ron's side was a constant lesson to me in how it was done. We'd always carefully prepare before any meeting but, if he then sensed a weakness in the other team, he would improvise and up the ante! I had to pay close attention. He'd also pre-arrange staged walkouts and outbursts, all to strengthen Westbank's position. This worked well when the Westbank Band Councillors were involved; they knew the drill. So when Ron gave the signal (usually a sighed "this is not enough"), one would go ballistic at the table, ranting about "sell out," "peanuts," "disrespectful to my people," "bullshit," before storming out. Ron would then, with a sad face, try to pick up the pieces, usually successfully. But this didn't work quite as smoothly when Ron was negotiating a Specific Claim for another Band whose two Councillors were a part of the negotiating team; they weren't quite as tuned into what was required. At Ron's pre-arranged signal, one of them did go berserk — but seriously berserk, pretty well out of control! The Deputy Minister on the other side sat white-faced, looking straight ahead, perhaps fearing for his own safety, while this vehement railing continued. By the time this seemingly incensed Councillor had left the room, accompanied by his fellow Councillor, Ron had to call a 30 minute recess to "let things calm down." He told the Deputy Minister that he was going to try to coax his negotiating team back, but there had to be "a more positive atmosphere." And Ron succeeded once again!

Ron and I shared thinking as to what was needed for the Bands: economic development and self-government. For the former, he was pre-eminent. For the latter, getting away from the *Indian Act*, he was watching closely as I worked with the Sechelt Nation in its endeavour to become the first self-governing Band in Canada, achieved in 1986. During those intense years of struggle, Sechelt was lambasted on all sides for its allegedly diminished concept of self-government. The native organizations and prominent Band leaders maintained a constant barrage of criticism. In British Columbia, only two groups spoke out in support of Sechelt: the Nisga'a Tribal Council and the Westbank Indian Band. At a conference held in Saskatoon to discuss Native self-government, I was so impressed when Ron went to the microphone, confronting a sea of hostility, and praised Sechelt's right to self-determination — "it's for them to choose." The Sechelt people never forgot that moment and recognized Ron as a true friend. Chief Stan Dixon subsequently invited him to his wedding where I was the best man, and we were like The Three Amigos! More seriously, last July when I delivered the eulogy at Chief Dixon's funeral, his widow made some highly favourable remarks to me about Stan's heartfelt appreciation for Ron's loyalty and support.

From all of this, one might have expected Ron's way forward, on behalf of his people, to have been smooth sailing. But the hostile forces, those unaccepting of an Indian equal, were making evil plans. Almost unprecedented in Canadian history, there was an attempt made in 1982 to assassinate him when a hired thug beat him with a steel bar when he opened his front door. It was in the headlines on the B.C. news that evening, and it sounded as if Ron had been seriously hurt. I called Fred Walchli right away, and he assured me that it was the assailant who was most hurt, having been shot by Ron in a scenario more akin to a Bruce Willis movie than a recognizably Canadian incident! What perplexed me in the ensuing months was the widespread lack of sympathy for Ron. People just did not seem to comprehend the sheer outrageousness of an attempted murder arising from a business dispute fuelled by racial animosity. Why no outcry? In fact, the tide appeared to be going the other way. As said in the book: "After September 1984, I saw that the failed physical assassination attempt morphed into another even more determined attempt at character assassination as my name began to be raised inside the House of Commons in relation to a series of increasingly bizarre set of accusations." These accumulating allegations culminated in a Royal Commission headed by Judge John E. Hall which, after months of contentious testimony, found there to have been no problems at Westbank "of a serious criminal nature." So there was Ron Derrickson, after all he had accomplished, fighting not just for his reputation but also for his very life. Yes, "Two Worlds" indeed.

My hope for my friend Ron's book is that it will allow the Canadian public the opportunity to learn about the motivation arising from his formative years; his drive to succeed; his dedication to his people; and to dispel the shadows that have marred what deserves to have been a dazzling legacy.

— GRAHAM ALLEN

CHAPTER 1

Homeland

The flight from Kyiv, where I have business interests, to my community in the interior of British Columbia is close to 12,000 kilometres. With stops in Amsterdam and Calgary, it takes 26 hours from the time my driver, Volodya, picks me up at my flat near Bessarabska Square to when I arrive at my Westbank office in the B.C. Interior. It is a flight I take back and forth several times a year, often after months-long stays. But each time I arrive on the last leg of the trip from Calgary to Kelowna, I feel a surge of energy as we pass over the towering peaks of the outer Rockies and begin our descent onto the Interior plateau, where my Okanagan people have lived since time immemorial. My Indigenous territory is part of me. It belongs to me and I belong to it. Or rather, what's left of it.

My company CEO, Cathy Hellyer, who started working with me more than 30 years ago, or Tara Trottier, director of operations, who has also been with me for more than 25 years, meet me at the Kelowna airport. On the ride into this city of 132,000 people, they fill me in on the latest business developments. They are both smart, no-nonsense women who also have a great sense of humour, and they are a large part of the success of the RMD Group, the holding company for my commercial and residential real estate and other business ventures.

The airport is on the other end of town, so while we chat, we pass through the heart of the city, where my great-grandfather once owned a major part of the downtown area before he was cheated out of it by locals working with a corrupt magistrate.

The Westbank Reserve is on the west side of the William R. Bennett Bridge spanning the narrow section of Lake Okanagan. It is one of a few tiny pieces of the once vast Okanagan territory that remains under our control. I was born and grew up in a shack without plumbing or electricity on the hills overlooking the lake. My earliest memories are of kneeling in the field, gathering vegetables alongside my mother. And, when I was older, riding our horses along the ridge with my brother Noll. As a young man, I ranched these lands and for more than a dozen years, in the 1970s and 1980s and again at the turn of the century, I was chief of the Westbank First Nation.

Both sides of the road cutting through the reserve are now crowded with stores and businesses on leased reserve lands in deals I negotiated to bring income into what was once the poorest reserve in Canada. During my first 10 years as chief, I increased the band's leasing revenues by more than 3,500 percent. I fought for every advantage for my people so we could have the economic development we needed to give a future to our children. But I always fought for more than that. I fought and I continue to fight for the land and the resources on our greater Okanagan territory, which encompasses thousands of square kilometres in the B.C. Interior.

My political commitment today continues as a grand chief, but the occupation on my passport says *businessman*. Although it would be more accurate to say entrepreneur. I am a hunter and gatherer of business opportunities and today I run more than three dozen businesses under the RMD Group umbrella. And I am not shy about being successful. I have a nice house and in good weather I drive my Rolls-Royce Phantom to my office, which overlooks the Two Eagles Golf Course & Academy, one of the businesses I operate through the RMD Group. Outside the building, 25 Coastal Salish totem poles rise from the surrounding grassland. The office itself has become a kind of Indigenous art gallery with paintings, sculptures and carvings from Indigenous artists from British Columbia and beyond. When I step inside, I am always reminded of the beauty of my people and their amazing talents. How we have endured the waves of oppression that were released against us again and again.

Inside, I am greeted by Lisa Harding, my administrative assistant, and then with great, almost insane enthusiasm by Molly, the Bichon Pomeranian owned by my controller, Tanya Culling. Molly rushes up to me, madly barking her welcome. I have always gotten along well with animals, but in Molly's case I confess I have also courted her affection a bit by keeping a supply of dog treats in my desk drawer.

With my businesses in Ukraine and here in Westbank, I live in two worlds. But that is not unusual for a North American Indian who always lives simultaneously in our world and the white world. Most in my generation started out in one-room shacks, and our dealings with the white world that surrounded us were generally difficult. Very early on we had to decide whether to try to stay out of trouble by keeping our eyes down and not challenging the racist authorities — or stand up for ourselves and face the attacks that this would inevitably bring. I chose the latter, and I have never regretted it. But I have certainly paid a price.

At this point, you might be thinking that I am going to tell you a story about how I, as an Indigenous person, was personally victimized by this oppressive world, by racist laws and by an abusive state. While this is very much the stuff of our history, that is not exactly the story I want to tell you. My story is not a litany of complaints but a list of battles I fought to carve out a place for myself and for my people in the world as it is, and doing it on my terms. I did not advance by doing the white man's bidding, as some of our people have done — those Native business people who rose to prominence by becoming a compliant brown face in front of white puppeteers, or those Indigenous leaders who were rewarded by Canada for surrendering land or sovereignty to the state. That was not my way. My allegiance as an Indigenous leader and an Indigenous businessman has been to my people. And unlike some Indigenous people who make a few bucks, I will not now turn on our people to lecture them about pulling themselves up by their bootstraps. I know that for so many, history has conspired to rob them of their bootstraps and their boots.

This book is designed to provide not so much an antidote to, but more a completion of, the Indigenous stories that have come before, which I find sometimes slip into the overly pious. As a businessman, I like to give the straight goods. I will not avoid any of the controversies I have been involved in while taking on establishment interests, including the attempted character assassination on my life and work through a Royal Commission called by the Mulroney government, and a real assassination attempt by a hitman hired by a group of Kelowna-based businessmen who held Indian land leases at unacceptably low prices. Yes, that happened — and yet I'm still here! I will also give some of the behind-the-scenes activities in working with my late, great friend Arthur Manuel in trying to unsettle Canada. I will describe how this fight was never an intellectual game but a fight that me and my family have been engaged in for the past century and more.

I will not hide who I am, even though I know that some have found my directness, determination and my bouts of arrogance hard to deal with. But it wasn't my goal to be loved or even liked by the white man. At some point in my life I said the hell with it, I am as smart or smarter than any white man and I am not going to go through life with downcast eyes. Or downcast anything. From the first moment I stepped into a white classroom as a six-year-old Indian kid, I understood that I would have to fight or submit. And very quickly I learned that there were a lot of whites who would not hesitate to use every advantage, every underhanded trick to steal from us. At a very young age I determined I would not hesitate to use the same tactics against them to fight for myself and my people. I did not pull punches in my career and I will not pull my punches here.

Finally, I will admit to you one other fact that goes against the grain in Indigenous memoirs. I had tough battles — everyone does and especially an Indian who has the gall to step forward and insist on moving himself and his people up in the line. But as someone from the Coyote clan, an animal that is both trickster and helper, I will admit to something that straight-up activists rarely admit to: I had a hell of a lot of fun along the way. I have given and received my share of lumps, but I have embraced life to the fullest and often enjoyed the battle as much as — or even more than — the rewards of victory. So I promise to give you a true story of a life in battle, blow by blow, and the story of a people who have endured and who fight on, without trying to dress up the truth — and also, without apology. You can make of it what you will.

CHAPTER 2

Stories My Grandfather Told Me

Indigenous kids don't need history books to tell them who they are or where they come from. For that we have grandmothers and grandfathers. And the stories my grandfather told me about our history were not at all about passive suffering and acceptance. They were about fighting for our rights until we were knocked to the ground, then dusting ourselves off and getting up to fight again.

My grandfather lived in a shack that was almost identical to our own just a few miles from us. That was how it was in those days for everyone in our community. We struggled to survive by farming our small plots of land and working off the reserve as fruit and vegetable pickers or at some labouring job to earn a small amount of cash to buy the other necessities.

As well as being a man of boundless patience and affection for his grandchildren — and later for my own children — my grandfather Mickey Derrickson was a font of wisdom. He was born in 1887, only 75 years after the first whites had appeared anywhere on our territory and seven years before the first white birth was recorded on our side of Lake Okanagan. From this vantage point, he had a glimpse of the land and our life as it had been before the invaders arrived and had seen how, step by step, they had stolen our land and attempted to steal our future.

He had a clear view back to the time before the whites arrived. He told me once that as a young man he had gone bear hunting with old Chief Tomat, who was born in the 1840s and lived into the 1920s. The old chief told him all about how they lived and what the country was like before the miners and the settlers arrived. Chief Tomat said that the land looked all raggedy compared to what it had been. This was about 1912, and Tomat said in his youth, the trees in the valleys towered over the land, nothing like the small timber that replaced them; and wild fruits and edible roots were readily available almost anywhere in the tall grasslands, which were waist-high but had in the intervening decades been grazed to stubble by cattle or uprooted entirely and replaced by cropland. He told my grandfather this and much more when they went on a bear hunt with other community members, as had been the custom of our people. In a 10-day period they took 14 bear. Old Chief Tomat, my grandfather said, was an amazing hunter. He would stop when he saw a sign and dismount. And he would follow the paw prints, the droppings and the tree scratchings until he met the bear he was searching for. And they would come together like it was already fated for the bear and the man.

That is how it had been in the old days. But even back then, you could see that change was on the way. Only one year after that phenomenal bear hunt, Chief Tomat found the whites at his door-step and literally stealing his water. It was in the summer of 1913 when he looked out his window and saw an Indian Affairs agent by the name of Brown standing in front of his irrigation ditch, which took waters from the local creek down to his garden lands. Beside the Indian agent was David Gellatly, the white man who a few years earlier had usurped the common land alongside the reserve to grow tomatoes.

The Gellatlys had appeared out of nowhere. In 1888, a white guy called Billy Powers had claimed land next to Chief Tomat and built a log cabin. He stayed only a year and then disappeared, but because he was white, the area took his name and became known as Powers Flats. A year after he disappeared, the Gellatly family showed up and moved into the Powers' house on Powers Flats, which henceforth would be known by the local whites as Gellatly Flats. The Gellatlys were apparently from Scotland and had spent some time in Ontario before heading west to take advantage of the "free" land, our land, that was being given away by the British Columbian government.

The irrigation ditch that the Indian agent had given to the Gellatly family was only 75 feet from Chief Tomat's barn and he went out to see what the white men were doing there.

The Indian agent told him that they were going to siphon off water for Gellatly's tomatoes. Chief Tomat protested. He told him that this was reserve land and his father had built that irrigation ditch 60 years earlier. The Indian agent shrugged off his protests and told him that if he interfered with Gellatly's irrigation he would be put in jail. The next day, workmen came and built a flume that siphoned off every drop of water from the creek, leaving Chief Tomat's irrigation ditch completely dry. That, my grandfather said, was the point at which he understood that the whites really did want to destroy us, to wipe us off the face of the earth, stealing the water that we needed to irrigate our vegetables to feed ourselves. My grandfather admitted that these were the hardest times but he was determined to fight for his share.

When the whites first arrived in our world, people in our area didn't believe that such a being could really exist. This "white man" seemed like an unlikely invention by storytellers, not only because of their skin colour but because of the magic that was associated with them.

As it turned out, even the *idea* of the existence of white men brought trouble to our land. The rumour of their appearance across the mountain passes sparked a war between us and our Lillooet neighbours.

This is the story my grandfather told me: At around the beginning of the 1800s, Pelka'mulox was leading our people. An important Okanagan chief whose name means Roll Over the Earth, Pelka'mulox had defended our territory from a Secwépemc invasion from the north and then went on to forge a peace and friendship treaty with them, and finally a close alliance. He had also formed an alliance with the Blackfoot people on the other side of the Rockies and he would lead summer trading parties to Blackfoot country. On one of these annual trips, he was told by the Blackfoot of "white men" appearing on the prairie. He was skeptical at first, but when some of the Blackfoot said they had met these strange men on the plains, Pelka'mulox insisted on seeing for himself. He went with the Blackfoot into what is now northern Montana and he met two Northwest Company traders. When he returned to the Interior, our people were gathered at their late-summer fishing spot on the Fraser beside the Lillooet people. In the evening, Pelka'mulox announced to all who were present that the longstanding rumour of the approaching white men was true, that he had seen two of these men with his own eyes. Some were amazed at the news and others were skeptical. The Lillooet chief was one of the latter. He insisted that the Okanagan grand chief was lying about the existence of these mythical creatures. The argument between them grew heated to the point where the Lillooet chief stood up, drew his knife and killed Pelka'mulox. With his last breath, Pelka'mulox pleaded with his brother to take care of his son N'kwala and to avenge his death.

This occurred sometime in the first years of the 19th century. But it would have big repercussions later and symbolizes the discord that the arrival of the whites brought to our lands. In dealing with them, we would try to tame people who often seemed like crazy beasts to us and then we would try to slay them. But no matter what we did, they kept coming.

The first was David Thompson, who in 1811 came down the Columbia River and cut through our territory on his way to the coast. Later that same summer, an American group of fur traders arrived from the south and built a trading post near the mouth of the Okanagan River and then a second post at L'Anse au Sable, across from us on Lake Okanagan at the site of modern-day Kelowna.

Pelka'mulox's son, N'kwala, had taken over as Okanagan chief after his father's death. His birth name was Hwistesmetxe'qen, Walking Grizzly Bear. But the fur traders gave him the name Nicolas. Our people then took on that name in a form we understood, so we began to call him N'kwala. Whatever you called him, Hwistesmetxe'qen or N'kwala, he eventually became recognized as not only the grand chief of my Okanagan people but also chief of the Nicola Valley peoples and also of the Kamloops Band of the Shuswap people.

N'kwala developed good business relations with the white traders. Our people provisioned their L'Anse au Sable trading post in return for useful European knives, axes and cooking pots. The whites has so much confidence in N'kwala that during the winter of 1814–15, he was asked to watch their post over winter. When they returned in the spring to find everything in order, they made him a gift of 10 guns and a supply of ammunition.

This is when the war over Pelka'mulox's death finally occurred. When Pelka'mulox's brother heard about this gift, he went to his nephew to remind him of his father's dying request for revenge. N'kwala accepted this obligation and formed an alliance of neighbouring peoples — Secwépemc, Stu'wix and Upper Thompson — to attack the Lillooet (St'at'imc) Band, whose chief had murdered his father. In 1815, an estimated 500 warriors swept through the mountainous Lillooet Country all the way to the valley of the Lillooet

River, the country of the Lower Lillooet or Lil'wat, driving the people into exile in the woods away from the salmon-rich streams of the region for a generation.

This battle made N'kwala into an important war chief, as his father had been. And like his father, he travelled widely, visiting with the Blackfoot and even taking part in the buffalo hunt with them and joining them in battle. He cemented his leadership in the traditional way by taking on wives from allied nations. He is reported to have had more than a dozen wives, drawn from Okanagan, Sanpoil, Colville, Spokane, Shuswap, Stu'wix, Thompson and others, and fathered some 50 children, so that many people throughout the Interior of both British Columbia and the adjoining regions of the United States are descended from him. It should be noted that multiple wives were not common in our society, where marital fidelity was the norm and where both partners had an equal right to leave the marriage at any time. But it was a practice among political leaders to solidify alliances and to symbolize the family of Nations we belonged to.

Throughout this period, N'kwala also kept the trust of the white traders, which was rare among the Interior tribes. At the time, whites were clearly afraid of us, as you could see by the way they surrounded their post with a palisade and four-pounder cannons. They had reason to worry. The same summer they appeared among us, a group of American traders had been attacked in Clayoquot Sound by the Tla-o-qui-aht people after one of their Elders had been insulted. A full battle erupted with dozens of deaths on both sides — although most of the Indigenous deaths came not as a result of the fighting but of a suicide bombing, with the detonation of the explosions from below the ship after the Tla-o-qui-aht had boarded it to finish off the remaining whites. There were also early and then rapidly escalating skirmishes throughout the region with Indigenous peoples trying to expel the whites before they secured a foothold in their country. But these clashes did not deter them. They kept coming in not one but two rival gangs of fur traders, the

Northwest Company and the Hudson's Bay Company — who at one point erupted into warfare between them, attacking each other's trading posts like rival drug gangs.

The fur trade did resemble the modern drug business in that it was incredibly lucrative. The Okanagan fort amassed, in that first season alone, 2,500 beaver skins that they paid for with about 12 cents each in trade goods, and which they would sell on the London market for $7.50 each. That's a 6,250 percent profit — a margin that today is comparable to the astronomical profits heroin street dealers bring in, compared to the pennies they pay tribal people in Afghanistan for their poppies. Our people were taken advantage of on the business side because we lacked information of the true value of our goods — always a fatal flaw when you are trying to do a deal and something that is sadly repeated today by the fools who are negotiating away our land rights for a pittance.

The Okanagan people's conflict with the whites did not come with the fur traders, however. They came much later, when the fur business was replaced by the mining invasion. During the fur trade years, when the whites were few, they tended to behave themselves. They passed up the lake and then used our ancient trail along the west side to pack their trade goods on mules and horses north to the fur trading country. For those travelling in canoes, the favourite camping spot was across from us at L'Anse au Sable. The traders worked hard to keep up good relations with our people because they were passing over our lands and they came to rely on us for the fish and game we sold them along the way.

So N'kwala's strategy of working with the traders was not without benefits in those early years. It managed to get for our people things that were useful — horses, guns and iron cookware (although in the case of horses, we generally unhooked them at night and rode off with them rather than going through the purchase route). The whites were not a threat to our independence or cultural practices because the traders generally kept only a couple of men in a post to amass furs and distribute trade goods. After a time, many of these men married Okanagan women and settled among us, so we ended up being of more an influence on them than they were on us.

But by the 1840s, this generation of relatively peaceful co-existence in our part of the Interior was coming to an end. In 1846, Britain and the U.S. signed the Oregon Treaty, which somehow allowed the British to retain the northern part of our territory for the Crown and the Americans to seize the southern part of our territory for their republic. By then, the first settlers were already arriving from the south and our people were becoming increasingly worried by what was then a slow-motion invasion. When the Yakima people began resisting the onslaught of white settlers in Washington state, many of our young men went south to join them in an attempt to stem the tide before it moved up into the Okanagan.

Our local peace was finally shattered when gold was discovered in the Interior in 1856 and all hell broke loose. Thirty thousand white gold seekers flooded our territory from California to work the bars of the Fraser between present-day Lillooet and Hope. Many or perhaps most came overland via the Okanagan and Kamloops, or else by a more southerly cut-off via the Similkameen River, through what was by then known as Nicola's Country.

By 1858, our people were literally up in arms against this new invasion. The first conflict came in June, in the southern part of our territory when runners arrived at our spring fishing camp with news that 30 miners with 70 horses and mules were approaching from the south. When they appeared on the other side of the river, our people called out to warn them not to touch our fishing gear. In the evening, all of the women, children and old men were quietly sent away to the hills, while the remaining men built large fires to warn the trespassing whites that we were there and we were watching them.

At dawn, the warriors moved down from the hills and discovered that the miners had fled, leaving behind them some of their horses and mules and some of their packs. Four young men were sent to follow them and keep an eye on them as they passed through our country. Our men followed them on the trail over the mountain and up the river to my great-grandfather's community of Ashnola. There, they saw the miners kill an old man who had ventured out to speak with them. So our warriors lay in wait during the night and shot arrows and killed two of the miners who were sitting by their fire.

They knew that the miners would be after them for this act of vengeance, but they were determined not to let strangers come onto their land and murder our Elders.

But the miners continued to come in greater and greater numbers. A month later, a large force of well-armed men entered our territory with a pack train of 300 gold seekers, after ascending the Columbia River Valley from Oregon City. They approached one of our villages at the south end of Lake Okanagan. Our scouts had warned the people of their advance and we withdrew to the hills. From a distance, they watched the advance guard enter the village and shoot a number of barking dogs, then entered the huts where we had stored 50 to 100 bushels of dried berries and nuts for winter use. They filled several of their sacks with our food, then dumped the rest into the lake, destroying our winter supply.

Our warriors followed the pack train as it moved up the west side of the lake. In the morning, after the miners broke camp, our young men paddled across the lake to search the campsite for anything of value left behind. But there were 25 miners hiding in the gulch near the campsite. Three or four canoes with seven or eight of our young men in each landed. After they were on the shore searching the camp-site, the miners opened fire, massacring a dozen of our unarmed men and wounding a dozen more. Only a few managed to escape.

These conflicts also took place in Westbank. Sometime in 1858, a group of miners came across a group of local men near our camp at what is now our reserve land. They ambushed them, killing six. Our warriors were sent after them along the trail, catching up to them at the north end of the lake, killing all 12 of them. The place where our people were killed is today known as Dead Man's Creek and the place where we exacted our revenge is called Whiteman's Creek.

Our people were also involved in the Fraser Canyon War in the western part of our territory and the McLaughlin Canyon battle in the south. The Fraser Canyon War began when a young Nlaka'pamux woman was raped by a group of French miners. The Nlaka'pamux retaliated by killing several of them, decapitating them and dumping their bodies in the river. The bodies were eventually found circling in a large eddy near the townsite of Yale, terrifying the thousands of miners lining the riverbanks between there and Kanaka Bar. The miners organized themselves into military regiments and marched against our communities, threatening to kill every single Indian in the Interior. They rampaged up the west bank of the Fraser Canyon, destroying our food caches, but our people had withdrawn to Camchin to assess the situation. While our Okanagan people were holding an assembly with leaders of the Nlaka'pamux and allies from the Secwépemc (Shuswap), two of the miners' regiments were wiped out in a nighttime gun battle. This was not due to our attack, but to a panicked reaction to a rifle falling over and misfiring, causing the two groups of whites to rain fire on each other in the dark with only two survivors left standing in the morning.

At the same time in the south, our people were trying to choke off the invasion of our country from the source, at the McLaughlin Canyon, where the old Brigade trail ran parallel to the Okanagan River just south of what is now Tonasket, Washington. The canyon is a perfect place for an ambush, with hundred-foot rock walls on either side of the narrow trail. We hid along the rock walls and waited for a wagon train of 160 miners to approach. Fortunately for the miners, the ambush was sprung too early. Someone from our side fired before the wagon train was fully inside. Six miners were killed and nine wounded, but the rest managed to escape back down to the river. The miners took another route north and a small party of Okanagans followed them, sniping at them and stealing their pack horses at night.

But the white man could not be dissuaded from gold. They proved again and again that they were willing to die for it.

In 1860, the colonial government in Vancouver was stepping very carefully, unsure if they had the military capacity to actually hold the lands they claimed, and so the governor refused to grant official lands to the settlers. Because of their fear, the first land commissioner, William G. Cox, was told by the colonial governor, James Douglas, to "grant all lands claimed by the Indians" and offer them the "exclusive Indian rights to resources on reserves of land of whatever size and location they demanded." When Cox arrived in our territory in 1860, our people paced out the necessary boundaries for our exclusive use lands, choosing the good bottomland that allowed us to retain our village sites, our fishery locations and garden plots, and provide both a hunting territory and a good base for winter-ranging our livestock. We were willing to make room for the newcomers, but we required ample lands for our livelihood and to preserve our way of life. The whites, who were unable to subdue us by force of arms, had no choice but to agree.

But this deal did not last. When our people were weakened, the vultures circled back to pick apart our flesh.

The biggest blow came very soon after the land grants were made. During the spring of 1861, we had heard rumours of a strange sickness on the coast — smallpox, which had been brought to the colonies from California by the gold miners. The following year, it moved up the Fraser Valley, beginning as a mild illness, headaches, body aches and general weakness on the first day. Then, small round blisters appeared on the face, arms, legs and inside the mouth, and within days these blisters began to swell with fluid and an agonizing death followed. Within a week, all of the caretakers and all in the lodge with the stricken would fall ill from the smallpox virus, which could be caught by touching a sick family member or even caught from the air.

The smallpox epidemic was the biggest disaster to ever hit our people. It wiped out whole villages. At first we buried our dead, but as the death toll got out of hand, the survivors simply piled up the corpses in mounds, covering them with branches from trees or in some cases leaving them to decompose where they fell. By September 1862, miners reported coming upon villages where all of the inhabitants had died of smallpox. One group reported that they ignored the bodies and dug up the potatoes from the nearby fields before leaving our dead where they had fallen. That disaster, more than anything else, ended our resistance during this period. With up to 90 percent of our populations wiped out in some areas, we were in an extremely vulnerable position. And the whites did not hesitate to take full advantage.

Part of the new forces of destruction came from the priests, who had arrived in our area in 1859, but with the smallpox epidemic devastating our communities, they went into overdrive trying to weaken us spiritually, by enlisting the survivors into the Christian cult while, at the same time, new laws were enacted in Victoria allowing settlers to claim or preempt our land. This resulted in a flood of settlers into the region, with each family allowed to preempt 320 acres of land. The whites rapidly seized the fertile bottomlands with access to water and began cattle-ranching operations. Soon they had taken up all the best lands and they instantly began to agitate for the government to seize what remained of ours. In 1865, to accelerate the process of genocide, the priests opened up a residential school at the Head of the Lake for Shuswap and Okanagan Indian children. All elements of European society, which were to both inspire and impinge upon the Indian economy and culture, were in place by the mid-1860s. And for the next 50 years, the settlers were relentless in stealing, piece by piece, our land and water rights. That is the story of our people and to understand my family battles and my later battles as chief, you have to understand that these were the defining forces of our existence.

CHAPTER 3

Riding the Bucking Bronco

My grandfather grew up under the occupation. And to under-stand the rage of the local whites against me in later years — to the point of trying to assassinate me in 1982 and continuing with their character assassination attempts for another five years after that — you have to understand how they controlled us during the times of my grandfather and father. It was the world that instantly attacked any Indian who refused to stay silent on the reserve while the Indian agent controlled every aspect of our lives. If an Indian stood up for themselves or their people, they would be immediately struck down by the authorities, who worked hand in glove with the local white settlers to keep us in our place.

My grandfather spent most of his childhood and youth in the southern reaches of Okanagan territory. His mother, my great-grandmother, was born on her father's land, which is now part of the townsite of Kelowna. She met a young man from the Ashnola reserve, one of the sons of Chief Ashnola John, and she moved with him down to his community on the Similkameen River. My grandfather was born there in 1857.

Ashnola John was from the earlier time. He was known as a fierce fighter who had been involved in the Nez Perce wars, and local whites claimed that he had the scalps of three white men in his cabin, though my grandfather never confirmed this. At any rate, they were not in Ashnola for long. The marriage didn't work out and when my grandfather was still a boy, his mother took him down to live south of Tonasket, near the Colville reservation on the U.S. side of the boundary. It is a place of true pan-Indianism, with not only Okanagan but people from 12 Nations gathered there, including the Nez Perce war refugees.

My grandfather lived near the McLaughlin Canyon and as a child he played there with his friends. He remembers that during this period, you could still find arrowheads and lead shot in the ground from the ambush of the gold miners there, and someone had even dug up a skull with a snapped-off arrow through it that the locals identified as a missing man in the battle by the name of Frank Hughes. In the summer, my grandfather often returned to Ashnola to stay with relatives, and from there they travelled north in late August to pick hops in the fields north of Vernon.

These trips were among his fondest childhood memories.

Picking hops and other crops in the fall was a great collective endeavour not only of our people but our allies the Nez Perce, and they would travel north through our territories in large caravans of men and women on horseback trailed by pack horses with the children set on top of the tents and camp gear. This colourful parade was written up each year in the local press, although in their typically racist language:

> From as far south as central Washington they come,
> riding their "cayuses" and leading or herding along
> the pack-horses loaded with blankets, food and
> cooking outfits, camping by lake or stream, wherever

night finds them. . . . It is interesting indeed to watch them file by — the "squaws" with their varicoloured garments and the "bucks" with their deerskin coats and chaps.

When my grandfather was young, the caravan was still led by Chief Joseph, the Nez Perce leader who was already a living legend for having led his band of 700 men, women and children in a 1,900-kilometre-long battle with the U.S. Army in his attempt to join the Lakota people in seeking refuge in Canada.

It was a turbulent time and although my Okanagan people had been devastated by the smallpox epidemic only 15 years earlier, many of the surviving men had gone south to join our traditional allies in the Indian uprisings. There were many Okanagan, like Ashnola John, who fought beside the Lakota at Little Big Horn in 1876, and many more who fought alongside Chief Joseph and our Nez Perce at Colville the following year. In one of the most daring Okanagan raids on the U.S. military, they stormed a fort and freed our women and children who were being held there. When the Nez Perce were forced to surrender short of the border, many of the Okanagan fighters were able to slip through the U.S. Army encirclement and cross back into Canada. There is even a strange story of one of our local people, who had been arrested by the Americans, escaping north. He did not have shoes, but he managed to steal a cow and ride it all the way back up to Lake Okanagan.

So Chief Joseph was already a living legend at the turn of the 20th century when he would lead his people north for the annual hops harvest. My grandfather would travel to the harvest with his mother and the Ashnola people and he remembers seeing the still-proud Chief Joseph leading the Nez Perce caravan on a white horse followed by up to 200 band members. They would travel on the high ridges above the lake, where they could camp along the way and hunt deer for extra rations. At the Coldstream Ranch where they picked hops, their presence gave the place a powwow atmosphere.

During the day, they worked hard with whole families in the field filling the wooden boxes with hops. The boxes were six feet long and three feet deep in the shape of coffins, and my grandfather said that it took a long time to fill one up. When they were full, the men would haul them to the foreman, and for each full box they would get a round ticket with a hole in it that they would attach to a string around their neck. At the end of the season they would exchange these round tickets for cash payments.

After the long days in the field, everyone would retire to the open-air camp of hundreds of people; deer meat and wild vegetables would be cooking on open fires and there would be a celebratory atmosphere with singing and dancing. My grandfather told me these were among the happiest times of his childhood and he recalled the hops-picking excursions as being almost like family vacations.

My grandfather made his first visit to his mother's territory as a young man in 1910. At the time he was making his living as a rodeo rider in the American northwest and in southern British Columbia. He recalled he came to the Kelowna Stampede, as it was called, because the competition was not great, so it should be easy money.

It was while he was there that he met the woman who stayed in his mind after he returned to the Colville Reservation at the end of the fall. As it turned out, his mother passed away that winter and the following spring my grandfather travelled north to be with his mother's people, and in particular with that young woman who had caught his fancy the year before.

This time he stayed on and they were married. He moved onto the Westbank Reserve and he remembered that that first year was extremely difficult. He had only a few dollars and a horse. He had to fish on the lake in the winter to feed the family and he sold a few fish in town to earn some money to buy flour, salt and tea. Still, it was a hungry winter. And in the future he could not let up, because of the demands of their growing family. Eventually, he and my grandmother would have nine children, seven boys and two girls.

In those early years, there were still only a few whites on the Westbank side of the lake. The main non-Indigenous landowner was still the Gellatly family, which had moved in to take possession of the bottomland as soon as it became available. Thanks to Chief Tomat's stolen water, Gellaty became known as the "Tomato King of the Okanagan" for his industrial-sized production.

A few years after my grandfather arrived on our land, orchard trees were planted and the early fruit business began. The place remained sparsely inhabited, though. The first store wasn't opened in Westbank until 1915 but it didn't amount to much. My grandfather said that for the first couple of years, you could have bought everything in it for $10 and still gotten change back.

During this period, Mickey Derrickson was still "stampeding" at the local rodeo and you can find write-ups about him in the local newspaper that show that while he won all of the man-to-man competitive events, he was only awarded second places in the "judged" events.[1] The white judges would not allow an Indian to beat a white boy when they were keeping score.

According to my grandfather, we managed to get ours back in the betting circles for the straight-up races-to-the-finish, where the judges didn't count. He remembers bringing ringer horses up from the south to compete and entering them with a bareback rider. The whites would bet heavily against the Indian kid riding bareback, with just a light blanket on the horse, but when the race started, the bareback rider would fly through the field to the finish lengths ahead. The challenge then was collecting on the bets and my

---

1 *Kelowna Record*, 25 September 1913.

grandfather recalled that they would bring the biggest and strongest young Indian guys from the villages in the area to stand beside the white bookies as soon as the horses were out of the gate. They would stay there until the bets were fully paid.

These were rare victories. In the day-to-day, we faced the heavy weight of racism on all fronts. This could be seen most clearly in the newspapers of the day. Our people were almost always characterized as drunks and our community as a "hotbed of vice and drunkenness which has long been a festering sore on the other side of the lake . . . whisky which sets their savage brains on fire."[2] In some cases, we were even accused of "stealing white children" in the type of blood libel that was used in Europe to justify deadly pogroms against the Jews. They would use any slur against us as an excuse to persecute anyone who stepped out of line. Our leaders were especially vulnerable. As you will see, if they complained about injustices against us, they were immediately deposed from office and threatened with jail.

All during this period, our people were being corralled on smaller and smaller parcels of land.

The lust of the local settlers for our land, to crush our spirits and to steal everything from us, was so great that it astounded even white outsiders. When Gilbert Sproat, one of B.C.'s first land commissioners, visited the Okanagan in the 1890s, he found in his discussions with the local whites "the angry utterance of men steeped in prejudice. Like most forms of prejudice, the settlers' was nurtured by ignorance, or, at least, by a selective retention of information about the Indians." One of the most telling experiences that Sproat had as reserve commissioner was his inability to gain accurate information about the Indians from settlers who lived in their midst. He was, for instance, told on many occasions that land was wasted on us because we were incapable of building irrigation ditches, when Sproat could plainly see "ingeniously

---

2 *Kelowna Record,* 7 March 1912.

constructed Indian ditches several miles in length" all through the valley, sometimes even visible from the spot where white settlers were telling him that Indians were incapable of building them.

One of the first acts when I became chief in the 1970s was to commission a detailed 400-page study of how the whites managed, through self-serving legislative and legal manoeuvres as well as outright fraud, to steal our lands from the original Cox grant until we were left with the tiny portion that we have today. The study is a lesson in the profound dishonesty and rampant fraud of our white neighbours. I will give you some examples here so you can understand how our land was outright stolen by local conspirators and how Indians were beaten back whenever they tried to protest the injustices — often using the same tactics that were used against me when I was chief 50 years later.

The insatiable greed for our remaining lands began as soon as we became weakened by their diseases in the 1860s. As early as 1865, our reserves were reduced to a fraction of their previous size after J.C. Haynes, the local Justice of the Peace, argued that the reserve awards were excessive and "beyond the requirements of semi-nomadic Indians." Haynes even went as far as denying the authority of Governor Douglas's emissary, William Cox, to grant us our land in the first place. Illegally, in the absence of the majority of band members, he slashed our lands from approximately 200 to about 25 acres per household — with an estimate of only 10 arable acres. In the stroke of a pen, we were suddenly condemned to a century of poverty. Under the new regime, Indian rights to the land off-reserve were impeded as they now needed the permission of the Lieutenant-Governor-in-Council to preempt land. With Indian holdings reduced, white stockholders moved to acquire the newly available bottomland as the nucleus of their livestock operations.

British Columbia entered Confederation in 1871 as an almost-bankrupt apartheid government. When it became part of Canada, banks had refused to lend it any more money and it was already $1 million in debt. Its population at the time was stated as: "8,576 whites, 462 coloured, 1,548 Chinese and a number given as more than 25,000 Indians." But only the whites would get to vote and their primary economic activities would be stealing Indian land and profiting from cheap Indian labour from the recently impoverished Indian communities in the agricultural sector.

In 1880, to ensure we could not rise again, the settler government categorically denied Indians the right to purchase land off the reserve. In 1888, our local Okanagan Commonage Reserves contained a total of 188,582 acres, more or less, and Indian rights to these reserves were stolen and replaced by 3,238 acres across in the Tsinstikeptum Indian Reserve. No surrenders were taken, no compensation was paid to the Okanagan Indians and the exchange of lands was not published in the *British Columbia Gazette*.

Our land base was eroded again in the 1890s, when the government allowed white settlers to purchase land immediately adjacent to various reserves, thereby eliminating our access to Crown lands lying beyond. Further reductions were recommended by the McKenna-McBride Commission of 1912–16, resulting in the Penticton, Westbank and Spallumcheen reserves being reduced by 14,060, 1,764 and 1,831 acres, respectively, and the Nkamaplix Reserve by the loss of various small outlying reserves.

This did not stop after they had reduced us to lives of hunger on our drastically inadequate lands. In 1911, the year my grandfather arrived from our southern territory, the B.C. minister of lands calculated that while "there were 147,000 acres of land in the Okanagan Agencies, only one-third of that land (50,000 acres) would be amply sufficient for the use of those Indians." So the local conservative association petitioned the Dominion government and the government of British Columbia "to take such proceedings as may be necessary to re-adjust and reduce the acreage of the Indian reserves in the Okanagan."

In such a desperate situation, our chiefs tried to fight back. But the white corruption ran to the core and any chief who stepped forward to speak for his people was quickly unseated by the government.

These incidents from early in the century are important to understand because they were in my grandfather's time and they set a pattern that was still in effect two generations later when I became chief. One of the most blatant examples of this corruption was in 1908, when Mr. W.A. Lang, a local businessman with strong connections to the Conservative Party, tried to steal all of Reserve 5 from us. He drew up the papers for sale and they had "Chief" Isaac Harris sign them. The only problem was that "Chief Harris" was not a chief, he was not even a member of the band or of the Okanagan Nation. He was the son of a white father and Lillooet mother and he had no more right to sign over our land than I would have in selling the Brooklyn Bridge. This was done in secret in October 1908, and Lang and his Conservative Party fraudsters then tried to force the actual chief of the band, Pierre Nequalla, to approve the deal, with the quiet backing from the local Indian agent, who was in on the fraud.

Chief Nequalla said he was brought into Vernon, B.C., by the Indian agent who told him if he didn't sign the document, Isaac Harris would be officially made chief. In a letter to the superintendent, Chief Nequalla said Isaac Harris received money that should have gone to the band and that Isaac Harris had never been voted into the Okanagan Band as a member because his father was a white man and his mother was a Lillooet Indian.

But the fix was in. The superintendent, a Mr. Irwin, replied on March 8, 1909, that Pierre Nequalla had several times been convicted of intemperance and that the band members wanted him removed. Then Chief Nequalla was said to have "voluntarily resigned" rather than be deposed, and Isaac Harris was deputized to act as interim chief. But once again the band resisted and at an election held on March 1, 1909, Baptiste Logan was elected chief.

The fraud continued with the Isaac Harris backers claiming that at a band meeting, a decision had been taken to sign away the land. The new chief was caught completely off guard by this. Chief Logan said he had left the meeting where it was discussed with about 48 others because they did not understand what the meeting was about or why they should sign away their land. Logan then objected to the phoney Chief Harris being on the reserve and the community voted 23 to seven to evict him.

This was only one of a series of similar attempted and successful frauds against our people during this period. A few years later, a local politician, who was working with Lang and other local businessmen, claimed to have a petition of band members calling for the cancellation of the reserve. Old Chief Tomat knew that it was useless to complain to Indian Affairs — who were obviously in league with the fraudsters — so instead wrote a letter to the local paper, with help from a friend of the Okanagan people, James Christie, where he denounced a new effort at stealing Indian land.

"We, the Band Indians," the letter said, "protest against our reserves being taken from us. We have no other lands, and have no other means of supporting our families, and have no other grazing for our stock. We understand that Mr. Lang claims to have a petition from us asking to have the reserves cancelled. We have not signed a petition, and if he has presented a petition with our names attached, it is not ours and is false."

The press intervention had an immediate effect, because it was picked up by the opposition parties and made an election issue. In the Kelowna paper, it was reported that the Conservative candidate Price Ellison of Vernon was "noticeably ill at ease" when he tried to answer the charges made concerning the sale of the Westbank Indian reserves to Mr. Lang.

The Conservatives were nonetheless re-elected in Victoria and the premier, Richard McBride, became a personal champion of all of these shameful Indian-land frauds throughout the province, writing the federal government to complain of "the large excess acreage held on account of Indian Reserves in British Columbia, and to the necessity, in view of the rapid increase in the white population, of having immediate readjustment of all reserves, so the excess acreage may be released to the province."

Locally, the elected Chief Logan still refused to sign over our people's land and the consequences were the same as befell Pierre Nequalla. The local Indian agent warned Chief Logan that if he didn't sign over the land, he and all of the objectors in the band would be sent to jail. Chief Logan refused and on June 21, 1912, Privy Council Order No. 1712 approved the removal from office of Chief Baptiste Logan of the Okanagan Indian Band on the grounds of intemperance and incompetency, and he was declared ineligible to hold office as chief or councillor for a period of three years.

We know all of this because it was later reported in the newspapers by James Christie. Christie had wisely sent the letter to not only the local paper but to newspapers across Canada, and it attracted such attention to the issue that it was partially responsible for the striking of a new Royal Commission on the land frauds being committed across British Columbia. There was a surge of hope when this occurred, but those hopes were dashed when, on October 7, 1913, the Royal Commission arrived for a hearing in Westbank and the man sworn in as the Commission interpreter was none other than Isaac Harris, who had played a central role as the phoney chief in the original fraud.

The final blow came in 1916, when the McKenna-McBride Commission made its ruling to cut off sections of 22 reserves in B.C., including the Penticton Spallumcheen and Westbank reserves. In the case of Westbank, we lost 1,764 acres, which were taken from us illegally because federal law had stipulated that Indigenous peoples must agree to any change in the boundaries of their reserve. This was another theft and it would be recognized as such by Canadian courts some 70 years later when I was chief of the band.

As for Isaac Harris, he was still alive when I was a child, but he was already a little crazy from syphilis. His bad karma was apparently passed on to his children, who were all a bit nutty — one of them literally wore a tinfoil hat to try to stop the bad thoughts that were raining down on him, and a number of others suffered long and painful illnesses. It was a cursed family, and I sometimes think some of our ancestors had worked a bit of black magic on Isaac Harris for his attempt to steal our lands.

But when Isaac Harris was out of commission, there were always other local whites who were willing to take his place. Despite the fact that hundreds of B.C. Indians enlisted to fight for the empire in the First World War, and even raised money throughout our reserve lands to support the war effort, when the war ended this was ignored by the locals, who lobbied instead for the seizing of the last lands we had been allowed and giving them to the returning white war veterans. This bordered on obscenity when the local Kelowna paper described the plan submitted to the Honourable Arthur Meighen, minister of the interior in Canada, for the "Dominion government secure tract or tracts of land in the district of Kelowna — more than 2,000 men having enlisted from this district who will desire to settle here on their return — and provision for them should be made on Indian reserve and other lands now lying idle around Kelowna."

The insane reasoning for this had already been covered earlier in the paper when an editorial argued that "sentiment must not blind us to the fact that our boys have fought for the Indians as well as for us, and those (Indians) that have fought side by side with our men will surely share whatever good thing is given to them, so I feel they also should be willing to help in this matter (of Indian veterans surrendering their lands to white veterans) and not play dog in the manger."

This was the same bizarro world that my father was born into — where our reward for putting our lives on the line alongside whites in the trenches of Europe was to surrender our lands to the whites when the war was won. These are the type of people who would also come after me 50 years later as band chief, when I started to fight for justice for my people.

Behind my election was the unrelenting push of the local whites working for more than a century to defraud, legislate or outright steal our remaining land from us. We were despised by them, attacked by them, insulted, jailed and, in many cases, treated like subhumans by them. All because they wanted our land. They wanted all of it and they knew that without our land we, as Indigenous peoples, would simply disappear. That was the goal. But their animosity was not only because of the land they still wanted, it was because of the land they had already stolen. To even look at us reminded whites that they were occupying someone else's country. That is why they hated to see us in the town. We reminded them of their ongoing crime and raised the possibility, however remote, that some day we might rise up and seize it back. And they understood that the only way to remove this shadow cast over them was to remove us completely and thoroughly from the land. Force us to abandon our territories while we slowly disappeared into the body of the under-class in their cities. Slow but effective genocide. But no matter how much they beat on us, we would not surrender. And for Indigenous people today, this is the source of our greatest pride. We did not, we will not, surrender.

CHAPTER 4

Lessons from the Onion Patch

Like my grandfather, my father, Ted Derrickson, understood that everything was, ultimately, about the land. Growing up in the 1920s, when the whites were still aggressively pushing us into smaller and smaller spaces, he told me that land was the only thing that had real value. The rest was decoration.

My father was born in 1919 and grew up in the hardscrabble world where survival was the only goal. He met my mother, Margaret Schoven, at lower Similkameen at the Allison ranch in the late 1930s. She had been abandoned at the age of two at St. Mary's Mission in Omak, Washington, and she was planning to become a nun in the Sisters of St. Anne Order. But when she met my father, she fell in love and her plan to enter the nunnery quickly faded.

Their first child, my brother, Noll, was born in 1940. I was born a year later, on October 6, 1941.

As a child, my earliest memories are of working in the vegetable garden with my mother, squatting between the rows and weeding the onion patch. The land gave us life itself. Along with a market garden, we had a few chickens, milk cows, pigs, goats and a few horses. Because my father and grandfather hunted, we had fresh meat — deer, moose and grouse. In fact, we ate extremely well, not only because of the provisions we had but because my mother was an excellent cook. She could turn the simplest ingredients into a feast.

Even though we ate like kings, the house was far from a palace. It was heated with a wood stove and lit by kerosene lamps. The bathroom was the outhouse behind the house and bathwater was heated on the big kettle on the stove. Because my father went into the bush to work in the lumber camps for cash, we had things like tea, flour, sugar and baking powder. We were, by Canadian standards, dirt poor, but when you are young you don't notice these things. Even looking back now, I don't really remember poverty. I remember instead the flickering yellow glow of the kerosene lamp at night and feel the warmth from the crackling wood in the stove.

My mother and father were both hard workers. Neither of them would tolerate laziness and we were expected to treat our Elders, and in fact everyone, with respect. And because they had little, they were always frugal with themselves. When I was growing up in the late 1940s, my father was driving an old, battered 1932 Chrysler pickup that had a loose ignition wire, so you could start it by kicking the fender. This frugality did not extend to helping others in need, like the Japanese internees who came to live among us, and their arrival in our midst was one of my earliest memories.

Waves of Japanese began to arrive in the Interior during the early war years and my father allowed them a place to stay on our land, a few hundred metres from our house, and helped them set up a camp and to build a packing house. This was in April 1943, and the Japanese remained among us for several years after the war because their land and property on the coast had been confiscated and they had nowhere else to go.

Their presence had been welcomed by the white farmers as a cheap labour replacement for the young men, including many young

Indigenous men, most of whom were once again being sent overseas when they reached their 18th birthday. My father was very aware of what was going on. He had a Japanese friend, Hidido Yamada, in Rutland, a rural community outside of Kelowna, who came to him just after the Pearl Harbor attack, and the subsequent storm of anti-Japanese racism it caused, and asked him if he could put his land in my father's name until the furor settled down. Fearing — as it turned out, correctly — incarceration and the seizure of their lands, many Japanese did the same thing and many whites agreed to put their land in their own name. But then unlike my father, many of these refused to give it back after the war.

Even though the Japanese were welcomed as cheap labour in the fields, laws were immediately enacted to keep them out of Kelowna and any possible contact with the whites beyond the farmers for whom they worked. When one Japanese family arrived with the intention of staying a couple of days in the city while their mandated internment camp was being set up, they were immediately set upon by local vigilantes and forced to flee. From then on, Kelowna was officially listed as a "closed town" to the Japanese.

Indigenous people, on the other hand, tended to have good relations with the Japanese. After all, their situation seemed not so different than ours — they had been stripped of their rights and their lands and corralled in monitored camps that resembled our reserves. When I was a boy, I would go down to visit them. I even learned a few basic phrases in Japanese, and they gave us sweets that I had never tasted before. They had their own marvels, like outdoor hot tubs, and they seemed grateful for our friendly reception of them, given the contempt and even hatred they faced during this period from the white world. My mother would go down to meet with their women and she watched them prepare their strange foods, until they no longer seemed so strange and she began cooking Japanese dishes for us.

Our good relations with the Japanese were not repeated with the local whites. As a community, we had been forced to retreat into ourselves and that was our final protection. We were confronted by the meanness of our situation only when we went into town or on those occasions when the police pushed their way onto our reserves to look for people breaking their racist liquor or game laws.

Despite the hardships, there was a lingering but well-hidden magic in those times. In the literal sense. We had stories of little people, only a foot-and-a-half high, who co-inhabited our land at Dead Man's Creek, and although I have personally never seen them, I know people who have.

They also figure strongly in our stories and many strange things are attributed to them. When the miners were killed at Dead Man's Creek, they were hung in the trees upside down by their boots and left as a warning to the others if they came back onto our territory. But when our people returned a week later, they saw that the bodies were stripped bare and even their boots were gone. Our people saw this as the work of the little people.

Little people were known as master thieves. There were many instances of people in camps in that part of the bush finding articles stolen right out from underneath them. But there were also many instances when people stranded in storms or injured on the trail would find food or extra clothing appear before them. In one case, a local woman was travelling with her infant child when a late-fall snowstorm hit. She huddled in the dark night with her child when suddenly a fire flamed in front of her with enough firewood to last the night. Little people had a kind of Robin Hood morality. They took from the rich and gave to the poor.

There was also a magic of a darker kind. I remember when I was five years old, when my brother was off to his first day at school, I walked with him down to the road where he was to catch the school bus. As he climbed into the bus, he told me to go home. I walked along the shallow creek with the stepping stones and my father was near the creek burning tumbleweeds. I stopped, because I liked the sweet smell. Suddenly, out of nowhere, a medicine man from Colville appeared before us. I hid behind my father. The man was hunched over and obviously old, but he didn't have a wrinkle on his face and he had a staff decorated with feathers and fur. My father and him spoke in Okanagan. It was about my uncle Bill, the black sheep of the family, a big tough guy, a boxer and a wrestler who always seemed to be one step ahead of the law. The old man told my father that Uncle Bill, who local whites called "Indian Bill," had stolen $10,000 from a guy in Colville and thrown him off the bridge and killed him.

I remember my father asked, "Are you going to hurt us?"

The old man said no, but that my father's brother would shrivel up and die at the age of 65 like the tumbleweed when touched by the flame, and his son, who would try to cash his pension cheques, would also shrivel up and die. Then the man disappeared.

My father and I never spoke of this and I do not believe he ever spoke of it to his brother. I watched in later years as the old man's prophesy came true, and this has given me another reason to respect the magic of my people.

When times were really hard, my mother would join my father to work in the lumber camps as a camp cook, but my grandfather and grandmother were always there, in their small house about a 20-minute walk from us. Me and my older brother Noll visited them often, and I had this game that I played with their tame goose. I would approach the goose very carefully from behind and swat it on the butt and run like hell for the house while it chased me, squawking furiously. I would, to my grandmother's amusement, come flying through the screen door just ahead of the goose. She would laugh and say, "It is going to get you one day."

It never did, but I stopped playing the game when I was about six years old and Granny suddenly passed away of a heart attack. It was a shocking moment for me. I remember afterward still going up to the house to look for her, believing that she must be there somewhere, hiding from me. It took a long time to accept that she was gone forever.

Even with my grandmother gone, my grandfather continued to play a major role in our lives. We loved to go hunting with him — he was a master. We would leave with a small pack of tea, flour, baking powder and lard, and maybe a hunk of triple-smoked bacon for breakfast, and head into the hills. When it was time to camp, my grandfather would lead us to one of his traditional spots and he would undo a rope from the branches of a tree and lower down his cache of cooking utensils and teapot. We would sometimes have only dried meat and gathered greens the first night, but more often than not we would supplement that with grouse or fool hen we shot along the way — generally shooting two, one for roasting and another to make soup with. We would hunt until we shot a deer or a moose, butcher it on-site and haul the carcass home to be shared among the family and friends.

These were not just food provisions for my grandfather — the trips were more than a visit to nature's grocery store. He took hunting and its responsibilities very seriously. I remember his anger when I was older and he learned that me and my cousin Dave had gone on our own little commercial hunt and shot seven deer and sold them to white folks for $25 each. Those deer were not things that could be bought and sold, my grandfather told us. They were on our land to feed our people, and as long as there were still hungry people on our land, it was a sin to take them.

This was one of the very few times he showed anger at me. Generally, we just enjoyed each other's company, the old man and the kid. We played cribbage and he would beat me every time, often holding his nose for the last couple of hands when it was clear he was going to skunk me.

I would try to best him in everything and rarely, if ever, succeeded. He was a master at gardening as well as hunting. The summer that I was 11 years old, I bet him $10 that I would get a ripe red tomato in my garden before he got one in his. I watched as his tomatoes outgrew mine by a noticeable margin, and then I hatched a plan. I got up very early one morning, at first light, walked to his house, snuck into his garden and carefully cut his near-red tomato from the vine and brought it home to quietly integrate it into my most advanced plant. I waited until the sun had fully risen above the hills and, enormously pleased with myself, headed back to my grandfather's house and, barely able to control my enthusiasm, brought him over to see the ripe tomato in my garden. My grandfather had not said a word to this point. Then he agreed that it was the first ripe tomato, but he said he would be more impressed by it if he hadn't watched me crawling around his garden at dawn and stealing it off one of his tomato plants. The old man was impossible to beat. I had to pay the $10 bet.

Later, my grandfather showed me how to nourish and care for the plants, and our family started a lucrative side business selling packed tomatoes for the Alberta market, some years selling 200 boxes, with my father picking and my mother and I packing. This was mainly my mother's project, though. She remained a religious person all her life, but she also had a very good head for business and we were always looking for ways to earn a little extra money for the family.

These country pleasures were mixed with much darker elements in our contacts with the white world, which was often shaped by the laws that made it a felony for Indians to purchase, possess or consume alcohol. On Saturday nights, the white world would come to us when the city police would drive onto the reserve and kick in a few doors to find out if any Indians were drinking and, if they found them, roughly arrest them, often with a beating, and haul them off to jail while they "confiscated" their money and alcohol. Most of the people accepted this as a difficult fact of life, like the bitter winter storms, but my great-uncle Hank Macdougal decided he had had enough. He set up a shotgun in a cabin to fire if anyone tried to break in, and when the police came for him, it fired and killed one of them. He quietly disappeared to the southern part of our territory after that, but as a result, the local police no longer came on to the reserve and were replaced by the RCMP, who of course were no better.

On Sunday mornings, the local priest would be in our community to tell us we were hellbound savages and our only hope for salvation was to jettison our own culture and adopt white ways.

I discovered very early that these ways were not something anyone would want to adopt. My brother Noll and I were among the first Indians from our community to go to a white school in Westbank, rather than to St. Mary's Residential School in the south. I entered school the year after him, and in first grade we faced a level of racism equal only to that of Black kids in the American South. Teachers and staff treated us coldly and the white kids were openly hostile. It was so traumatic that our parents pulled us out after one year and sent us to the residential school, where at least we would not be targeted as the only Indians in a white world. But residential school, with its harsh discipline and hunger, and unrelenting assault on our culture, was worse, and after a year there, my parents made the choice to send us back to the Westbank school.

So that became my schooling. As Indians, we were made to sit at the back of the class and we were expected to remain invisible. When the teacher asked a question, you could sit with your hand up all day and never get called upon. In the schoolyard, I soon learned that I had to fight back with my fists, as I was not willing to accept the dominance of the white kids.

I am sure the teachers and the other kids considered me a tough little boy, and outwardly I was. But it also took a toll on me. I remember that I felt bad a lot of the time because of the way I was treated, and even today it pains me terribly when I hear of Indigenous kids committing suicide at a very young age. I remember that I spent many nights when I was nine or 10 years old thinking of this — an escape from the rage and humiliation we faced in the white school.

In the late 1940s, the only white kid who hung out with us after school was Harry Lewis, an older boy who was mentally disabled. He lived up by Shannon Lake and he would come down and I remember we gently teased him at first, but then began to make a real friendship with him. He was a profoundly good-hearted person and someone who had a finely developed moral sense. I remember once when we were discussing siphoning gas from parked cars, he became very upset because he said it was wrong to do that. He was so angry at the thought that he seemed prepared to fight us if we actually tried to carry out the plot. He died at a fairly young age, but his brother's wife, Dooley, later told me that the family was very appreciative of how well the reserve kids treated Harry. Especially compared to the cruelty of the white kids.

Our treatment by the whites, both children and adults, continued to be unforgivable and too often violent. Which was how I was finally ejected from school.

My formal schooling was cut short in grade nine. Originally, I was enrolled in a university-bound program, but halfway through the year the principal, whose name was McLaughlin, removed me from the university program and put me on the trades track, which made me think the whole schooling thing was useless, because I could simply leave school and get an apprenticeship if I wanted to enter one of the trades.

But I continued for a couple of months, until what started as an uneventful morning of the class saying the Lord's Prayer. As soon as we finished the lines ". . . and forgive us our trespasses, as we forgive those who trespass against us, and lead us not into temptation, but deliver us from evil," the school principal, who had been waiting at the back of the class, came up behind me and grabbed me by the collar. Apparently at the end of the previous day, he discovered that someone had carved what looked like *rd* in one of the desks and he had decided that it must be me. While holding my collar, he slapped me and marched me out of the room to the school office, all the while berating me for damaging school property.

I was 15 years old and physically quite strong from working on the farm and even though I was resisting, he managed to drag me to his office. Finally, I wrested myself free. When he shoved me into his office, I said with a force that even surprised me, "If you touch me again, I'll kill you."

It was my declaration of independence. I had experienced the injustice of the system on a day-to-day basis and like a growing number of kids of my generation, I decided I would no longer accept it — no matter what the price.

The principal reacted in an instant rage, slapping me hard on the side of my head. I reached for the inkwell on his desk and hit him with it on his head, drawing blood. He went down. I kicked him once and I headed out the door, leaving the school for the last time, feeling a mixture of exhilaration and terror at what I had just done, but knowing that I could never go back.

So that was the end of my high school education. When I explained what happened to me, my parents only nodded. This type of injustice was by then expected from whites. They were worried about my future, but they did not criticize me for fighting back.

I did have one final school experience. In the late 1950s, the federal government introduced a plan to educate Indian kids in more advanced farming methods, no doubt as a method to try to keep us on our reserves. It was a six-month course at the University of British Columbia and I was among the handful of young people selected to attend. The course was interesting — I had been working around the farm since I was three years old, so the concepts all made sense to me, and I would later even get a chance to employ some of them.

The campus had been built in the 1920s on land stolen from the Musqueam people in the point of land at the head of Burrard Inlet and the Strait of Georgia, now rightly recognized as part of the larger Salish Sea. The university was small by today's standards, only a few thousand students, but it was still pretty imposing to a kid from the reserve, with its architecture modelled on the old stone buildings of the great eastern universities. My stay there taught me not to be overly impressed by these types of grand symbols that white society uses to cover its emptiness, and to see that the so-called elites it was meant to serve were certainly no better than us.

Probably the most important result of this period was that I met fellow Okanagan Len Marchand. He was a senior at the agricultural school then, and when he heard that an Okanagan kid was in the dorm he came down to see me, to say hello and make sure that I had a change of clothes and other incidentals needed to get by at the school. Len, who would become a lifelong friend, went on to become Canada's first Indigenous MP when he was elected as a first-wave Trudeau Liberal in 1968, and later broke new ground as a cabinet minister and then a senator. My friendship with him also resulted in me drifting into the Liberal Party in later years, which would lead me into some very strange political territory.

After the stint at the UBC, my formal academic education was finished. I was, willingly or not, enrolled for the next several years in the school of hard knocks and lived through a very unsettled period.

I worked first at a series of farm labour jobs, locally or in the U.S. picking fruit. One of the local jobs that allowed me to explore the entrepreneurial side of my personality was picking potatoes for a grower, Milton Reece, whose family had moved onto the reserve cut-off lands in the 1920s. The work was back-breaking and when I started, the crew I was working with was about half Indigenous and half poor whites. After a few days, I noticed that the whites tended to be slow and lazy and it was the Indian guys who were carrying them. At first I saw this as another burden. Then I saw it as an opportunity.

At a lunch break I asked the other Indian crew members what they thought of us telling the owner, Milton Reece, that we could take a contract on the whole field, get rid of the whites and do their share of the work in less time. The other guys thought it was worth a try and at the end of the shift I went to Reece and made the offer. We would get extra pay and he would make a few extra bucks if we took over the whole job ourselves. Milton heard me out. He was a decent guy who always treated us with respect. "OK," he said. "Give it a try."

We did, picking up the pace, and fairly easily covered the work of the lazy whites and made a good profit for ourselves in the process.

This moment tied together much of my learning up to that point. Indigenous people could get ahead if they stuck together and played it smart. In the rigged system, you might have to be twice as smart and work twice as hard as white men to get ahead — fortunately, as the saying goes, that was not so hard to do.

After working some months in the orchards and farms of the south, I went north and worked in the bush for the logging companies. I was given the tough, dangerous job of a choker setter, hauling logs with high-tension cables with a special choker harness and then running clear while the cables snapped into place. I was very lucky that there were other Indigenous guys watching my ass in a job that could leave you with serious injuries from the flying cables if you simply stopped in the wrong place after running away.

At the end of winter, when the forests were closed for spring break-up, I headed down to Vancouver, still a teenager with no clear idea of what I wanted to do with my life, but with a vague plan to make enough money to buy some ranchland back home and try to make a go of it raising cattle.

In Vancouver, there was very little work for an unskilled Okanagan kid, but it wasn't long before I met others like me, young men with no prospects, and I saw what they had to do to survive. One of these was a group of shoplifters who specialized in a kind of made-to-order shoplifting. They would canvas people on the streets for items they wanted and negotiate a price, then go and steal the item. I fell in with them and to survive the winter, I became an order-taker and price negotiator. If someone wanted, for example, a leather coat, I would pass on this information to the shoplifting team and they would go and get it at Eaton's or a specialty boutique. They would bring it to me and I would take it to our client and negotiate the best price I could get for it. It was not something that I liked doing, but it was keeping me alive.

I escaped this street gang life when I was able to get what I thought was a more legal job as an elevator operator in a big Vancouver hotel. But elevator operators in Vancouver in the 1950s were tied into the system of bootleggers and taxi delivery, and businessmen knew when they wanted an after-hours drink they only had to give the order and a delivery address to an elevator operator and the delivery would be made. I joined in on what I saw as this harmless trade, but I was not very good at it, because I was arrested for bootlegging three times over the next two years. On the third offence, I faced the possibility of doing time in the provincial jail and I knew it was time to get my life in order. When I appeared in court for that third charge, I told the judge that I was sorry for what I had done and, in a flight of fancy, added that I had already begun to get my life on track by enrolling at Van Tech, a trade school.

The judge picked up on this. "Bring back to the court proof that you are enrolled at Van Tech and I will give you a conditional discharge."

That was excellent news — except for the fact that I had not even approached a trade school or even had an idea of what trade I might do. When I left the courthouse, I went directly to Van Tech to do a retroactive enrolment. But I was surprised to learn that the school was filled up. No spaces open.

I pleaded with them for a spot — after all, my freedom depended on it — and I must have made an impression, because a week later I was told that they had an opening in the welding course. I hurried back to the court with proof of enrolment to have my charge dismissed.

This was the end of my unsettled period. I became a tradesman and over the next several decades I would also be a rancher, a politician and a businessman and I would never lack for work. I am proud to say that I worked hard on every job I had. And I liked all of them, even welding. The principles of oxyacetylene and arc welding are simple enough, but making a good, strong, clean weld is more an art than a science and it brought me real satisfaction in doing it well.

CHAPTER 5

Only the Land Matters

My first job as a welder was with Wagstaff Hoists, and that came with membership in the welders union, which eventually allowed me to travel in B.C. and northwestern U.S. doing service work for the company.

By this time the economic boom of the 1960s was in full force, and I found I could work anywhere. I got welding jobs on oil pipelines and at pulp mills all over the country, working eight hours on and eight hours off, often seven days a week, for six months.

I was sending money home and my father was using it to buy land, which was cheap at the time — you could buy a section of 12 acres for a $1,000 an acre. Slowly I saved the money I would need to purchase land and cattle, not knowing at the time that land values, especially near Lake Okanagan, would grow to $500,000 an acre.

These on-reserve land purchases sometimes surprised people who think Indian land is always held in common by the band, but in our community and most others in the B.C. Interior, we had a mix of public lands and a system of internal ownership managed by certificates of possession. In his own life, my father not only held on to his family land, he purchased the certificates of others who wanted to sell. This was not something understood by my mother, who saw it as a waste of money. But my father knew that everything, finally, is about the land and he was always very ambitious with regards to having a large land base. In fact, I can remember people in our community used to jokingly call him "the Commissioner" and "the Baron" because he had amassed all of this apparently useless land. Some of this land would later increase in value because of leases he made with outsiders, but some of it wouldn't. It didn't matter to him. Land, he believed, was a value in itself.

"It is the only thing you can count on," he drummed into my head since I was a child, "Land always has value and it will always be there tomorrow."

The land in Westbank was at issue in another way during this period. At the end of the 1950s and into the early 1960s, we still did not have our own reserve — we were part of the larger Okanagan Band. Getting control of our own band was a major issue in our community throughout my childhood, and my parents were very involved in the lobbying efforts with the Okanagan Indian Band and with the Department of Indian Affairs to have the Westbank Reserve recognized as separate.

The reserves in our territory had originally been established in 1888 by Peter O'Reilly, an appointed reserve commissioner for British Columbia and our lands were included as part of 10 "reserves" grouped under the administration of the Okanagan Indian Band. The main reserve, Okanagan 1, is located at the head of the lake near Vernon, 30 kilometres from Westbank. At the time, our band lands were described as Okanagan Indian Band Tsinstikeptum Reserve 9 and Tsinstikeptum Reserve 10 and a smaller, uninhabited Reserve 8 on the Kelowna side of the lake.

Although we shared a common language and culture with the Okanagan Band, the distance between us was a natural division. Historically, Westbank always had their own chief, which Indian Affairs called a sub-chief to distinguish him from the recognized Okanagan Band chief. But our political representation on the Okanagan Band Council consisted of one lone councillor. There was a feeling of general alienation among our people and a suspicion that we were not receiving our fair share of funds provided by the Department of Indian Affairs.

In 1957, a group of residents of Reserves 9 and 10, which included my parents, petitioned the Indian agent at Vernon for a separate status for Westbank. They noted that in addition to problems caused by geography, there were philosophical differences between the Okanagan Band Council and the band members at Westbank. Some members residing on Reserves 9 and 10 were anxious to take greater economic advantage of their proximity to Kelowna. They wanted to lease their lands for commercial purposes and this movement increased after 1958 when a new floating bridge was built joining the Kelowna and Westbank sides of the lake. The floating bridge was the first of its kind in Canada, because it allowed for sailboats to pass underneath through the lift span. More importantly, it connected Highway 97 from the west side of the lake to the east, and this would figure largely in future developments when the province built the connector, 97C, to Merritt to give the region quick access to Highway 5 to Vancouver.

The Okanagan Council was generally opposed to the long-term leasing of reserve lands. The reason was because they had excellent farming lands, so renting to outsiders would not give them any advantage. I knew all of these issues well because from our earliest days, my parents took me and my brother to the band meetings. I can't say that it was always voluntary on our part — sitting in the community hall listening to our Elders drone on and on about band business was not tops on our lists of things to do on a weekday evening — but I think me and my brother absorbed more than we realized, because both of us would go on to become Westbank Band chiefs.

By 1960, the pace of development in Kelowna and the surrounding Okanagan Valley was rapidly increasing as Kelowna developed into an important commercial, industrial and service centre in the B.C. Interior. With its mild climate and wealth of leisure activities, Kelowna also began to emerge as an important centre for retirement. So its need for satellite communities increased even further. With the construction of the new bridge, whether we liked it or not, this expanded Kelowna was suddenly at our doorstep.

The first proposed development that caught the interest of many in our community was leasing part of our unused reserve land for a Kelowna college site, which would bring badly needed revenues to the reserve with a minimum of intrusiveness. People of Westbank were generally favourable to the plan, but the chief and council of the Okanagan Band were still hesitant to commit themselves to long-term leasing and they remained unenthusiastic about the project.

My parents were part of the group that travelled to Vernon to lobby the Okanagan Band Council to move on the college proposal and to ask the Okanagan Band Council to increase Westbank representation from one to two councillors. But the council refused both requests.

In 1962, the final push for an independent Westbank Band was on. A committee of Westbank members including my parents, Ted and Margaret Derrickson, as well as Norman Lindley, Mary Anne Eli, Francis Swite and Bert Wilson was struck to demand that Indian Affairs finally recognize Westbank as a separate band. The committee convinced Indian Affairs to hold a referendum on the issue. Voters at the head of Okanagan Lake outnumbered those at Westbank by approximately four to one, but even so, the results of the vote were close — 49 percent in favour to 51 percent opposed. The result was so close because while 90 percent of the eligible voters at Westbank had cast ballots only about one-third of the eligible voters on the other Okanagan reserves had. But that was enough to narrowly defeat the resolution.

In 1963, the Westbank committee insisted that Westbank's 90 percent turnout and virtually 100 percent support of the resolution among its voters was proof enough that the government should go ahead with the partition. Finally, the government relented. On October 18, 1963, pursuant to the provisions of Section 17 of the Indian Act, the federal government provided for separation of the Westbank Band from the Okanagan Band. Westbank's lands would include Tsinstikeptum Indian Reserve Numbers 9 and 10 and Mission Creek Indian Reserve Number 8.

Norman Lindley was elected the first chief for Westbank with my mother, Margaret Derrickson, and my uncle, Harry Derrickson, elected as councillors. The first five years after separation were very much learning years. Most of the time was devoted to establishing an administration that could manage the growing social assistance, education and housing programs, which were at the time being transferred from the jurisdiction of the department to local band administrations. In Westbank, the pace of development had not been as great as may have been anticipated at the time of separation and many of us, especially the young people, were getting impatient for more action on the economic front.

Instead, there was a zigzagging on the issue that began in 1965 when band members voted to permit leasing throughout Reserve 10. This was done to accommodate a plan referred to as the "Grosvenor Laing Development," an ambitious proposal for developing the entire territory. My father was one of the architects of this plan and he worked closely with the private developer to get a good deal for our people — even though he only had four and a half acres of his own land involved. But the deal was too far ahead of its time and Indian Affairs, which was then reluctant to see Indigenous people actually making money, blocked it — to my father's great disappointment.

So, finally, only minor developments occurred on Reserve 10 during this period. A portion of waterfront had been leased for a marina development, and another small parcel adjacent to the bridge had been leased for a retail enterprise. Okanagan Regional College Council had leased a substantial lot for a college site in 1965, but relinquished it in 1973 without building the school.

Part of the problem was that the band did not have the planning infrastructure and the by-laws in place that would allow it to move forward on leasing to secure benefits for the people. By 1968, this was becoming apparent to the younger generation, who were pushing for a more aggressive development plan with an infrastructure that could maximize benefits. This was the message my brother Noll put forward when he stood for chief against Norman Lindley that year. Even though he was only 28 years old, Noll defeated him in the band election. The people of Westbank, then one of the poorest reserves in the country, were demanding a better future.

I had also begun to get serious about my own future, spending more and more time in the community laying the groundwork for a ranching operation, and less and less working on welding contracts. Finally, I was able to use my savings to buy a ranch off-reserve, a full section of land with 25,000 acres of grazing rights and a small and neglected herd of cattle.

I bought a second section of land on the reserve and a further 14 head from one of the women band members, and I added to the herd whenever I had a little extra money. So I had two ranches to run, meaning I often found myself needing to be in two places at once. This was further complicated by the fact that they were an hour-and-a-half drive apart.

The pace was gruelling. I got up at four in the morning and I wouldn't be home until late into the evening; and of course ranching is seven days a week. The cows have to be fed at dawn and they have to be fed again in the evening. I was virtually alone in this. I even learned to artificially inseminate the cows and turned that into a separate business. As I told a reporter, "Try handling 40 cows in heat, and you'll find out what work is."

The work paid off. Within two years I was grazing 750 head of cattle and running myself ragged to keep them healthy and the ranch in the black.

Looking back, I still don't know how I found time for my passion during the period: speedboat racing. I have always been a bit of a thrill-seeker and my outlet at this time became boat racing, which I happened upon by accident. I was looking through the local classified when I saw a "hydroplane speedboat" for sale. It piqued my curiosity because I had no idea what a hydroplane speedboat even looked like. I called up the guy who was selling it and went to see the boat. I was immediately struck by the beauty of it. What attracted me was the fact that it had been conceived, designed and built for one thing and one thing only: speed. The push for speed determined its size, shape and weight, with no thought for comfort or practicality. I asked him if I could take it for a test ride. We put it in Lake Okanagan and after a few moments of puttering around with a near-idling engine, I opened it up. It flew, barely touching the water in the stern with the bow and most of the boat completely out of the water. I was hooked.

It was a pleasure to speed around on the hydroplane, which was called *Little Warrior*, and I quickly proved it was the fastest boat on the lake. It wasn't long before I wanted to test it in action. I began to travel to races in the B.C. Interior and the northwestern U.S. I discovered that *Little Warrior* was competitive and I became an increasingly skilled race driver — I won more races than I lost. But on the professional circuit there were a number of boats that I could not beat. *Little Warrior* simply didn't have the power. I had proof of this after I acquired a new boat and sold *Little Warrior* to Richard Kruger, a driver who was always coming second behind me.

He decided he would break my record of 206 km/h, and pushed it to 207, which is when *Little Warrior* blew up in the middle of the lake.

The new boat was built with Jimmy Hutchison — a small, wiry and good-natured guy who was one of the masters in B.C. hydroplane design and construction. Hutchison had also been a champion and record-setter on the professional circuit, and after watching me race he told me that I had something that could make me a champion: fearlessness. Over time, we became friends and together we built a new boat, called *War Canoe*.

It was a magnificent craft. With *War Canoe*, I quickly outran the local competition. By 1969, I was racing all over North America, and by 1970, I was North American champion in the America Power Boat Association hydroplane category, amassing what the APBA referred to as "an astonishing 11,763 points in one season," breaking Hutchison's own record and setting one that has remained unchallenged to this day.

Looking back, I think hydroplane racing was my version of my grandfather's rodeoing, and like him, I finally had to set it aside because I had a family to support.

I was 24 years old in 1965 when I married a Kelowna girl, Peggy McBride, who I had met at a city park dance when we were still teenagers. Our first child, Doug, was born in 1967, and our daughter, Kelly, was born in 1974. While they were growing up, I had to be at home more. When Peggy and I were married, we first lived in a 25-foot trailer across the lake at the Pandosy trailer park in Kelowna. We were still there when Doug was born. Soon after, we rented a house on Water Street, but I was determined to move back onto the reserve and build my own home. Which I did. Literally. I had put all my money in the ranchlands, so I built that first house myself with a little help from my grandfather and old neighbour who had the type of basic carpentry and building knowledge I needed to complete the project on a shoestring budget. Often I didn't even have the money to buy basic materials, and I remember going to the local construction sites to pick up odds and ends of lumber that they were going to throw out or burn and picking up the dropped nails from the ground and straightening the bent ones. In the end, I built the house with $17,000 and a lot of sweat equity.

It wasn't much by today's standards, but I remember the house fondly because Dougie and Kelly grew up there. And they tell me of their happy memories. The backyard in the house was full of fruit trees — peaches, plums, apricots, several kinds of cherry trees — as well as a vegetable and flower garden. Kelly remembers spending her days in our little orchard and says she rarely wanted to go in for lunch, because she would be eating from the fruit trees all day. Probably because I had many childhood memories of surviving the final months of winter on leftovers from the previous year's potato crop, I always made sure we had a big garden to feed ourselves, generally with many baskets left over that me and Peggy would take around to people on the reserve who were still struggling.

Weekends, we would go over to my parents' house for dinner and a night of music with family and friends. My mother would cook a feast and afterward my father would bring out his fiddle and banjo and someone would drag out a laundry tub drum and we would have a real hoedown, with family and friends drifting in during the night to share in the plentiful food and the music. It was there that my daughter, Kelly, showed her musical talent, really from infancy. She would hum along to the music before she could speak and by the time she was three years old, she was belting out songs with my father, who was a brilliant musician and someone who really felt the music he played. Sometimes he would play the fiddle and you could see tears in his eyes.

I spent long days during this period working alone on the ranch, although the kids liked to hang around when they could. But ranches can be dangerous places for kids and especially for Kelly, who had a serious allergic reaction one day — I think it was from being too close to the horses. I found her turning blue lying in the straw outside a horse stall. The hospital was more than 15 kilometres away, so I ran inside with her and laid her down and I could see that her throat was completely constricted. I had to reach down and pry her throat open with my fingers to get her breathing again. Of course I forbade her from coming to the ranch or from riding horses, but a couple of months later she began to sneak out at night and somehow managed to overcome the allergy and rode Smokey, a horse we kept in a small corral outside the house.

I still had to watch every penny at this time. When I started ranching, I had nowhere near the $100,000 I needed for equipment and I had to buy an ancient tractor for $2,000 and take it into my shop to get it running. I bought my second 40-year-old tractor from an old guy who told me that he had to sell it, because he had kept it in the garage for 30 years while his wife's car was kept outside and she finally told him that either the tractor goes or she does. "It was," he said, "a difficult decision," and he hoped he wouldn't regret it later, but he had decided to sell the tractor.

I had some help when I was on the road during racing season but for the most part I worked the ranches alone — up at 4 a.m. and in haying season working until 11 p.m. In later years, Dougie, even though still a child, would come out to work with me during the haying. I felt a bit guilty years later when he told me he went to bed every night after working in the tractor with sore legs, because he had to push down on the clutch with two feet and all his might to change gears. But this was how I was raised by my father — to be disciplined, to persevere, and no whining. My son had taken on the same values. He would rather live quietly with the aches and pains than make a fuss.

My income in these years was heavily dependent on the market. I would fatten the heifers for a year or two, depending on the prices. In the summer, I had grazing rights to 28,000 acres of Crown land and along with the herd, I had up to 25 bulls to ensure the numbers increased every spring. My cows were known in the region for their shiny hides, which I managed to get by mixing molasses in with their feed, which I bought for $12 for a 45-gallon barrel.

My only vice during this period was speedboat racing. In everything else, I was a worker and a saver. I never went to a rodeo or powwow until I was in my fifties. I lived with my cows and because I had so little help, I had to train them to herd themselves. Especially my lead cow, which I taught to come whenever I called, and she always brought the rest of the herd behind her. Even old ranch hands found this cow's devotion unusual. I remember one fall when I was selling off a large section of the herd, the trucking guy, Norm Dias, arrived in my yard, and when he saw the cows far out in the field he reacted with impatience. Why didn't I have the cows ready for transport? he asked. He didn't have all day to sit around and wait for me to round them up and bring them in. He quieted down when I shouted out to the field and after a few minutes my lead cow came trotting in, bringing the herd in behind her.

I was surrounded by white ranchers at the time and I was concerned about my relations with them. But as someone who was brought up to lend a hand, I would never hesitate when I saw their strays to round them up and bring them to my barn and feed them until the neighbour had a chance to come and pick them up. I knew that I was accepted by the white farmers when I housed 17 of a neighbour's cattle for a full month before he arrived to pick them up. The next day, trucks arrived with an enormous gift of 12 tons of hay to repay me for my trouble.

I went into the horse business when I saw that horses that were thought too mean to tame were being sold dirt cheap at the market. I would buy them up, take them in and in three months have them ready for riding. Taming horses, I had learned as a kid, could be accomplished by playing on even the wildest animal's sense of curiosity. I would approach the wild horse in the stall without looking at it and sit quietly while I reached into my shirt pocket to scrunch a piece of paper. The horse would try to figure out what the sound was and where it was coming from and would become quiet while it contemplated the strange noise. Then I would reach deeper in the pocket where I had stashed a carrot. When I moved the carrot to the tip of the pocket, it would smell it and then move closer to me. Soon I would be feeding the horse the carrot and after that, when I came into the stall, he would come over for his carrot. I ended up with a herd of about 20 wild horses that I trained to be gentle enough for kids to ride. And many of them I would then sell at a profit.

I was putting everything I had into the ranch during this period, but I also kept my eye open for other business deals. When I heard a defunct mining operation was selling off 50 diesel and gas generators and pumps, I bought the lot, made some repairs and sold them for a tidy profit of between $100 and $2,000 each, depending on what state they were in. I was gaining confidence in my entrepreneurial instincts, but as in everything — from business to speedboat racing — you are going to crash sometimes. As a guy from the Indian side of the tracks, I was determined to prove that I could compete with the whites. When I got involved with a group of four Kelowna businessmen in a deal for a parcel of 80 acres of land, they were kind enough to give me my first lesson in doing your homework before you go in with strangers on an irresistible offer, when they skinned me for everything I had. In the deal, they got every cent of the $88,000 that I had saved to that point, when one of them pretended to be my friend and assured me he was looking after my interests. Next time I looked, they were in possession of the land and my $88,000 and I was left with nothing. That is when I realized you cannot trust anyone to look after your interests except you yourself, and never go into a deal before you have a precise knowledge of what you are getting for your money. In the end, I was left poorer but wiser and my only recourse was to accept the loss — and to seek my revenge with a visit to a local medicine man to ask him to put a curse on the guys who took my money.

Lessons like these helped me to recognize that business was not going to be a well-regulated game of softball. The only way to win was to play hardball all the way. This was confirmed to me when my father rented a large section of good grape-growing land to a local wine company. When the lease came up for the five-year renewal, they refused to negotiate new terms, as our contract called for. Instead, they tried to sell their operation to a New York company. I told them that until we came to terms on a new lease, they would not have access to our lands and parked a tractor across their road access. The New York company then said forget it — settle with the Derricksons or we won't do the deal. So they were forced to negotiate and I got from them a new long-term lease, with $80,000 in back rent and ownership of the equipment in the field.

One of the deals that would have enormous implications for me down the road came in 1968, when I was approached by an RCMP officer, Leonard Crosby, to lease eight and three-quarters acres of land I had purchased with money I made on my welding contracts.

Crosby wanted to build a trailer park and the land he was interested in was a section of Reserve 9 land that overlooked Lake Okanagan. We agreed on a 50-year lease, with the rent for the first five years set at $800 a year, after which the rent would reflect "the increase, if any, in the market value of the unimproved land." To determine the amount of any increase, we had a standard clause calling for "the locatee and the lessee, each selecting one arbitrator, and the two arbitrators choosing a third and the decision of the majority of the three arbitrators shall be final." These were the terms that I agreed to with Crosby, but in the paternalistic system of the time, the lease had to go through the Department of Indian Affairs for approval. It was a time when every part of our lives was still controlled by Indian Affairs, and we needed permission from the regional office of the Department of Indian Affairs even to sell our garden produce in town. I found this humiliating. Crosby, who likely knew something of the history of the Department of Indian Affairs colluding with local crooks to steal Indian land, found it comforting.

In 1971, Crosby leased more of our family land for his growing trailer park and he was able to retire from the RCMP on the substantial revenues that it brought him. But from the beginning, he seemed to resent every cent he had to pay to Indians for any reason. As an RCMP officer, he was used to giving Indians orders and breaking their heads if they stepped out of line, and he did not like the idea that he was now in business with us. We would see this again and again as Crosby tried to bring the government, in the form of the regional office of the Department of Indian Affairs, in to support him and to chastise us. Unfortunately for Crosby, his timing was bad. In the mid-1970s, the department was, for the first time in its history, run by someone who was a decent man.

Fred Walchli became the director general of the B.C. branch of the Department of Indian Affairs in 1972, and he was almost unique among Indian Affairs officials in showing genuine respect for our people and an openness to changing some of the Department's ugly ways of the past. Because of this, he, too, would find himself caught in the crosshairs of several furious trailer park owners and led by Mr. Crosby in front of a Royal Commission that was mandated to look into my affairs.

The battle between me and Leonard Crosby and the other white trailer park owners I would come to represent began in earnest in 1974, when we had to settle on a new rent after the first five-year period. But it would continue for more than a decade, and would involve an actual assassination attempt against me.

After the initial five-year lease, the value of the land Crosby was leasing had increased significantly with the expansion of Kelowna onto our side of the river and the development of surrounding band lands, so I had upped the rent to $2,675, which was still a great deal for him, considering the profits he was taking in. But Crosby expressed outrage at the increase and he went to Indian Affairs to demand that they put me in my place. When they refused, he threatened to pull out of the lease and I said, fine, I will buy you out and repossess the land — this was the same deal I had originally sought for my grandfather from the vineyard. But of course Crosby was bluffing. Even with the rise in rent, he was still making a bundle. The proof of this is that when push came to shove, he signed a new lease — which I had gladly offered him a way out of — with a new clause that was fairer to me. It provided for setting lease rates based on applying bank prime rates to appraised land value at a time when land values were shooting up. It also provided that "the level of income being generated by the tenant from its use of the land will be taken into account." Under the new regime, Crosby had to pay the increased value or 20 percent of the revenues, whichever was greater. Crosby signed, but from then on, he treated me like his mortal enemy and he went on to enlist the association of trailer park owners to fight against me. And it was from within their ranks that an assassin was hired and the later libellous campaign against me was launched. While it was about trailer park leases, in reality it was about the fury of local whites when they were confronted by an Indian who refused to back down and assume the subservient posture they expected of us. I was simply demanding a fair deal for myself and local families like the Tomats and Wilsons, who were also renting lands to trailer park owners, something that up to that point had always been refused us. And for that they would come after me with a vengeance.

CHAPTER 6

Finding My Footing

While my family was engaged in the struggle to gain reserve status for Westbank in the early 1960s, we were also linked to the larger provincial and national Indian movement that was beginning to gain traction in the 1970s. One of the links was our support for the great Secwépemc leader George Manuel, Arthur Manuel's father, who in the late 1950s and early 1960s was a rising regional leader in Andy Paull's North American Indian Brotherhood. George was from Neskonlith Reserve across from Chase, B.C., and on weekends, when he was off from his job as boom man on the South Thomson River, he would travel the Interior preaching the gospel of resistance that called for self-determination and self-reliance for Indigenous peoples and fought for our long-denied land rights. When he was in the Okanagan, George often stayed overnight at our house. We would feed him and my father would pass the hat around the community to try to help him on his way.

George Manuel's support grew throughout the 1960s and by 1969, he was recognized as one of the most forceful leaders in the country. When the federal government released its infamous White Paper that threatened to remove our Indian status, George Manuel was catapulted into the role of president of the newly formed National Indian Brotherhood to fight it. That same year, a group of young radicals, which included his son Bobby, launched the Union of B.C. Indian Chiefs to fight on the land question in the province, where very few of our people had ever signed treaties. The union was pushing a radical plan at the time to make our people completely independent from Indian Affairs and the Canadian government and return to our status as self-governing Nations.

That spirit was going through our community as well, and there was a sense that we needed to seize the day. Despite having won reserve status for Westbank in 1963, five years later, not very much was happening. We remained one of the poorest reserves in Canada. The young people would meet at the local greasy spoon and talk about what changes we wanted to see, but it seemed that our community was still going nowhere. A few of us had gone down to Victoria to the Indian Affairs district office to see about the new economic development programs, but our council was not seizing the initiative. And it was clear from the attitude of the bureaucrats we dealt with that it would take strong community leadership and real determination to shake the apples from the tree.

My brother Noll was at the forefront of this little informal group of young community members. It was typical of him that while others were renting their land to outsiders to develop, he was launching his own business to compete with them — in his case, building his own trailer park to compete with the Crosbys and their ilk.

Noll was always a man of action. In 1966, when he was a newly elected band councillor, he made an important gesture by going out to Peachland Creek to fish for salmon in a symbolic protest of the fish and game law restrictions on our people. When he caught a Kokanee, he was arrested by the fish and game warden and hauled off to jail. He was never put in the cell, because the Anglican priest prevented it. And there was already a crowd of people and TV cameras outside, so the police quickly booked him for illegal fishing and set him free with a court date. I remember feeling very proud of my brother at that moment, and his case became an important one in Aboriginal rights, travelling all the way to the Supreme Court along with Bobby Manuel's case, in which he was charged with hunting deer without a licence.

It was in 1968, when our impatience at the council's wheel-spinning under Chief Norman Lindley reached its limit, that Noll decided to run against him in the band election. It was on a platform of pushing the type of development programs in the community that would lift our people out of poverty and make us once again economically self-sufficient.

To Noll's surprise, he won the election. Norman Lindley accepted defeat gracefully and he even agreed to stay on as a councillor to work with my brother. Later they would have a falling out over a rumour that Noll was up to something with Norman's wife — the usual reason for feuds in small communities everywhere and for all time — and even though the story wasn't true, it wasn't until Norman was an old man that he learned that Noll was innocent and went over to apologize to him. These accusations weren't that unusual for Noll, because he was a very handsome young guy and always received more attention from the local ladies than he could handle. He really was the type of person that attracted attention in a political sense as well. You could see this at any public event, when journalists would gravitate to him. Noll was also an original in every way. He even used a different spelling of our last name "Derriksan" because he thought it fit better with the Okanagan language.

As chief, Noll became one of the founders of the Union of B.C. Indian Chiefs, but his priorities were local. He was determined to forge ahead in laying the groundwork for future band development and started the process of building the community infrastructure that was necessary for moving forward.

A new band development strategy was put together with a policy framework that would allow the band government to move ahead on development projects. According to this new policy, designated reserve lands should be used as the basis to establish a viable economic and social environment for the community, and employment opportunities for band members would be one of the key objectives. In land rentals, both band and private transactions would be encouraged.

Indian Affairs responded by asking that the band adopt a policy of having a portion of revenues from private land leases shared with the band, but this caused considerable controversy. After much discussion, the proposal was put to a vote on October 21, 1971, and by a decisive tally of 44 to two, band members decided that locatees should have the right to retain all revenue from land leases.

The most important achievement of Noll's stint as chief was the launch of the Westbank Indian Band Development Corporation. This would become the major income-generating tool for the band, and it was set up with an appointed board that answered to the council. With the development corporation in place, Noll started making preparations with the Lakeridge development group to develop and lease reserve land for a major housing development.

The plan Noll put together in 1973 called for the lands in Reserve 10 to be developed as a planned community, while Reserve 9 would be used for band housing as well as agricultural and recreational purposes. The Lakeridge Park development was the first big project Noll created. It began with the band leasing a large block of lands above Lake Okanagan to the Westbank Indian Band Development Company, which then undertook to develop the subdivision with a group of private sector contractors.

The development company would obtain revenue directly from subleases of individual lots. The project was to be financed by way of conventional financing, including long-term residential mortgages. It was conceived as a high-quality residential development, and that is how it played out. But not without some serious bumps along the way.

To make sure that the project had buy-in from the community, Noll held a referendum on it and in January 1974, band members voted in favour of surrendering 177.3 acres of Reserve 10 lands for a 99-year lease. It looked like the way was open and the first homes were already built when suddenly the whole project was put in jeopardy as the overheated Kelowna-area housing market suddenly went cold on the idea of buying long-term leaseholds on reserve land. When the banks saw this, financing immediately dried up and the project teetered on bankruptcy. Instead of bringing resources into the band, it was slowly sinking us deeper and deeper into debt. Noll's position became even more complicated when the trailer park he had launched on his own was also being squeezed for financing and was looking like it was going to default on its loans before it was able to fully open and begin generating revenue.

It was a tough year for him. He had easily won re-election in 1970 and 1972, but by the time 1974 rolled around, fears about the collapse of the Lakeridge development project sank him. He lost the 1974 election and was replaced by a returning Norman Lindley. But once again, Norman was not up to the task of solving the business issues faced by the community. There was a sense in 1974 that the community was adrift while it was slowly but steadily sinking from the Lakeridge debts.

I had been following Noll's adventures and later misadventures on council and I had a lot of sympathy for what he was going through. But in the early 1970s, my life was taken up by my ranch. In fact, my two ranches. I had purchased an additional 640 acres of ranchland at Salmon River with a lease on 28,000 of grazing land. This was all in addition to the 100-acre purchase and 20,000-acre grazing lease for Derrickson Cattle.

But in the late summer of 1975, all of the hard work and extraordinarily long hours literally paid off. Beef prices reached a historical high that summer and this coincided with a high point in my herd. When I counted my heifers and multiplied that number by the price offered for beef, I realized that I could make a fortune if I sold it off. I also looked at revenues I was making in some of my leases and entrepreneurial endeavours and I made a business decision to sell my entire herd.

It took 25 double-cattle trucks to clear out the herd, with some heading to Alberta and others down the coast. I also sold a large portion of my ranchlands. The New Democratic Party had passed the Agricultural Land Reserve Act in 1975, which limited the sale of agricultural land, but there was a loophole that allowed you to sell a minimum of 60 acres at a time. Fortunately, there was a market for this size of holding in the back to the landers, an outgrowth of the 1960s hippie culture, who were flooding into the Okanagan region. So I subdivided much of the Salmon River ranch into 60-acre parcels and sold them to the young hippie families, making sure that each parcel had enough trees on it to build a log house and a barn. In the end, through the sale of the cattle and the farmland, I made $1.6 million — the equivalent of close to $10 million today. For the first time in my life, I had the capital I needed to begin to seriously develop my lands and business interests.

One of the things I did that would pay great dividends later was increase my purchases of land along the rocky shore of Lake Okanagan. The land was not considered at the time to be of great value, but over time, as I acquired up to a mile of lakeshore properties, it would become my greatest wealth generator.

It was not only through leasing, though. Over time, I would develop a very lucrative marina and fuel stop and in the 1970s, I operated the Pier Pub, one of the busiest bar/restaurants in the Okanagan, on land that I purchased when I was only 19 years old. The restaurant got its reputation from the unbelievable deals I would offer, like $9.95 for a pound of king crab and five-cent chicken wings. I made money because I bought king crab from an Indigenous fishing company up in Alaska and I charged for extras, like French fries, which I spiced up with a bit of cajun seasoning so beer sales soared. That was how the game was played, and I was good at it. I am still in the restaurant business through the bar and grill called Nineteen, which I own as part of the Two Eagles Golf Course & Academy.

At the time that I was selling my ranches and experimenting in new business opportunities, the B.C. Interior was caught up in political turmoil. B.C. native youth had begun a series of massive protests against the colonial system and the paternalism of the Department of Indian Affairs. On May 1, 1975, Indigenous activists in B.C. launched simultaneous occupations of Department of Indian Affairs district offices in Kamloops, Williams Lake and Vernon.

The Kamloops takeover, led by Tk'emlúps te Secwépemc Chief Mary Leonard attracted 100 supporters from the 25 bands in the Thompson-Nicola region, while the Williams Lake takeover drew 160 participants from the 15 bands in that area. Support quickly spread across the province with occupations at the Bella Coola and Nanaimo offices beginning shortly after. Organized locally to promote a wider single goal, activists planned for the occupations to continue until the federal government agreed to negotiate on the land issue, and until Department of Indian Affairs permanently closed its offices and ceased to exist. This insurrection spread quickly to the DIA offices in Winnipeg, Vancouver, Regina and Ottawa.

In Kamloops, the occupation turned into a complete shutdown of the office when the Public Service Alliance refused to cross the Indigenous picket line. As the shutdown continued, DIA offices began to see the situation as permanent and began to arrange for district staff to be retrained and relocated to other government agencies.

By September, activists succeeded in closing the offices in Kamloops and Vernon with DIA transferring administration to the 30 respective band councils throughout the Thompson River and Kootenay-Okanagan districts. Ultimately, the occupations and resulting disruption to DIA services allowed many communities to envision governance unfettered by Department considerations, and this was a powerful boon to sovereignty.

The occupations also extended to the regional Department of Indian Affairs office in downtown Vancouver, where Indigenous leaders and activists and 100 AIM members from across the province came together to shut down the regional office. The *Vancouver Sun* described the Vancouver or "Black Tower" occupation as noisy but peaceful, with an AIM security force maintaining order by allowing Department staff to move freely, banning drugs and alcohol from the premises and restricting the occupation to Department offices only.

Viewing all of these occupations as expressions of Indigenous sovereignty, participants argued that, in the absence of fully functioning offices, Indian Affairs no longer had a purpose, and its budget should be returned to the bands to administer. As a step on this road, the Union of B.C. Indian Chiefs urged their members to refuse to administer DIA programs and services on their reserve. Instead, they demanded the resources to design and implement their own programs in their own way.

This could have worked as a pressure tactic, but in their enthusiasm to get to direct action, the UBCIC organizers skipped a few crucial steps. In immediately refusing government funding, they left the most vulnerable in their communities — those who depended on government assistance — without the basics of survival. The spirit of the protest was good, but the adults seemed to have left the room when it came to building a transition period into the process, where they could demand a step-by-step transfer of wealth, settlement of land issues and the community investment needed to rebuild Indigenous economies after a century of the most devastating colonial control and enforced poverty.

In Westbank we were watching this very closely, especially when our people closed the Vernon office. My brother Noll at the time was not impressed with the activism. But I liked what I saw in the spirit of resistance, even though I recognized that at the time, we were not ready to make a great leap forward. We had to learn how to make measured steps first.

One of the important outcomes from this was that the Department of Indian Affairs was suddenly taking our immediate issues much more seriously and were accelerating transfer of programs and services to the bands to administer. They were also increasing economic development programs as a way to get buy-in from the less radical band leadership, and they largely succeeded in marginalizing the radicals and using their bag of goodies to stabilize the situation.

In Westbank, we had one enormous economic problem and that was the stalled Lakeridge development. Again, as an economic chief, Norman Lindley was out of his depth. He had been unable to move the development forward and the delays were driving the community deeper into debt every day. I spoke about this with many in the community and they were looking for someone with business sense who could either get the development moving or, if it wasn't salvageable, take action to kill it and repossess the land. Noll was definitely not running. He had done what he could and now he was struggling with his own business interests.

I looked closely at the finances. The Lakeridge development plan called for housing 9,000 people on 173 acres of the Reserve 10 lands. The target date to get things moving had been May 1, 1974. But it was already approaching autumn of 1976 and the development was frozen. The community debt had passed $3 million and it was still climbing. In these circumstances, it was not surprising that no one had put their name forward to run for chief. Who needed the aggravation? And who could afford it?

The sale of my herds and my ranch made me one of the most financially comfortable people on the reserve. I could afford to take on the basically unpaid job and I was urged to do so by many in the community. Perhaps as a substitute for death-defying risks of hydroplane boat racing, I agreed to put my name forward.

In the end, I would be elected and re-elected five times during that initial run and I would manage to transform Westbank from one of the poorest to one of the most economically successful bands in Canada, increasing its revenues by 3,500 percent in my first six years in office. But as mentioned, being band chief turned out to be a death-defying act for me that was capped off by a Royal Commission into my affairs. Even for a speedboat champion, this would turn out to be one hell of a ride.

CHAPTER 7

Entering the Fray

A week before the election, when council nominations were closed, I was the only one on the ballot for chief. Looking at this optimistically, I thought it must mean that the people in my community knew I was the man for the job — cleaning up Westbank's finances and getting the major projects moving so they could begin to lift us out of poverty. Part of the encouragement I felt came from the support I received from Norman Lindley, who I replaced in the job. Even though he didn't have the business skills, Norman was a strong community pillar and remained a friend and a confidant until the day he died.

But in my more clear-eyed moments I knew that the reason I was unopposed on the chief's list was that no one wanted the job. No one wanted to captain a ship that was foundering in debt and sinking under the weight of the Lakeridge housing development of half-finished houses with no prospective buyers and the credit tap turned off.

On election night, I went to the school gym where the voting for the two councillors was taking place. I was happy to see that my cousin, Bill Derrickson, and Albert Wilson Sr. were elected — Albert in particular. He had no political experience, but he was a salt-of-the-earth guy and I knew that he was someone I should listen to because he would represent the many people in our community who were struggling to survive the day-to-day. That evening when we met after the vote, I told him, "Albert, if there is something we are doing that you don't like, just tell me and we won't do it."

I kept my word and he did a great job in keeping the council real. Unfortunately, he stayed for only one term because, he told me, the political life was not for him.

Billy Derrickson was also an asset. He was a very good administrator and was responsible for our social programs. After a certain time in council, though, he became less disciplined. When he was receiving honorariums and expenses from both the band and from the government, I insisted he pay the band back. When he refused, I had no choice but to force him to resign. But typical of Billy, he then showed up at my house with his brother and his father to fistfight me on the issue. He was no better a fighter than a politician, and his father and his brother had to carry him home.

One of the things that disturbed me about the election was the extremely low turnout. It was apparent from the people I spoke to that the community had little hope that we could succeed. That was one of the worst problems we faced. Deep in their hearts, Indians in Canada generally believed the horrible racism that had been oppressing them for the past century. We believed that the white man was, indeed, better than us, that we were incapable of succeeding and our poverty and wretchedness was not the result of the fact that 99.8 percent of our land was stolen from us. We were under occupation from a heartless imperial power, but the feeling was that it was caused by some inadequacy in ourselves. This, after all, is when the oppressor really wins — when they convince the oppressed that their wretched condition is entirely their own fault.

In Westbank, the brief hope of the Lakebridge development was already dashed in most people's minds and they were thinking, how were we so stupid as to think we could accomplish anything? You could see this in the way our people dealt with the white man, with fear and the belief that the white man was smarter than us, to the point our people kept their eyes on the ground when we were forced to speak to them. From my earliest days, I refused to show this fear, even if I felt it. I have always looked everyone in the eye, and I think this was seen as an affront by many racist white people who expected an Indian to cower before them.

By the time I took over in October 1976, the community was again stuck in this sense of apathy and fatalism that had made us so easy to control for most of the 20th century. But despite the low expectations of those around me, I was determined to do a good job. I have a competitive spirit and the fact that others had failed before me didn't disillusion me but spurred me on. Just like in business, it is never the money that inspires me. It's the challenge of finding solutions to problems and turning a losing proposition into a winning one that gives me the rush. Money, as they say, is just how you keep score.

I certainly had not signed on to be chief because of the glamour of the job. At the time, the band council office was a rundown trailer with an oil heater that gave off a heavy petrol smell and threw black soot over everything. My first salary was under $500 a month and I knew the job would take all the time and all of the skills that I could bring to it. So I would arrive at the trailer at 7 a.m. each weekday morning and leave, on many evenings, at 10 or 11 p.m. I quickly learned that there were no "after-hours" for a chief. You were on call seven days a week, 24 hours a day, from distraught mothers of missing children, band members with emergency health needs, parents worried about kids picked up by the police and all the weddings and funerals in the community.

As band chief, your time is no longer your own. My friend Arthur Manuel wrote about this in *Unsettling Canada: A National Wake-up Call.* "As chief, you are expected to be present in the lives of band members from cradle to grave. This includes celebrations like graduations and weddings, and sad events like funerals. The chief is called when a band member is arrested and when a band member succumbs to despair and commits suicide. You are responsible for housing your people and for difficult issues involving child welfare, and for dealing with racial attacks on your children in white schools. And for so many other issues that it is impossible to list them — everything from protecting archaeological sites to hosting visitors."

One issue that I saw needed attention as soon as I began was the gaps and inconsistencies in the business regulations on the reserve, some of which allowed many of the outside renters to take advantage of us. But before I could begin to address the longer-term issues I had to face the immediate one, the elephant in the room — the Lakeridge development.

The few houses that were constructed were simply not selling and cost overruns on the project had led to the banks turning off the credit lines. At the time, we couldn't even pay the interest on our debt. What was needed was either some dramatic action to get the project relaunched or to abandon it completely and file for bankruptcy. This last was not a course of action I wanted to follow, but it was one I was prepared to take. I had to do whatever was necessary to get this financial millstone off our necks.

Indian Affairs had encouraged the Lakeridge project through its new economic development fund, and I went to Vancouver to meet with Fred Walchli, the regional director general of Indian Affairs, to look at the options. What I found in Fred, to my great surprise, was an ally and eventually a good friend. At the time, he was in his early forties and a career civil servant. He was from Prince George, but he had worked for the City of Kelowna before joining Indian Affairs in Alberta and had risen rapidly to become the Alberta director general before being transferred to the head job in B.C. At the time, downloading programs and services to Indian control was the official objective at Indian Affairs, but it was more often than not carried out at the most superficial level — transferring responsibility but not power. This made it very frustrating to deal with them, because they gave you an open path through the laws, then strangled you with restrictive policies and regulations. It has always been my complaint that Indians are controlled by 5 percent law and 95 percent policy.

Fred Walchli understood this, and he was willing to cut back on the restrictive policies to give you breathing room where you could do what you had to do. This immediately became apparent on the Lakeridge file. In our meeting, I laid out all the possibilities and told him we had to act fast and take a big gamble if we wanted to save the development. Otherwise, we should just put it into bankruptcy and move on. Fred surprised me by letting me know that I was the boss — if I wanted to try to save the development, he was happy to give me a free hand to act. I could shape the deal and write up the leases in any way that would help me move the properties. Legally, he had to sign them, but that would be it. He would sign any of the third-party deals that I made.

After the Walchli meeting I tried to buy time with the bankers and other creditors by quickly selling two of the completed houses at fire-sale prices — less than $100,000 each — to give me the money I needed to pay the interest on the debt. With that in hand, the bankers and creditors agreed to give me time to try to save the rest of the project and they freed up a little more money to restart construction.

I knew that the problem in selling the units had been the reluctance of home buyers to buy a house on reserve land — something that was a new concept at the time. What I needed was some kind of distraction. So I began putting together a package of bells and whistles that would divert their attention from the reserve issue and put it on the great product we were offering. In relaunching the promotional campaign for the houses, we offered five years of o percent interest on the mortgages. Each house would include a dishwasher and a compact washer/dryer and, the icing on the cake, a Volkswagen in the driveway. All of these things were easily paid for by a modest bump-up in the 20-year mortgage price, but for the buyers it seemed like a load of free stuff. Almost overnight, people forgot about the fact that they were buying into a house on leased reserve land, and focused on the packet of goodies I was offering.

The houses began to move. Not at a crawl, but in a flash. Suddenly, we were shipping out the 99-year leases 10 at a time for Fred Walchli to sign. That first year, we sold 159 units — that's more houses than were sold in the rest of the Okanagan district combined that year — and we completely cleared off our $3 million debt with total revenues of around $10 million. Lakeridge, from being a drag on our meagre resources, was transformed into an important revenue generator.

The effect was like a tonic on our community. The sense that we were perennial losers in the white man's game instantly began to change. Our people had set up the deal and finally had made it a success. Without help from outside. This was not charity, this was our initiative and it gave us the first taste of what self-reliance felt like.

With the Lakeridge project returning dividends, I turned my attention to ensuring we had the infrastructure in place so the community could fully profit from the land lease opportunities. My objective was to establish a land-use policy framework and provide a process that would serve as a guide to the band council, locatees and developers. To accomplish this, I began to research the types of by-laws we would need to create a framework of law and ensure consistency.

This process had been started under Noll with the creation of the Westbank Development Company, and we extended this in our new strategy, which encouraged economic development not only by the band, but also by individual band members and outside commercial interests. Our new strategy called for cash flow that was generated by the band to be used to finance improved social programming for the membership. We also put a priority on close liaison with the surrounding non-Indian communities so we could share in regional development. Above all, we determined that all band affairs (business and government) would be operated on a sound businesslike basis.

An important part of this plan was our priority on membership involvement in the affairs of the band government. This was essential in our parallel community planning process — that along with aggressively developing our economic interests on lands designated for that purpose, we included the conservation of all of the existing natural features of the reserve, in the development of a functional community that met both the spiritual and physical needs of our people.

For this to work, the membership had to be involved in all decision-making and we made a conscious effort to ensure this. Weekly band council meetings were open to all band members. In addition, general band meetings were held three or four times a year. At these meetings, policy issues were discussed, reports were provided by the chief and councillors on their areas of program responsibility and the membership was encouraged to question, to voice opinions and to make suggestions. When we reached the point that we were able to make annual cash allotments to the membership, the criteria for eligibility was that they had participated in the affairs of the band. So, the woman who came each week to criticize everything we were doing and denounce the chief and the councillors at every turn would get a cash allotment, but the guy who took no interest in the band affairs and never showed up for band meeting would not. That is how much we valued participation in band affairs.

We continued to expand the list of band-owned companies and set up two companies related to the Lakeridge development — Lakeridge Realty and Lakeridge Management. A spinoff from that was the WIBCO Construction Ltd. We also set up the Sookinshute Utility Co.

The band adopted a firm policy of business discipline to manage these assets. Books of financial accounts were kept current and the band auditors provided monthly statements for the council on Indian-owned businesses, both band- and individually owned.

The one area where difficulties were arising was in the lands rented for trailer parks. I was having to deal with the resentful Mr. Crosby on a too-frequent basis, even though I had offered to cut him loose from his misery by buying out his lease. Both he and the York family, who rented land from Noll for their Westview Village Mobile Home Park, always seemed to be simmering, and at times seething, with unhappiness at having to deal with Indians. What they refused to accept was reality. The land surrounding Kelowna was increasing in value significantly every year, and that meant that at the end of the five-year period of most leases, the increases would be substantial. These values were set by market forces, but it was painful for the local racists to be forced to give a fair price to Indians.

But my biggest headache at the time was the Toussowasket trailer park owned by my brother.

The property, at the edge of Reserve 9 adjacent to Highway 97, had originally been incorporated by Noll and my mother in 1971, but Noll didn't start to develop it until after he was out of office. In 1974, he hired Heritage Realty Projects Ltd. from Vernon to oversee it and Heritage Realty proposed that financing be provided by means of an Indian Economic Development Fund (IEDF) loan, as well as a loan from the Federal Business Development Bank (FBDB). Heritage was controlled by a guy called Weir, who had previously been the land use officer at the Vernon district office of the Department of Indian Affairs, so he had an inside track on the Indian Affairs development money and understood that the Kelowna area had a big market for mobile home parks. Using his connections, Weir managed to secure financing with the FBDB in the first security position and IEDF in second.

But Heritage quickly ran into cost overruns, and when the first part of the mobile home park was completed, the debts were mounting. Worse news came when the booming mobile home market went bust because of excess capacity. This was a temporary situation, but it happened at the worst time, when the now debt-heavy company needed to begin bringing in revenues to keep it afloat while construction on the rest of the park was completed.

The debt obligations at that time were substantial. There was approximately $195,000 owed to the IEDF and approximately $170,000 owed to the FBDB. Noll had guaranteed payment of all of the former and a part of the latter. The amount of money he contributed to this project by way of equity injection was $40,000, in addition to providing the land to the project that at the time had an uncertain value.

The crisis for Noll came in the beginning of 1977, when Indian Affairs refused an additional $50,000 in emergency financing to the project because, as they saw it, "the present financing exceeds the projected ability of the project to pay both principal and interest."

Up to this point, I had nothing at all to do with the project and I was happy to keep it that way. My first impulse when I looked at the situation was to suggest to Noll that he simply declare bankruptcy and wrap it up. He would lose his capital, but he would have the land back free and clear of debt.

But then Fred Walchli showed up at my office. He had refused Noll the $50,000 loan but he did not want to see the project go under. The reason was that the FBDB loan was the first time the federal bank had made a loan to a project on Indian land, and he wanted to make sure that they didn't burn that source of capital for the future. He had seen how I had turned around the Lakeridge development and believed I could do it with Toussowasket.

I still favoured Noll simply pulling the plug, but Walchli had been good to me and I agreed to help. But I was also distracted during this period by the death of my grandfather and the break-up of my marriage.

I would miss my grandfather greatly. In his later years, I would take him across the river to the local rodeo and he was often visiting me and my children, his great-grandchildren, at my house. Both of my children adored him. He liked to tell the story of Kelly asking why a village Elder died.

He said, "He died because he got old."

Kelly replied, "Well, why aren't you dead then?"

He roared with laughter. His life was, indeed, coming to an end. But he kept his sense of humour and vitality until his final days.

My strongest memory of him during this period is an amazing hunting trip that began and ended in his driveway. Me, my uncle Curley and my uncle Richard had met at Grampa's house on a Saturday morning to go on a hunt with him. While we were having tea, Curley went out to saddle the horses. A few minutes later, he returned and motioned us outside. A big bull moose was standing at the end of the driveway 100 feet from the house. Old Mickey took his rifle and laid it across the saddle and shot. The bull moose dropped to the ground.

"I am so old," my grampa said, "the great spirit has to send the moose to my door." We spent the rest of the morning cutting up the animal and filling up freezers around the community with the meat. That night we feasted, but a few days later my grandfather was gone.

Later, I would hear from my uncle Dave the bizarre news that Mickey Derrickson was not really my grandfather. According to my uncle, he couldn't have children and that all of the children his wife, my grandma Julia, bore were from different men. Uncle Dave said that the man who fathered my father was a guy called Brady Steel. Whether true or not, for me, this changed nothing. Mickey Derrickson was my grandfather in every way and I miss him still.

This was the time of personal losses. My marriage was also on the rocks in this period. I remained on friendly terms with my wife and a good father to Doug and Kelly, but to be honest, I probably wasn't a great husband.

After the marriage, I embraced single life again and it was a time when women and men were breaking out of old relationship moulds. The extent of this kind of socializing hit home to me one morning when one of the office secretaries asked me where I lived, because I seemed to be arriving from a different direction every morning. That was how it was in those days, but people were not judgmental — nothing like the furrowed brows and finger-wagging that we subject one another to today. People were less afraid of both pleasure and pain and accepted life on its own terms.

CHAPTER 8

Building a Future, Fighting the Past

The Toussowasket deal was one that would come back to haunt me. The rescue package I put together with Fred Walchli to save Noll's mobile home park was not designed to save him, but to save the Indian Economic Development Fund and Federal Business Development Bank funds that were tied up in the deal. The plan called for Indian Affairs to loan the band funds to buy into Toussowasket and in return, Toussowasket would sign over half of the park to the band. This would give Noll the capital to complete construction and get the operating revenues he needed to keep afloat while things picked up in the local real estate market. In return, the band would get equity in the company that it could sell later at, presumably, a profit and pay Indian Affairs back in full, with bank interest, on their loan to us.

At first it was Noll who refused to go along. Harold Derrickson, who was on council, and I went over to Noll's house to present the plan. Noll said he did not want the band meddling in his affairs and he certainly did not want to end up in a business partnership where the band moved in and took 50 percent of his property. The argument grew heated and he threw us out. My brother is the type who often has a strong initial reaction, but if you give him time to think about it, he will usually come around. So he contacted my other counsellor, Brian Eli, and said he would, finally, discuss the possibility. When Brian told me this I said, fine, but I'm not going over there again. So we made the deal with Brian as the middleman who would negotiate with Noll, then come back to me for approval. The first agreement that Brian negotiated I wouldn't agree to. He kept running back and forth until we had something hammered out. And one of the conditions was that Noll would not handle the invested funds. They would be handled directly by the band.

The final deal included not only the parcel of land the trailer park was on, which was Lot 32-2, but it also included the part that was not developed, 32-2-1, and an option to acquire Lot 33-1. A contribution agreement was entered into between the Department of Indian Affairs and the Westbank Indian Band, whereby the Department agreed to contribute to the band up to $300,000 over a period of three years. The band agreed to undertake liability for 100 percent of the IEDF loan and to undertake liability for 50 percent of the FBDB loan and 50 percent of Noll Derriksan's guarantee. The band would do the deal through the Westbank Indian Band Development Company, which would be the actual purchaser of the half interest in the lease.

It was a deal where everyone won. Noll did not have to declare bankruptcy, so the government funders were paid back on their loans and the band eventually got its investment back through the sale of its interests back to Noll when the market picked up. And on the land swap, the band would exit the deal with a parcel of land that today is worth $200 million. All this was done in close association with the Department of Indian Affairs — in fact, much of it was done at their behest. But the deal would come back to haunt me when a group of our white renters began to feed stories to the press of the Derrickson brothers siphoning off Indian Affairs funds to their private businesses, and the whisper campaign against me began.

The initial source was not hard to identify. In September 1981, the band sent a bill for development fees, road and other improvements that benefited their property to Crosby's Park Mobile. The bill was based on an amount calculated in the band by-law for development fees, and in the case of Park Mobile it came to $14,500. The trailer park renters association went ballistic. They not only refused to pay but they began a full-frontal attack on me within Indian Affairs and in the press.

Even in this initial period, it had some effect. In the spring of 1982, we were scheduled to receive the first $200,000 investment for the Toussowasket deal. But an Indian Affairs official in Ottawa, Ernie Hobbs, sent a telex to Walchli in Vancouver advising him not to disburse the remaining funds under that agreement until the matter had been fully reviewed. This was a potential disaster for the deal, because we were only two weeks from the end of the government's fiscal year and if the funds were not paid out before April 1, they would disappear and there was no guarantee they would be reallocated the next year.

I called on Len Marchand, who was no longer in Parliament and not yet in the Senate but who still had a lot of clout in government circles. Along with support from Chief Antoine from the Coldwater Band and Chief Moses from the Lower Nicola Band, we met in Walchli's Vancouver office for a conference call with Hobbs, where Walchli and I described the architecture of the deal. By the end of the call, Hobbs was satisfied and he said Walchli was free to release the money if he received an OK from his boss, Donald Goodwin, who was the assistant deputy minister of the Department. Walchli got the OK and the money was paid out just days before the end of the fiscal year. But for me, it was a warning shot that people were working inside Indian Affairs to block me.

During this period, I was slowly putting together a team of people I could trust. One of my real estate go-to guys was an independent appraiser named Rod Cook, who worked with Kent Macpherson Appraisals, and who I would consult when determining rents and mortgages. He was young and very bright and good-natured even though I would argue with him every step of the way, trying to get him to up his appraisals. Part of his good nature, I suppose, came from the fact that he won every argument we had and they would generally finish with him saying in exasperation, "My job is to appraise what is actually there." If I kept pushing, he would remind me that his AACI accreditation, which referred to the Accredited Appraiser Canadian Institute, "did not mean mean Appraised According to Client Instructions!" Once, when I persisted, he even called me a "bonehead." I liked him because he was always straight with me, and when he came up with a number, it was solid. He could back it up with a mountain of paper.

Another consultant who I could trust completely was Graham Allen, the Vancouver lawyer who looked after the band's leasing issues and who lobbied with us with DIA to increase our control over band finances. I had met him around 1979, when I became involved in the so-called Alliance of three other bands — Musqueum, Squamish and the Sechelt — who were also trying to wrest greater control of their affairs from the government. Graham was the legal advisor and then counsel for the group, and he also came in to serve as the legal counsel for us in Westbank.

We were part of a very hard-working crew and the band office could, at times, be a high-pressure situation. But in my life I have always tried to keep things on the lighter side and part of the survival mechanism in the office was to make sure that everyone had their say. My job was to make the final decision, but I wanted people who had a point of view and weren't afraid to speak it. Although even those limits were tested. I had an excellent secretary, Deborah Bergen, and when she was preparing an urgent report for me, I kept interrupting her as I recalled other urgent things I needed her to do. Once, she threw up her hands and said, "Ron, will you fuck off!"

The air went out of the room and everyone waited for my response. Deborah was looking at me fearfully. But of course I understood the pressure she was under, and what a difficult balancing act it was to keep up with her inhuman workload.

"Deborah," I said, "This is it! Show some respect. Next time, it better be 'Fuck off, *sir.*'"

The office relaxed. That is how I always wanted it: everyone working hard, but supporting each other as we went along. And making sure there was time for fun.

Certainly there was enough to keep us busy. Throughout the struggle to keep Toussowasket afloat to pay off its government debts, I was looking at the whole issue of reserve leases and quickly saw that both in the band leases and the individual leases to outside interests we were getting hosed. Part of the reason for this was that our leases had to be approved by Indian Affairs and they were approving fire-sale leases on our lands. Our people accepted this in a system that had always told them that they were dumb and whites were smart and we could never really stand up to them to demand more. So I began to lobby on behalf of all leaseholders for getting rid of the land and leasing authority at Indian Affairs so we could reset all of our leases to something that approached fair market value.

The white tenants fought just as hard on the other side, fiercely lobbying Indian Affairs to preserve the system that so massively favoured them. This meant that we were always in court. Graham would fly in from Vancouver for a day or two a week and leave burdened with leases and other files, and would often accompany me in my most difficult and sensitive negotiations to try and get us the right to run our own affairs.

To push the issue along, I enacted a resolution creating our own in-house director of lands to set rents on our reserve, a measure that was quickly disallowed by the Department. But we insisted we would no longer accept their system and we were supported by an article that was published in a Vancouver newspaper that said that the provincial rentalsman had no right on Indian reserves. As the headline put it, "B.C. Rentalsman Scalped by Indian Act." I sent the article around to the renters on our land and announced that I would represent the lease owners in their negotiations with their tenants. As one report put it, this led to "howls of outrage" by the renters, particularly from the mobile park owners who began accusing me of trying to bankrupt them so I could take over their businesses. This was nonsense. I only wanted a fair deal for our people. It was only later, when the trailer park renters actually took out a contract on my life and hired an assassin that I decided to be done with them and I turned their fears into reality.

The head of the Westbank Mobile Park Association was my own troublesome renter, Leonard Crosby. In what turned out to be an ominous move, a flurry of complaints were lodged with the local Conservative members of Parliament and with the Department of Indian Affairs, where Crosby made sure I was personally targeted. The offensive began in the local media, where suddenly dark motives were being attributed to everything I did to try to improve the life of band members. Then, to my surprise, local Conservative MPs, like Cariboo-Chilcotin MP Lorne Greenaway, began to denounce me in front of the Standing Committee on Indian Affairs in Ottawa, zeroing in on the deal with my brother's trailer park as proof of my perfidy:

"So here is Noll Derriksan, obviously one of the favourite sons of paternalists in Vancouver. He is having a lot of trouble repaying his loan. In fact, he has not made a payment on it, either in principal or in interest. So the situation gets rather difficult and dicey. Then you get a lawyer who suggests as [Noll] is not only unable to repay your loan, but is also having trouble satisfying his other creditors that you make another loan, this time to the Indian band. Incidentally, the chief of the band at that point is the brother to Noll, Ron Derrickson, whom I see has received money from time to time, at least in one instance to travel with you to Ottawa. I see an expenditure of $4,000 travel expenses to that particular person. The notion was kicked around, that the department should make another loan, this time to Ron Derrickson, on behalf of the band.

This is the story I got, so you might be able to fill me in. If that is true and that coincides with facts, or if it is even close, you know, of course, that this is highly irregular, if not illegal, in terms of the constraints of the Financial Administration Act."

Fred King, Conservative MP from Okanagan–Similkameen, continued the attacks, accusing me of illegally raising the rents on the non-Indian leaseholders, moving to darker accusations that I was stealing money from the community and from Indian Affairs, and he began to demand that the Department of Indian Affairs carry out a forensic audit on all of the band's activities. DIA Minister John Munro resisted, saying he could not call an inquiry on the "flimsy stuff" the opposition was raising as evidence against me and pointed out that Westbank was thoroughly audited every year and always received a clean bill of health.

But the opposition was relentless on these types of ad hominem attacks, which were picked up and added to in the local press, until the government relented and commissioned and promised to publish an extensive review of the band under my stewardship. When the report, entitled "Some Indicators of Change in Westbank 1971/72–1981/82," was published, it gave no solace to my detractors. In fact, the report showed that the band had made a great leap forward under my and Noll's leadership, and it pointed to my term as an example of dramatic progress for the community.

When the report looked first at our planning process, it noted "that the Westbank plan compares most favourably with that of any other community in British Columbia. The approaches employed by Westbank could be used as a model for other communities in the province." It was particularly impressed by our "sound balance of commercial and people development; our twenty-year phased approach to development; and the incorporation of the community plan into the Band by-law structure."

In community housing, the report showed that in my six years in office, the number of Reserve Housing Units more than doubled, with the average age of homes on the reserve now only four years old. The average size of the houses increased from 800 square feet to 1,100 square feet. All of the houses on reserve now have full services of electricity, septic tanks and running water — an increase from 25 percent of the homes to 100 percent. The percentage of houses with telephones increased from 20 percent to 100 percent. Fire protection went from 0 to 70 percent.

The band housing had all been done under my term. I had gone to the Bank of Montreal to get the financing for our house-building spree and the Western Canada director, who was one of the rare women leaders in the system, took a chance on us and lent us the money. By March 31, 1982, 24 new band homes were built and the pace continued throughout my term. By 1986, the number of band member housing units had grown to 84, from 26 in 1972.

Taking care of our people was really what I was about. And when I did bend the rules it was to make sure we had the community supports that our people needed. For example, Indian Affairs refused my project to build a high-quality retirement home for our Elders, but I found the money elsewhere and built it anyway. On a smaller scale, I pushed the program limits to get Norman Lindley a housing grant that he might not have been totally eligible for. Looking back, these moments — supporting your people — were the most satisfying part of being chief.

The government report found we had achieved similar gains in education and, in an area I am most proud of, caring for our children. The report confirmed that even though our on-reserve population had increased by 60 percent — which had been caused both by a high birth rate and people moving back to the reserve to take care of the new services we were providing — we had seriously reduced not only the percentage but the sheer numbers of our children who were taken away under the Family and Child Services Act. Part of this was the fact that the economic advances helped stabilize families, but also the band council was very active in finding on-reserve placement with friends and relatives for children in crisis families. This was all part of the new spirit of self-reliance that was part of our message to our community.

In fact, the DIA report found we had made this kind of leap forward in almost every area, with an astounding gain in the economic indicators for the community.

We had increased band employment, in the administration and through Indian and non-Indian companies and off-reserve, by a combined total of more than 400 percent. We had gone from one band-owned business to nine and more than doubled the private Indian-owned businesses on the reserve. Our total leasing revenue had increased by an incredible 3,500 percent, from $37,000 in 1971 to $1,296,000 in 1982, with most of that increase coming after 1977, from band-owned leases that increased from $22,000 in 1972 to $830,000 in 1982.

The scope of the economic miracle that we had managed could be seen simply by looking at the band budget. In 1972, band own-sourced revenues were $5,000. By 1981, band revenues had risen to $2 million and in the 1982/83 budget they were expected to almost double again to $3.8 million. Before I took over, the Department of Indian Affairs contributed about three times as much money as we took in to the band budget. By the end, the ratio was reversed, with band-owned revenues making up three times more in our budget than the Department's contribution.

In its conclusion, the report identified "leadership" as the most important reason for these dramatic advances. As the report put it, "Since the establishment of the Band as a separate entity the elected leadership has worked consistently with the membership to establish a policy framework for development. This has succeeded in large part and as a result, despite the buffeting the Band did not lose its sense of direction." More specifically, the report found that "since the mid-1970s the Band has elected a tough-minded, goal-oriented Chief and Council that have demonstrated the will and the competence to reach established objectives."

The report could not have been more positive toward my years as chief, so it was devastating for my opponents — those on the reserve and especially off-reserve with the mobile home park association. But even before the report was published at the end of 1982, my enemies had realized that they would not be able to bring me down simply by lies and unfounded accusations. They would have to use much more direct methods.

And that is when they decided to hire a hitman.

CHAPTER 9

Assassination Attempt

In the summer of 1982, I could feel the hatred rising around us. In trying, at long last, to get a fair deal for ourselves, and in having real economic success in the Lakeview development, we had kicked the hornet's nest of racism and anger that had been hovering on the edges of our dealings with whites for the past 100 years.

During that period, as we saw countless times in the past, when a chief stood up to the local white establishment, they were swiftly and mercilessly deposed by Indian Affairs working hand in glove with local business interests. When the whites wanted to steal from us, local businessmen worked with Indian Affairs and the courts to seize our land. To see Westbank Indians rising and demanding a fair deal from their land was appalling to the local whites. Earlier in the century, when leaders like Chief Pierre Nequalla and then Chief Baptiste Logan stood up for our rights, they had simply gotten the local Indian agent to step in and remove them. But now I was upsetting their applecart and no one was coming to depose me, so the local rednecks were in a panic.

I had already had a sense of this a couple of years earlier. When the tenants association began to denounce me in the press, the local police chief, Inspector Collins, made an unannounced visit to my office to discreetly warn me that he had heard that some were planning to frame me with some crime to bring me down, and that he was even sounded out about taking part in the scheme.

In mid-August 1982, I was interviewed by the local paper and I pointed with some alarm at the growing anti-Native sentiment in the Okanagan that was dominating the white media and really getting out of hand. The article, entitled "Anti-Native Mood Hovers Over Okanagan," described the "vicious attacks" against me personally in the local media. I tried to dampen the flames by admitting that my own fierce commitment to my band and to band autonomy may have contributed to that mood. But I told them that when I took over, the band was $3 million in debt and we were in danger of sliding back into abject poverty. I had to act decisively and all I was asking was that non-Indians who were living on Indian land comply with the law. Unfortunately, I said, too many whites were repulsed even by the thought of being governed by Indians.

By early summer 1982, a much more dramatic scheme than framing me for a crime was put in place. A number of the trailer park owners had gotten together to decide that if the authorities would not bring me down then they would have to take matters into their own hands. And one of them came up with a plan.

My first encounter with the plot was on August 21, 1982, when I received a knock on the door and was met by Mr. Richard Cooper, a thug from Edmonton, wielding a sharpened still bar, a two-foot-long piece of steel with a sword edge.

Instantly, blows from the bar were raining down on my head with murderous intensity. Blinded by my own blood, I managed to get up a couple steps and kicked him in the face and then ran upstairs and pulled a revolver from my gun cabinet and shot Mr. Cooper in the shoulder. He went down. Realizing he had brought a sword to a gunfight, he got up and stumbled back down the stairs. I looked through the window from upstairs and saw he was pulling out a sawed-off shotgun from his car, and so I shot him again from the window. He spun around and looked at me for a moment in the upstairs window. Then he leapt into his car and drove away.

I followed him outside but collapsed in the driveway, bleeding profusedly. By a miracle, my then-15-year-old son came up the hill from where he was living with his mother and found me. I thought I was a goner. I told him to take care of Kelly and his mother as I felt my life bleeding out. He called the ambulance and they came quickly. They bound my wounds as best they could while they rushed me to the hospital, where I received an immediate blood transfusion and 285 stitches on my head and arms where I had fended off some of the blows.

Later, I learned of the chain of events that led to Doug coming to my rescue. He had chores to do at the house and he was agitated and told his mother that he wanted to go up and see Dad. She insisted that he finish his chores first. Then the phone rang. It was my mother, asking if she had seen me around that day. Peggy said no. My mother said she didn't know why, but she was worried about me. It was then that Peggy dispatched Dougie to go and see if I was all right and he found me collapsed in the driveway.

The whole community was stunned by the attack, and I must admit I was having trouble processing it myself. The police captured Cooper as he was preparing to flee back to Alberta, with my bullet still lodged in his hastily bandaged shoulder, when a local motorcycle cop heard his description on the radio and arrested him in his motel parking lot. This was beyond anything I had imagined. But I knew, instinctively, from where it came. The murderous rage behind this attack had not originated in the mind of a small-time Edmonton hood. I knew with certainty that it came from somewhere within the association of trailer park owners who had been denouncing me to the local politicians and in the press with ever-growing intensity.

The police felt I was still at risk after Cooper was behind bars, because they kept a uniformed policeman outside my hospital room all of the time I was there and when I was released, they they took me under police protection to the Lake Okanagan Resort for several weeks more.

Cooper was initially charged with attempted murder, but before his trial in April 1983, he cut a deal with the Crown to reduce the charge to assault causing bodily harm with intent to wound and he received an eight-year sentence. He was released two and a half years later and he has subsequently applied for and was granted a pardon so his trial records have been sealed from the public.

But he was obviously just the hired gun. Suspicions immediately fell on members of the York family, owners of the Westview Village Mobile Home Park and close associates of Leonard Crosby, as the people who ordered the hit. Police arrested Larry Sr. and his two sons, Bruce and Larry Jr., for conspiracy to commit murder.

This is where we had arrived at. White trailer park owners trying to kill an Indian chief over land rents.

I believe many Canadians will have trouble understanding this. How could a rental contract, which both parties have freely entered into, inspire attempted murder? What was galling to them was the fact that an Indian was demanding a fair deal and to receive the full value of our land. This was the source of their rage.

In this society there was never a real chance that a jury would convict the Yorks for trying to kill me — even though court documents showed that immediately after Cooper was arrested, there was a family meeting called by Bruce York that took place in Edmonton. The questioner was Justice Hall and the witness was a York family member whose identity was protected.

Q: What did they indicate had gone wrong in reference to this hit?

A: Well, at first they didn't know, they just announced that something had gone wrong and somebody had gotten shot.

Q: Were there any discussions at that initial meeting, if I could just take you back for a moment, in reference to the nature of the business transaction, or what type of relationship they were involved in with Mr. Derrickson?

A: Yes. There was some reference made to a lease on a trailer home, and that Ron had reneged on the lease and that they were out to get him, or something along those lines. It's been a long time ago.

This was all in court records. There was another meeting immediately after Bruce York and his brother Larry Jr. and his father Larry Sr. were charged with attempted murder for hiring Cooper to kill me. They met in Larry York Sr.'s home in an Edmonton suburb and Bruce York tried to convince his nephew, Larry Jr., to plead guilty to the offence to spare the rest of them. The meeting included Bruce and Murray York, Larry Jr.'s uncles, and the unidentified source who reported on the meeting under oath said that Bruce offered Larry Jr. $30,000 to $50,000 to plead guilty to ordering the hit. But Larry apparently told them that it was not enough. He figured he would have to do three to five years in the penitentiary and said that he would need more than $50,000 to do the time on behalf of the family.[3]

In the end, the payment to Larry Jr. wasn't necessary. The Yorks managed to escape prosecution when out of the blue another trailer

3 For the full Commission testimony on the role of the Yorks in the assassination attempt, see Appendix III.

park owner — in fact, the only non-white member of the trailer park owners association — emerged to take the blame. Mr. Gary Tsu, who I am convinced was not involved in the conspiracy himself, came forward to take the blame. The police suspected this, too, because even after he confessed, he was only charged with knowing about the hit beforehand, not planning it or carrying it out.

When I saw the way the Yorks were protected by the courts, I understood that if I was going to have justice, I would have to get it for myself. I launched a civil suit against them, which I won. Karma, in its most terrible form, also took over when I heard that Bruce York, who had moved to Armstrong, and lived nearby to the judge who acquitted him, ran over and killed his own grandchild with his tractor.

At the same time as the civil suit was proceeding, I finally decided to do what the trailer park leaseholders had been falsely accusing me of trying to do: bankrupt them. That was what they had continually told the press and the local MPs whenever I sought a modest rise in the bargain basement rents they were paying for our people's land. After the assassination attempt, I decided to show them what, exactly, trying to bankrupt them would look like.

I didn't tell anyone about my plan. Publicly, I announced that I had no problem with the trailer park owners per se, that my dispute was with the one family who was responsible and that I would seek to have good and productive relations with the rest. But then I quietly went about redesigning all of their leases to set them up from bankruptcy. The structure of the leases always called for them to run for 25 years, but with rental adjustments every five years based on the value of the land, together with improvements at the time of signing. But in the aftermath of the attempted murder, I pulled out all the stops. I gave them all new 25-year leases, which superseded and replaced all of the previous leases. The trick that I pulled was that they included a clause stating that the land would be appraised together with all improvements at the time of the signing of this lease. Previously, improvements they made to the land had been excluded from the assessment. When the leases came up for review in five years' time, the rents would skyrocket. And one by one, they signed without noticing the time bomb I had hidden within.

Five years later, when the first contract came due, I told them to be prepared for a 50 percent increase and they laughed, until I told them to read the lease. And one by one they understood that they had, in fact, agreed to a formula that, while completely legal and within my rights, would result in a massive and in fact unsustainable rent increase. One by one, they were forced to declare bankruptcy. One by one, they disappeared. And I had my revenge for their attempted murder.

For a time, I thought that was the end of it. The whites had come after me with everything they had, including a hired assassin, and I had beaten them back. With the glowing report from Indian Affairs on my leadership and my quiet revenge on the trailer park owners, I thought that finally I could refocus on the job ahead. And I was already getting involved in a great new potential revenue source for our people, in the newly released plan to double the highway through Westbank as part of the building of the 97C Connector to Merritt. This development would open for the Okanagan region a fast highway to Vancouver. A glance at the map showed there was no way that it could be built without passing directly through Westbank territory. I looked forward to the challenge of using our geographical position to get new wealth for our people. That was an important part of my job as chief. But while I worked at this, there were others in the shadows trying to tear it all down.

CHAPTER 10

Restoring Cut-Off Lands,
Building a Highway

I had, as it turned out, been overly optimistic in believing that I had put the personal attacks behind me and that I could refocus on the job ahead. But I was forgetting one of the cardinal rules of politics: friends come and go, but enemies accumulate. This storm had blown over, but there was another, even fiercer one on the horizon.

The accumulation of enemies is very much the rule in Indigenous politics, where you are making decisions that affect people at the most basic level — on social assistance, jobs and housing. In most communities, you overlay these sensitive decisions on all of the previous interpersonal and inter-family community conflicts.

These feuds came onto my council as well. After Billy Derrickson resigned, another cousin, Rose Derrickson, was elected to replace him. Rose was a staffer in the band on the welfare file and she was troublesome in both roles. The band wealth had reached the point where that year I was paying a $3,500 royalty to each band member from the success of our band businesses. At the same time, at Christmas, we gave every band member a free turkey. Rose, who was responsible for purchasing the birds, decided to go for a deal and bought a truckload of damaged turkeys to give to our people. I could not believe it. We were all about improving the self-esteem of our people and she was out there offering them one-wing or wingless birds for Christmas.

It was too late to exchange them, so I cut a cheque of $25 to each band member so they could go out and buy a proper Christmas turkey. As it turned out, this was a win-win for many of our people who, in a sign of typical Indigenous resourcefulness, used $5 or so of the $25 to purchase the missing wing or wings from the turkey parts section, and the rest to buy extra gifts for the kids.

The line of family problems after Billy continued when Rose was replaced on council by Harold Derrickson, whose strategy was to oppose absolutely everything I did. It became ludicrous when, for example, I would offer council's congratulations to a local sports team or welcome a new child into the community and Harold would vote against it. His do-the-opposite strategy failed miserably when he opposed me in the following election and received only a handful of votes. I think it was only two or three, but it was in that range. The worst part of this was that it meant that many of his own family members hadn't voted for him. He was not a guy with political smarts. I remember during one campaign he went to an Elder's place and they made some country food, deer liver or deer heart, and he was too fancy to eat it. He left it untouched on the plate, and of course the news went right around the reserve and Harold was sharply criticized for insulting the Elder. It was a big mistake politically, but also in the culinary sense, because the Elders were excellent country cooks and they knew exactly how to prepare each part of the animal. I always enjoyed visiting them during the campaigns, or any time.

Fortunately, during this period I had Brian Eli as well as Harold on council. Brian was smart and committed to the community and we developed into a great negotiating tag team, where I would play the put-upon chief and eager-to-please negotiator while he would play the unreasonable wounded Indian until we had wrung from our opponents every advantage for our people.

One negotiating session stands out in my mind because Brian really should have gotten an Academy Award nomination for his performance. It was in a meeting with the highways department, and while they set out their offer, Brian scowled and turned away, looking out the window while they continued nervously making their case. When they finished, he turned to me and said curtly, "You are finished as chief if this crap deal is the best you can do." Then he stood up and said, "I'm not wasting my time," and he and our own highways expert left the room. The highways officials looked at each other in stunned silence. Then at me.

"You have to do better," I said pleadingly. "My people won't accept this." They nodded. They understood. And then for the next hour they made concession after concession until we had everything we wanted and more. Then Brian and I met for a beer or two in the bar down the street to celebrate another victory for our people.

We fought for every dime with everyone, from private interests and public. One year, we managed to get $10 million from government from dozens of small grants and we even had to set up a special committee of people to spend all of the money according to the sometimes complex criteria under which we had received it.

My other great negotiating partner was my lawyer, Graham Allen, although we occasionally got lost in our own changing stories. As usual we met before another highways meeting to decide what we wanted out of it. When we arrived, I saw that our opponents were completely disorganized and I instantly upped our ask. Graham started to question my number when I gave him a swift kick under the table and he immediately shut his mouth. When I had them past our original ask, I went further and said if they added 25 percent to the amount, we would have a deal. So they did it and we accepted. But my instinct that they were disorganized was right on because the next day when we went to sign the final deal, they had forgotten that they had added 25 percent during the negotiations at the table, and the next day they went and added another 25 percent to the total.

I also worked with Graham on the self-government issue. Graham had put together the Sechelt deal, which called for them to withdraw from the Indian Act, and I backed them on this. At an AFN meeting, where chief after chief lined up to vote against the Sechelt, I stood up and told them they should be ashamed of themselves to put up barriers to any First Nation that wanted to follow its own path. My speech worked, because the vote went strongly for my side in the debate and this was noted by the Sechelt leadership, because they later presented me with a beautiful totem pole as a friend of the Sechelt people.

The success of my administration in doing these kinds of successful deals kept my internal opposition to a minimum. I was easily re-elected in 1978, 1980 and in 1982, immediately after the assassination attempt. The reason was not only financial. It was because the people knew that even though I was known as an economic development chief, I was one of them. This was brought home to me when I picked up a band member, Carter Abel, who was hitchhiking into town to buy groceries. Carter was someone who always seemed to have a rough go of it. A large part of this was his drinking problem, which often put him in dangerous situations. At the same time, he was known as someone who managed to survive scrapes that would have flattened other men. For example, he was once riding his bike along the highway when a truck barrelling by caught his bike in the wind draft and flung it under the wheels but tossed him into the grasses on the highway edge. The truck driver stopped and was relieved to see Carter miraculously unhurt, and the trucking company was happy to buy Carter a new bicycle. That's how his life went. He was tossed about by the winds but somehow, despite all odds, landed on his feet.

I remember running into him one time on Vancouver's East Side when I was driving by in my Mercedes with my girlfriend. Carter was in bad shape. He had obviously slept on the street and he was barefoot. I stopped to talk to him and after I introduced him to the woman I was with — who was white — I asked if he was OK. He told me he wanted to go back home, so I gave him $20 to buy shoes at the army-navy store and another $20 for a bus ticket back to Westbank.

When I drove him back home after his grocery run, it was just after the 1984 band election and he told me that he had voted for me because of the time we met in Vancouver. I thought he was talking about the $40 I gave him for shoes and a bus ticket, but he continued: "You were with a white woman and you stopped and introduced me. That is why I am voting for you, 'cause you are never stuck-up."

That was really how band politics worked. You cannot act in a high and mighty manner. My connection with the people rested not on the fact that I had business and management experience but that I respected them — because I was one of them.

You took care of your people not because you were campaigning, but because they were your people. When I met Carter in very rough shape on the streets of Vancouver, I introduced him to the woman I was with because he was one of our people and always deserving of respect. In retrospect, I think I was also testing her. To see if she was the type of person who could be respectful toward an Indian guy on the street, even if he was having a hard time of it. If she hadn't been, that would have been the end of it for us.

Still, I don't want to come off as overly pious. Because I am not and I never was. During campaigns, I would never promise something I could not deliver and never tried to buy people off with jobs, as some did. But I did enjoy the game and wasn't above packing my opponent's room with my supporters, who would mutter things like "Not true!" or, more colourfully, "In a pig's eye!" while they were giving their election speech. But this was not serious. It was more a version of the game I played as a three-year-old of slapping my grandmother's goose in the ass and running for the door. Just to raise a little hell.

As my colleagues can attest, I am not above playing pranks. Sometimes they came with a message. Like the one Brian Eli and I pulled on our economic development guy, Ian, a first-rate guy, an Irishman and former Edmonton police officer, who was very bright but also a bit straightlaced.

Brian and I had arranged to meet him at a bar in Vancouver before a government meeting, and when we arrived we noticed two girls working the street corner. I went over to them and said good evening and told them we were being joined by a bald white guy called Ian and asked them if they would pretend they knew him — like he was a regular client. And I slipped them both a tip.

The girls got into the joke. When Ian rounded the corner, they greeted him by name and embraced him while he, stuttering, tried to push them away. He had a wild look in his eye and he repeated, "I don't know you," and then to us, "I don't know them!" They continued to call him by name and insist that they missed him. It wasn't until later, in the bar, that he figured out that we had put them up to it, and he was noticeably less schoolmasterly after that, and we became good friends. Later, when he was faced with high tuition costs after his son had been accepted into university, he came to me to ask if he could borrow the money. "I will pay you back and I will always be loyal to you." He kept his word on both counts.

One of my favourite practical jokes during this period was one Brian and I pulled on Fred Walchli. We were meeting in Fred's office on a Thursday afternoon and on the way out for a drink afterward, I picked up a piece of his letterhead and put it in my briefcase. The drinks went late into the night until Brian and I, who were in much the same dishevelled shape as Fred, took him home in a cab and deposited him at his front door. In the morning, before heading back to Westbank, we typed up a letter on Fred's letterhead awarding Westbank a million-dollar development grant, signed it with a reasonable facsimile of Fred's signature and stopped by his office on our way out in the morning.

Fred was still shaky from the night before and surprised to see us — and even more surprised when we told him we were there to thank him and showed him his letter authorizing the $1 million grant. He blanched. Not remembering the night before, he said mournfully, "I'm going to get fired."

We played it a bit more, going on and on about what this money was going to mean to the band and he became more and more despondent. Finally, taking pity on him, we told it was all a joke and handed him back the letter. Now fuming, he slowly ripped up the letter and we headed out satisfied at a joke well played. He, not so much at the time. But when I saw him a couple of weeks later, he was amused by it and it became a milestone moment in our long friendship.

With Fred I could joke around, because he would always treat us straight. But with others in the Department, and with the people we dealt with from the province, I had to play hardball all of the time. I would do almost anything to get from them what we needed to build our Westbank economy. One of my favourite tactics with the provincial civil servants, when we were at a complete impasse, was to suggest that we meet a final time and continue the meeting until we had a deal. I would then suggest that we hold the meeting in Vancouver and I would always make sure it was at around 5 p.m. on a Friday, because I knew that the provincial representatives would have worked all week and all day Friday at their office in Victoria, rushed onto the ferry and arrived tired and hungry at the end of the day. We, on the other hand, would arrive in Vancouver in the morning and check into our hotel and rest and then have a good meal before the negotiating session began. When I saw the other side tiring, I would drive the negotiations further and further and by 2:00 a.m., when my opponents were almost punch-drunk with exhaustion, I would get everything I wanted and more for our community.

I looked for every advantage for my people. On one occasion, when a long-time highways employee, who I knew had not been so happy in his job, was retiring, I contacted him about his government briefing book. In complete confidentiality, I offered him $20,000 for it. He agreed and I suddenly had a copy of all of the government's highway plans for the next 10 years — which was like gold in my negotiations with them. To recoup the fee I paid for it, I contacted other First Nations that were negotiating highway right-of-ways with the government and sold them a copy of the book for a few thousand dollars, until I had my $20,000 back.

The stakes were particularly high in highway negotiation during this period because the government was moving forward with a key link that had to pass through our reserve. The Okanagan connector highway number 97C would link Kelowna to Merritt, where it joined the Coquihalla Highway heading south to Vancouver. At the time, to drive to Vancouver from Kelowna you had to first head south past Penticton and then wind your way west on the twisting Highway 3, a route that added 125 kilometres, and about 90 minutes' travel time, to the journey.

Building the Okanagan Connector would be a major transportation improvement and a major expense, costing $225 million in 1980 dollars. It was also a major engineering initiative in the mountainous terrain between Kelowna and Merritt, crossing 67 avalanche paths. Builders had to move sections of the Boston Bar Creek 15 times and the Coquihalla River three times without disturbing the trout spawning grounds. In 1984, there was a push to complete the highway for the opening of Expo 86 in Vancouver, and there were 7,000 workers employed seven days a week to build the route. To lessen the impact of the new road on wildlife, the Connector has a $10.5 million wildlife protection system. This features a 100-kilometre fence on both sides of the highway to keep deer and moose off the road. There are also 25 wildlife underpasses and one overpass to allow animals to roam freely.

What made the Kelowna-to-Merritt connector section an absolute political priority was that the highway had been a perennial campaign promise of Bill Bennett, who was not only the MLA for my riding, South Okanagan, but also the premier of B.C. from 1975 to 1986, a position his father, W.A.C. Bennett, held from 1952 to 1972.

The Bennetts stayed in power because they were masters of backroom deals. Kelowna was their fiefdom and it was certain that no highway deals would be done without their fingerprints somewhere on the contract. I knew that going to the first meeting with the highways department to plan the portion of the highway that ran right through our reserve, which called for widening the existing Highway 97 into four lanes. I brought a local map to that first meeting and told the highway officials that we would not go any further in the negotiations if the final agreement did not also reroute a local East Boundary Road so it would bring economic benefits to Westbank. When they looked at the map, the highways officials could clearly see that the proposed road would also provide direct access to a large parcel of land owned by Premier Bennett's family. To drive the point home, I said that Bennett would have to cede half the land for the roadway along the boundary and the reserve would cede the other half, so it was 50-50. The highways officials caught on very quickly and said that they were sure that this would be doable — in fact, they would guarantee it on the spot. The negotiators now had an important new incentive to do a deal, since the new road would dramatically increase the value of the Bennetts' land, while for us it opened up an important area that we would use for a new subdivision.

Because the highway was a special Bennett project, I knew that it would be drowning in dollars. As it stood, the siding to the existing Highway 97 was mainly scrubland, valued at a few hundred dollars an acre where it passed through the reserve, but I was not going to settle for that. I went to our band planning department and marked on the map where I wanted zoning for commercial and residential space, and told them to break up all of the land alongside the highway into individual lots that we could value at hundreds of times that amount.

The next time I met with the highways negotiating team, I brought with me a map of the reserve's 15-kilometre stretch of the highway broken into commercial and residential lots. When my interlocutors saw this, their white faces went even whiter as they had to shelve their quick $250-an-acre deal. This was going to cost them.

The negotiations were tough. They tried again and again to call my bluff on the division of the land into lots, but I told them it was not a bluff. Land values were not set only on the use of the land at any given time but on its potential future uses. And reserves do not, like municipalities, expand their territories with growing populations. Our land holdings are fixed and as our population grows, we have to use every square inch of our territory. And when that is used up, our people are simply forced out. So I would not relent on our land-use plan. Those lots were on paper then, but at some point in the future they would be necessary for homes and businesses and I was not going to agree to surrender these lands to the province for a pittance. They belonged to our children.

I watched as their exasperation grew. They knew better than to threaten us with expropriation, because overnight their whole highway would be blocked. So they had to deal with us.

They gradually upped the ante until, finally, they reached $20,000 a lot and they told me that was it. They didn't have any more cash to offer us. They had upped their original offer by almost 1,000 percent and the well was completely dry. I had busted them but I had still not agreed to their final offer. I knew we had been approaching this point and I was ready for it. "OK," I said. "If you can't pay more cash, then instead bring services all along the highway. Water, sewage, electricity. Run everything along the highway so we can plug into it. And we will have a deal."

This was the plan from the beginning. Get the most cash out of them and then force them to add services on top of that — this would be worth more than cash in many ways, because the infrastructure would be laid at the same time as the highway. We could immediately lease to commercial tenants who could build retail outlets along what promised to be a busy highway that would be used by the whole region and beyond as a shortcut to Vancouver.

In fact, that is what we accomplished. We succeeded in leasing out that land to five separate shopping centres and set new precedents for on-reserve developments in Canada. I financed this through a groundbreaking deal with the Toronto-Dominion Bank at a time when all the banks were refusing loans for large capital investments on leased reserve lands.

The TD deal is the one that I am perhaps most proud of, because it grew not out of tough-minded negotiations but from doing a good deed for a kid stranded at the Vancouver airport. Briefly, this is how it came about.

I was returning from a trip to Ottawa on a flight that went direct to Vancouver with a connection back toward Kelowna. While I was checking into my Kelowna flight at the Air Canada desk, I found myself behind a 12-year-old girl who was visibly upset. There was a problem with her ticket home to Toronto and Air Canada was refusing to let her on the flight or provide her with an alternative ticket. The kid was alone and frightened and I stepped up to the desk to ask Air Canada to do the right thing: let the kid on the flight, then settle the matter later with her parents. The counter person refused. I asked to see the manager. To my surprise, and, I might add, to my disgust, the manager also refused to accommodate the by-now crying child.

I told them point-blank: "You are horrible people." Then I paid $780 for the kid's ticket and in her relief she took down my name with a promise that her father would reimburse me. The next day, I phoned Air Canada and gave them hell and insisted that they apologize to the girl and her family for the way they had handled it. Then I forgot about it.

A few weeks later, I heard a gruff, unfamiliar voice asking my secretary if he could see Ronald Derrickson. The stranger, in his early forties, strode into my office and offered his hand. He explained that he was the father of the young girl who had been stranded in Vancouver and he had flown all the way from Toronto to thank me in person, and to repay me the money for the ticket. Then he handed me his card and said if there was ever anything he could do for me, just ask. I glanced at his card. He was a senior executive at the Toronto-Dominion Bank.

At the time, with the services in place from the highway deal, I already had the interest of a major Canadian developer in building a shopping centre for a fabulous amount in leasing revenues for the reserve. But the banks were refusing to put up the money. So I said to the TD executive, "There is one thing . . ."

He didn't flinch. He said he would look into it, and within days he got back to me to say, "I think I can help." And he did. TD loaned the money to the developers and we all made history together with the first shopping centre on reserve land. With the precedent set, we were able to build several more along the highway cutting through the reserve.

When the deal was signed, I knew that the future prosperity of Westbank was set. The revenues to the band that had increased by 3,500 percent in the 1970s and into the early 1980s would continue to increase at a similar pace for the rest of the decade.

The 1980s were, in fact, full of positive developments for the band. The second major advance came with the settlement, in 1983, of the cut-off lands dispute, which involved 22 communities, including Westbank, that had a total of 50,000 acres of their reserve lands illegally seized on recommendation of the McKenna-McBride report.

The McKenna-McBride land seizures had been patently illegal because Canadian law required a vote by band members before any reduction of territory was possible. But this was not done by our lawless governments. In Westbank's case, the seizures took place after the hearings where the infamous Isaac Harris was translator, and the exact amounts of the cut-offs were 50 acres from Reserve 8, Mission Creek, and 870 acres from Reserve 9, Tsinstikeptum, which was roughly a third of our meagre territory.

Our people had been lobbying the government for return of these lands for more than 50 years when, in 1977, B.C. committed to join Canada in negotiating a settlement. Finally, in 1982, B.C. passed the Indian Cut-off Lands Disputes Act, which paved the way for settlements of the disputes. Because much of the land had been sold off to third parties, the government offered us financial compensation that would allow us to buy new lands to replace those that were lost. For Westbank, I negotiated a $10 million payment that was earmarked for land purchase. On November 4, 1983, we held a referendum and the people of Westbank ratified the agreement with near unanimity.

With the money in hand, we looked for unused lands with significant economic potential and found them in the Gallagher Canyon area just east of Kelowna. As soon as we purchased the land, I applied to have them given reserve status, which would allow us to take full advantage of their potential, but this would turn into a very long process. Finally, I would have to return to politics after 10 years away to finish the job.

The mid-1980s continued to be an important building period. We constructed our modern band office, a three-storey building, taking the first two floors for ourself and renting out the third. Over time, as the band interests continued to grow, we took over the entire building.

I was also active in a number of band deals in the region where I was called in for my negotiating skills. Most notably by the Osoyoos Band, which hired me to negotiate the land cut-off compensation, which they had been trying to get for the past 100 years. Before the negotiations, I went over what they were hoping for — their best-case deal — and I said, OK, I'll get it for you, and they agreed that my fee would be a percentage of the total. The negotiations began at 8:30 a.m. on a Monday morning in the meeting room of a local hotel and to the shock and surprise of the band members, by 4 p.m. I had a deal for $14 million — an amount that surpassed their original ask. When the band administration saw how quickly I had closed, they tried to reduce my fee, but our agreement was solid and the $38,000 cheque for less than eight hours work came in the mail. As a bonus, I had drafted a development plan for them and 20 years later they were still using it, as Brian Eli discovered when he visited their office and saw a dog-eared copy on the table in their meeting room.

Another deal I am proud of during that period was one where I was negotiating on behalf of a woman Elder on the reserve who had to surrender land for a highway right-of-way. She had a small ranching operation, and even though I got her a good price for the land, the highway was cutting her access to the stream where she watered her cattle. Without it, she needed to set up, with a subsidy from the highways department, an elaborate pumping operation. In the deal, I negotiated for them to build an underpass for the cattle within nine years. And if they failed, the $1 million cost of the underpass would go directly to the Elder. Highways delayed and delayed and then seemed to have forgotten about it. But nine years later I received a call from our lawyer Graham Allen who said the nine-year anniversary of the department's promise had just popped up on his calendar. When I checked, the department had not built the promised underpass and they were forced to pay the woman a million dollars, which I understood she gracefully distributed among the needy in her community.

Another favourite negotiating tactic during this period was charging a premium for white racism. When I was negotiating and someone said something racist, I would show no reaction, but I would quietly add a penalty to the negotiation, something between $15,000 and $20,000 to my bottom line so they would pay in hard cash for their transgressions, even if they were unaware of it. (I hope some of my negotiating opponents are reading this and know now why my *ask* was suddenly raised in the middle of a negotiation and why I would settle for no less than the additional 20 grand.) I know that most of those who negotiate on our behalf today would not think of doing such a thing, and that is proof that they should not be negotiating on our behalf.

Such deals added to my reputation as a leader. The premier, Bill Bennett, who I had a respectful working relationship with, said at the local Rotary Club that he sent his people on a $300,000 negotiating crash course and when they came back, Ron Derrickson still cleaned out the store. At one point, Bennett even called me to ask me to advise on a negotiation, and in return he passed legislation that included Indigenous people in the province's fire protection act, which is something we had long demanded as a life-saving measure for our communities.

I took pride in my ability to get things for my people and there were few dull moments — I was always on the go. But at the same time, it was personally challenging and I remember this as the loneliest time of my life. The system was designed to suck you dry. And there were always people who no matter what you got for them, never seemed to be satisfied. In fact, the more you got for them, the more they demanded. During this period I was able to give each band member premiums of $3,500 and then $10,000 from band revenues — something that was unprecedented in Canada at the time. But there was that same group of perennially unsatisfied people who took the money and complained that it wasn't more. A number of these were my own family members.

This group was also the first to pounce when there was a stumble. And that came in my dealings with the Northland Bank.

In the 1970s, the Northland Bank was seen as a saviour for Western Canada, but it went down in flames in 1985, along with another Alberta-based financial institution, the Canadian Commercial Bank. The failure of the Northland would be used to spread panic on our reserve in the mid-1980s so I will take a moment to review what happened.

The Calgary-based bank was conceived as a regional bank that would service the needs of the mid-size commercial and wholesale operations in Western Canada. Its founders considered that the large national banks did not service the small business operations characteristic of Western Canada, so this was to be its market niche, with a focus on Western Canadian real estate and resource-based operations. Lending was to be in the commercial mid-market with loans ranging from $100,000 to $2 million, although the latter ceiling was removed in the second fiscal year. In the original descriptions of the bank, the founders announced that it was the intention that the bank should be a boutique bank for business rather than a supermarket for the general public.

I had some dealings with the bank when a Calgary amusement park I had invested in with my lawyer, John McAfee, was having troubles. It opened its gates during a serious recession in Alberta in 1982, but the bank had stood by us, allowing us to restructure in a way that at least saved the company — although in the end I lost money on the deal.

So I saw how valuable a regional bank like Northland could be, and while I was dealing with them in Calgary, I realized that the Northland could be the answer to many of the issues we in Westbank faced in the mid-1980s. In the period between 1982 to 1984, we were flush with cash with the moneys we received from the cut-off land settlement and the windfall I negotiated from the Highway 97C right-of-way. This should have put us in a position of new leverage with the big banks, but that was not the case. Every time we went for operating or investment loans, we were faced with stubborn resistance, leading not only to frustration but to missed opportunity. And as time went on, loans were getting more difficult to arrange, because the Federal Business Development Bank had announced they would no longer finance any type of development on reserve property, whether it was regarding an outside developer or a band business or individuals. So, the only resource for loans that we had available were the Department of Indian Affairs loans. With Department loans, there was a fixed number of dollars that they had available each year, and to get access to them was a long process. You were looking at maybe six to eight months to get a loan approved, and then under generally uncompetitive terms. So we were looking for alternate financing from outside sources and Northland offered a new door to knock on.

In late 1983, I began to explore the opportunities with them and I found them miles ahead of the other chartered banks when it came to offering services to Indigenous businesses and governments. Our long-time partner the Royal Bank, for example, had promised dozens of times to install a branch on the reserve and had finally reneged on the promise. In our initial talk, Northland was immediately open to these kinds of developments.

The bank also actively pursued us as clients. A Northland vice-president, Harold Bayard (Byd) McBain, and Martin Fortier, the bank's chief operating officer, made several trips to Westbank to meet with me and the council and make their pitch for the band, and me personally, to place a portion of our deposits with them and even invest in the future of the bank.

I was impressed by the numbers Fortier and McBain showed me and by my previous dealings with them, so I was inclined to move some of my own assets to the bank. But I wanted to be doubly sure before I committed the band's assets, so I had the two bank officials meet with my councillors, Brian Eli and Harold Derrickson, without me so they could question the bankers without my influence.

While the bankers were in my office, I called in the two councillors and left them alone to discuss the offer. They went on to have two more meetings with McBain and Fortier without me and they wrested a further concession from the bankers to set up an Indigenous loan office with its own policy for investing in on-reserve projects, before agreeing that depositing and investing a portion of our capital in Northland made economic sense for Westbank. I was personally convinced by the bank to put a large portion of my own capital in the bank.

Finally, as someone who likes to take a belt-and-suspenders approach to financial investments, I arranged with McBain and Fortier for the band to have a line of credit and loans equivalent to its investment, so even if the unheard-of happened — the collapse of a chartered bank, something that had not happened in Canada for more than 50 years — the band would be protected.

In 1984, I was invited onto the bank board and I remember I went to discuss this with Len Marchand, the Okanagan political groundbreaker who had by then been appointed to the Canadian Senate. Marchand checked out the bank and the people behind it and he strongly encouraged me to get involved. He said, "Ron, if they are offering you a seat on the board, take it. It will be the first time one of our people will be asked to become a director of a bank or any significant Canadian corporation . . . It will be great for our people and great for the band."

Then the earth began to shake. The recession hit the West in 1984 and the bank found itself with an uncomfortable, but still manageable number of high-risk loans. In August 1985, I was enlisted to work on the loan rehabilitation for a fee of $1 million a year, and to take on the job I resigned from my seat on the board. We were just completing the reorganization the following month when the government shut us down at the same time as it shut down the other Western Canadian bank, the Canadian Commercial Bank (CCB), which was, in fact, in real trouble.

The abrupt closing of the Northland was immediately questioned. As the *Globe and Mail* reported on October 23, 1985, a former auditor of the Northland indicated that the Calgary-based bank could have survived had the bank been given time to work out its problem loans. Liberal Senator David Stewart asked: "Did someone act too hastily in not allowing the Northland to recover?" Liberal Senators were in fact suspicious that the new Progressive Conservative government's handling of the CCB rescue helped to sink the Northland. Senator Jerry Grafstein said that "Northland was an innocent bystander that got sideswiped in the fallout from the government's effort to rescue the CCB. There were problems, but they were normal problems."

The Northland debacle would, however, play a major role in my standing. Neither the band nor I lost money in the end, but the bank failure added fuel to a smouldering fire that had begun building after the assassination attempt in 1982, and which was given a blast of oxygen by the election of Brian Mulroney's Progressive Conservative government on September 4, 1984. For the first time, my political enemies were able to come at me with the full power of the Canadian state. And they didn't hesitate to use it. Especially because at the time, my Liberal roots were showing.

CHAPTER 11

Character Assassination Attempt

As I mentioned, my friendship with Len Marchand led to my sporadic involvement with the Liberal Party of Canada, and in the spring of 1984, I was working as a volunteer on the Liberal leadership campaign of John Munro, who was the minister of Indian Affairs when Pierre Trudeau announced his retirement in February of that year.

Munro was an old-style machine politician from a working-class neighbourhood in Hamilton, Ontario, who had served as minister of labour in the Trudeau government before being moved to Indian Affairs in 1980. I had a good working relationship with him when he was Indian Affairs minister. He was a stand-up guy and when the local Progressive Conservative politicians were denouncing me before the publication of the 1982 report that had exonerated me, Munro always stood up to defend me.

When the Liberal leadership race was called for June 1984, Munro called me to tell me that he was running, and without being asked, I told him I would support him. So I went to work raising money for his campaign from business associates in the Okanagan region and donated a sizeable amount myself. When he hired a plane to visit Liberal delegates in the regions, I sometimes accompanied him, especially if he was going into an area with lots of Indigenous people, and I would speak at his rallies. I liked the guy. I believed in him and thought Canada could do with a straight shooter as leader.

I am not sure how much my support helped, because in the leadership election he garnered only 93 votes and dropped off after the first ballot, with John Turner beating Jean Chrétien on the second.

This foray into open Liberal politics in the spring of 1984 would come back to haunt me by the end of the summer. On September 4, 1984, Brian Mulroney led the Progressive Conservative Party to a crushing defeat of the Liberals under John Turner and this new development was part of the perfect storm that was heading toward me.

In fact, my opponents had never really given up their attacks on me. In 1983, after the assassination attempt and after the glowing 1982 DIA report on me, I was called in front of the Indian Affairs Committee, where Lorne Greenaway and Fred King were active members, along with Frank Oberle, a Conservative MP from Prince George–Peace River who was the committee's ranking opposition member. Both Oberle and Greenaway tried to attack me again for the Toussowasket deal with Noll, and it was difficult not to lose patience with them after all I had gone through. More ominous was that after I met with them, they invited Leonard Crosby to testify, and for several hours they not only gave him a national soapbox to sound off against us but actively encouraged him.

Frank Oberle revealed a lot about the mindset of the racist B.C. caucus that he represented when, after listening to Crosby's complaints about our leasing policies, he was not interested in questioning any of Crosby's assertions but instead seemed to be egging him on. Oberle said, "The fact is that you are dealing with some Indian people who exercise power and pretend to be a self-government for which they have no legal status. Is that right? Is that what you are saying?"

Crosby agreed, then told the committee that what he was asking for was "security of tenure" and by that he seemed to mean that he should determine what he would pay for what he saw as his right to occupy Indian land. Oberle indicated that he was in complete agreement and then speculated on "how to achieve that."

"I suspect that some of the regional officials here think [Ron] Derrickson is out of control. He is reading things into the Indian Act that are not there. The minister has been told by the Justice Department that he is becoming increasingly vulnerable in terms of the policy that he is dictating to his department and the statutes that are underlying his authority. I recommended to the minister that the band be put not in receivership but under trusteeship for a period for time until this situation is properly redressed. Would you consider that to be a reasonable action?"

Even this was only a partial solution for Crosby: "It might help to resolve the situation immediately, but we also have to bear in mind, what about the future?"

Oberle's remark suggesting I was reading things into the Indian Act on our leasing rights was a challenge to the expanded authority we had been given on leasing in 1977 after the closing of the DIA regional office in Vernon and transfer of some of the administrative powers to the band. This transfer included a freer hand in setting rents, which I was using to the fullest with support from Fred Walchli.

But for Crosby and his redneck backers the bomb went off in the spring of 1984, when the outgoing Liberal government passed us formal authority under Section 53/60 Delegated Land Management Authority "to manage First Nation land allotments, transfers, permits, approve leases and manage allotments." This meant we could administer permits, leases and licences under the Indian Act regulations.

This gave us the formal authority on leases that Crosby and Oberle had challenged in 1983. There were howls of outrage that spring when the Indian Affairs department granted me these powers and Crosby began to push the idea of some dark pact between Derrickson and the Department of Indian Affairs.

The field of battle dramatically changed in the fall of 1984 with the election of the Conservative government in Ottawa. Suddenly, the campaign against me personally, and against the right of the people of Westbank to control their own lands, went from slinging from the sidelines into the centre of government. They now held the reins of power. And they were damned determined to use them.

After September 1984, I saw that the failed physical assassination attempt morphed into another, even more determined attempt at character assassination as my name began to be raised inside the House of Commons in relation to a series of increasingly bizarre set of accusations. It became very clear, very quickly that this was part of an orchestrated campaign, with backbenchers planting questions with the new minister of Indian Affairs, David Crombie, that were heading toward yet another inquiry. In the fall of 1984 and throughout 1985, I could hear them coming for me like the deer hears the footsteps of wolves on the forest floor. But I had nowhere to run and nowhere to hide. In the end, this attempted character assassination would be far more damaging and far more painful than Richard Cooper's sharpened steel bar. Once again, when the truth was finally aired, I would still walk away without permanent damage.

By the spring of 1986, I was constantly looking over my shoulder, fearing another attempt on my life. It was the craziest of times. When it was announced that Princess Diana and Prince Charles would be visiting Kelowna on May 5, 1986, I was invited to be part of the greeting party as the chief of the band on whose traditional territory Kelowna sat. But I was visited beforehand by the RCMP, who said they had information that I might have intent to harm the princess. I told them that was ridiculous and if they had any serious concerns about that I would voluntarily withdraw from the invitation. They seemed satisfied and I did meet Princess Di in Kelowna. I brought small gifts for her sons and she said she was pleased by that. She said it was nice of me to think of her children.

Like everyone else who met her, I was charmed by her. What struck me most about the whole thing, though, was that the whisper campaign against me had progressed to the point where anyone could imagine I would harm visiting royalty.

In fact, it was no longer a whisper campaign — it was entering its final, public stage. Lorne Greenaway, the PC MP for the Cariboo–Chilcotin riding, was on his feet every week in the House of Commons with a new lie about me. To explain the fact that the DIA had repeatedly praised me and my leadership as exemplary, Greenaway also began to make dark accusations of a corrupt civil service that was serving the Liberals in protecting me. In April 1986, he appeared at the Indian Affairs Committee to make what a *Maclean's* magazine article described in the press as "stunning" accusations in "the most controversial presentation he has made in more than six years as a Conservative member of Parliament."

Greenaway charged that "officials in the Department of Indian Affairs," along with the man who is now the nation's highest-ranking bureaucrat, Paul Tellier, were covering up the "mismanagement of government funds" provided to the prosperous Westbank Indian Band. Greenaway told the committee, "It is a sad tale of corruption, fraud, attempted murder, extortion and, worst of all, a cover-up by departmental officials."

Greenaway, without providing any evidence of his wild claims, said that he had "obtained portions of a secret document on Westbank that would just curl your hair. We do not know whether department officials have been taking bribes or whether they have been intimidated." But the full story, he added, could not be told until all documents have been released — a quest he vowed to continue.

Greenaway's charges, made under rules of parliamentary immunity that protect MPs from libel action, left the Indian Affairs department "dumbfounded," said Assistant Deputy Minister John Rayner. Paul Tellier, deputy minister of Indian Affairs from 1979 to 1982 and by then clerk of the Privy Council serving the Conservative government, told *Maclean's* the department had conducted several reviews of the band, "none of which support the allegations being made."

Maclean's interviewed me about Greenaway for the story and I was quoted as saying, "What he is doing is slimy," and I told them that "Greenaway and other B.C. Tories have waged a vendetta against the band for the past decade."

In fact, access to information documents show clearly what I suspected at the time — that the character assassins were working once again with the white leaseholders of Westbank land. In a briefing note prepared for the minister in the late spring of 1986, which I recently acquired under the Access to Information Act, I found Indian Affairs officials summarizing six months of contacts with Leonard Crosby denouncing me and the Westbank administration.

There were 16 specific allegations and most of them involved what were clearly lawful rent increases on the leaseholders. For example, the lawyers for the trailer park leaseholders complained bitterly of the lease agreement they signed that made "provision for a minimum rent of $15,500 per year," which they thought was way too high, and were asking the government to intervene to reduce it to $6,000 — a measly $500 a month. Leonard Crosby followed up in a January 22, 1986, letter to the minister castigating them for giving the band the power to set rents in the first place.

As the Crosby letter put it, there had been a violation of the leases by a failure "to live up to the spirit and the intent of the contracts." Further, DIA had assisted the band in its "unethical and unprincipled" business practices and "the Band continues its tradition of abusing its authority to administer leases by using that authority to acquire assets."

While the local politicians were hammering me in Ottawa, a local businessman, Nicholas Kayban, was working behind the scenes to enlist community dissidents to their cause. And this would be crucial. A few redneck MPs and some angry trailer park owners were not enough to drag me down. For that, they needed to foment an uprising in the community and Nicholas Kayban was the shadowy figure who was given this job.

Kayban had grown up in the Edmonton area, in what for him was the appropriately named town of Weasel Creek, and had a curious employment record — head of security for Eldorado Mining in Uranium City, manager for Sears, owner of a wholesale menswear company, business development manager for Canada Trust, head of housing for the non-status Indians of British Columbia and owner of a natural gas company in Alberta. What he did have was close connections to the Progressive Conservative MPs who were working with the trailer park owners to denounce me in the press and his job was to build opposition to me within our community. Kayban would later be identified by Justice Hall as a major source of the slander and libel that engulfed me.

We see his handiwork in late 1985 and into early 1986 when Kayban brought together a group that included my cousin Larry Derrickson and seven other band members into a fifth column inside the community. He held several meetings in Kelowna at the home of Bonnie Thompson, which was located off-reserve. The meetings were attended by various members of my local opposition, including Robert Louie, my political opponent.

Under Kayban's guidance, Robert Louie and this informal group were shaped into the Westbank Indian Action and Advisory Council and Kayban worked with them to draw up a petition, which they brought out in March 1986. It was, as the judge later pointed out, full of inflammatory language and completely unsupported assertions — in fact, lies. Here is what Kayban came up with (the all-caps were in the original):

WE, THE UNDERSIGNED DULY REGIS-
TERED VOTING MEMBERS OF WESTBANK
INDIAN RESERVE 8, 9, & 10, HEREBY PETI-
TION THE MINISTER OF INDIAN AFFAIRS

AND NORTHERN DEVELOPMENT, THE HONORABLE DAVID CROMBIE, FOR IMMEDIATE REMOVAL OF CHIEF RONALD M. DERRICKSON AND Councillors HAROLD DERICKSON AND BRIAN ELI. WE BELIEVE THERE IS JUST CAUSE FOR REMOVAL IN THAT THERE ARE A NUMBER OF AREAS WHERE COUNCIL HAS CLEARLY FAILED TO REPRESENT THE BAND IN GOOD FAITH AND TO CONDUCT AFFAIRS OF THE BAND FOR THE BENEFIT AND ADVANCEMENT OF THE ENTIRE BAND MEMBERSHIP. WE FEEL AREAS WARRANTING GROUNDS FOR DISMISSAL ARE AS FOLLOWS:

1. FAILURE TO HOLD REGULAR BAND MEETINGS
2. MISAPPROPRIATION OF PROPERTY AND BAND ASSETS
3. ILLEGAL ENFORCEMENT OF BAND BY-LAWS SUCH AS "B.C.R 1981-03 BAND RENTALSMAN BYLAW" DISALLOWED BY THE HONORABLE JOHN MUNRO, MINISTER OF INDIAN AFFAIRS AND NORTHERN DEVELOPMENT
4. FRAUDULENT REPRESENTATION OF THE WESTBANK INDIAN BAND
5. FAILURE TO CONSULT WITH, AND ADVISE BAND MEMBERS OF BAND DEALINGS AND BUSINESS AFFAIRS. UNDER THESE CIRCUMSTANCES, WE DEMAND THE FOLLOWING:

1. THAT FURTHER CONSIDERATION
   OF SELF GOVERNMENT (BILL C-93)
   FOR THE WESTBANK INDIAN
   BAND BE DISCONTINUED AT THIS
   TIME.

It is telling that the one concrete demand in this fog of false-hoods, other than asking for my ouster, was that the government immediately discontinue Westbank's leasing agreement, which gave the band the ability to set rents. This, finally, what it was all about from the very beginning. The white rage at having to pay Indians a fair price for the use of their land.

Kayban took his petition to Ottawa, but he was unable to meet with Crombie. He delivered it instead to the bureaucrats at Indian Affairs, but nothing happened. So Kayban was forced to take it to another level. He invited Gordon College, an investigative news reporter for a Kelowna radio station, to the next meeting of the committee. As a result, on March 20, the above summary of complaints was issued in a press release — given to College. For me, it would become the basis of a successful lawsuit against 10 members of this Kayban-created Westbank Indian Action and Advisory Council.

A court would find all of the major statements defamatory, but at the time, the committee was on a roll and their flights of fancy reached new and breathtaking heights. According to Gordon College, he was told that there was "corruption at the local band level which overflows into the Regional level" and "That there was flagrant use of Band funds without consent of membership and that band Assets had been spirited away to foreign countries, such as Costa Rica, Miami (sic), Hawaii (sic), Switzerland. There was also illegal conduct regarding Band elections (bribery and intimidation)."

When these absurdities hit the press, I immediately called my lawyer and had him initiate legal proceedings against all of Kayban and his crew. Eventually, I would win what would be the largest amount of damages ever awarded in Canada, $410,000, for their libellous attacks against me, but of course that would be several years later.

At the time, Kayban and his committee were continuing to spread their poison. His next step was to lead a delegation to Edmonton to visit the Progressive Conservative MP David Kilgour, then the parliamentary secretary to the minister of Indian Affairs, so they could deliver their attacks on me personally.

After meeting with Kayban and his Westbank followers, Kilgour wrote to Crombie that "there are strong suspicions that Band members and DIAND employees have committed civil and/or criminal wrongs. Further DIAND is perceived as trying to 'cover-up' these questionable activities. Specific allegations include the following:

1. Attempted fraud — persons connected with the Band Council misrepresented the status of the Golden Acres lease in order to acquire a more lucrative lease.
2. Defamation — no further particulars are available.
3. Extortion — this appears to be connected with the above accusations of defamation.
4. There are two accusations of the Band publishing a false document and causing or attempting to cause other persons to act on it. (One accusation is from Golden Acres and one is from Park Mobile.)
5. Conspiracy between the Band and DIAND to circumvent British Columbia Supreme Court ruling. (Donaldson Engineering and Construction Ltd., an unsecured creditor.)
6. Conspiracy to commit fraud — the Band apparently attempted to obtain $60,000 from Acres Holdings Ltd. by reason of a purported development by-law requirement which in reality does not exist.
7. Welfare fraud — there is suspicion of a conspiracy between the Band and welfare person and/or Mr. Al

Monti (who reportedly collects rents on behalf of the Band Chief) to commit fraud. This suspicion was reported to DIAND (letter to Mr. J. Leask, September 17, 1984) but the matter was not investigated.

8. The band is suspected of using its position as a result of its section 60 authority to make secret profits."

In a kind of free-association addendum, I was also accused of being a welfare cheat, of stealing band money through the Northland Bank and there were catch-all mentions of "allegations of criminal activity which have been made include extortion and intimidation."

But there was far more to the meeting than what showed up in Kilgour's report to the minister. During the meeting, Larry Derrickson told David Kilgour that me and his own brother, David Derrickson, had murdered a band member, a descendent of old Chief Tomat, to steal his land. For good measure, he also accused us of the murder of a local white hippie who had gone missing in the hills a few years earlier — although I am not sure what motive they suggested for that one.

It was a stunning piece of news. Ron Derrickson was now a complete gangster. Fraud, theft, extortion, intimidation and now even murder. These reports went directly to the minister who contacted the RCMP and sent them in to investigate. But of course when the RCMP showed up on the reserve, Larry Derrickson and the dissidents suddenly disappeared. But before Larry headed into the hills to avoid having to answer the RCMP questions, he quietly warned his brother Dave of what he had done and apologized, saying he was "really only out to get Ron." The RCMP were left scratching their heads and asking around about a murder no one seemed to know anything about. Finally, they gave Dave a lie detector test on the killing and of course he passed it. It was bizarre. But by then, it was accepted as gospel in the Mulroney Department of Indian Affairs that my cousin Dave and I were gangsters who had turned the Westbank Indian Band into a criminal enterprise.

The Action Committee had done its job and when I formally launched a lawsuit against them, they faded into the mist.

But the damage had been done. In May 1986, Greenaway stood in the House of Commons to revive the old smear by requesting all of the information held by the Department on "Ron Derrickson or the Westbank Indian Band regarding Mr. Noll Derrickson, Toussowasket Enterprises Limited or the Mount Boucherie Trailer Park or any financial arrangements associated with the above (e) the Regional Director General for British Columbia of the Department of Indian Affairs and Northern Development and the Headquarters Economic Development regarding Mr. Noll Derrickson, Toussowasket Enterprises Limited or any official or employee of Toussowasket Enterprises Limited, the Mount Boucherie Trailer Park, Mr. Ron Derrickson, the Westbank Indian Band or the Westbank Development Company."

In June, Greenaway was back on his feet, this time with the resurrected talking points.

"In 1982, as a member of the Standing Committee on Indian Affairs, I became aware of a very serious case of impropriety involving the B.C. Regional Office of the Department of Indian Affairs and the Westbank Indian Band near Kelowna. It also became apparent that the chief of the band, Ronald Derrickson and his brother, Noll, were involved in some very questionable transactions and were receiving large amounts of money through the B.C. Regional Office, even though both men were known to be very wealthy. We wanted more information to determine if the Department was acting in an irresponsible manner and if, indeed, brothers Ron and Noll Derrickson were, in the words of the Honourable Member for Prince George–Peace River [Mr. Oberle], 'favourite sons' of B.C. Regional Director General Fred Walchli and becoming rich at the expense of other Indian bands and Canadian taxpayers.

"The Westbank affair is before the House once more and I sincerely hope the facts I and other members bring forward today will convince the minister of Indian Affairs and Northern Development

[Mr. Crombie], and this government, to seek a full inquiry under the Public Inquiries Act."

By June 25, they were ready to let the arrows fly. Fred King, MP for Okanagan–Similkameen, presented a petition "signed by 153 persons in the area of Okanagan–Similkameen, which calls upon the government to seek a full and impartial inquiry under the Public Inquiries Act to investigate fully all matters involving the Westbank Indian Band, most particularly its chief and council, and officials of the B.C. Regional Office of the Department of Indian and Northern Development . . ."

A few minutes later, Greenaway was also on his feet: "Mr. Speaker, on behalf of people of Westbank and Kelowna, British Columbia, I would like to table six petitions. They call upon the government to appoint a commission of inquiry under the Public Inquiries Act into the well-documented dubious activities with the compliance of the B.C. Region of the Department of Indian Affairs and Northern Development. I might add that there would be many, many more signatures on these petitions, but many people were afraid to sign."

The pressure on me during this period was enormous and I eventually blew up over it. It was in Vancouver at the Indian Affairs office, when I got into an argument with one of the regional officials, Jaimie Piez, who said to me, "You and your brother are nothing but crooks!"

I had had enough. My anger at the insane treatment I was receiving from every corner boiled over and I swung and hit the Indian Affairs official squarely on the jaw, sending him sprawling to the floor.

The police were there before I left the office and I was charged with criminal and not common assault, which does not normally carry a jail sentence, as you would expect when a punch is thrown in the middle of a heated exchange.

I thought then that I would be railroaded and given the longest possible jail sentence to put me in my place. Injustice was expected in these cases. I recalled that when I was around 20 years old, I was roughed up by a group of white guys outside the movie theatre and barely escaped to my car. But before I could get away, they surrounded me. I pulled out a tire iron to defend myself if they broke in and when the police arrived, of course I was the one who they threw in jail. This was the way the world worked. And I expected the worst after hitting that mealy-mouthed bureaucrat.

But the trial was a short one — and full of surprises. It lasted only from 9 to 11 a.m., with the charge dismissed by 2 p.m.

My worst fears had been confirmed at the beginning, when the Attorney General's office sent two of its top prosecutors to try to get my conviction, but the judge took notice of this, saying he really didn't like the look of this prosecutorial overkill and that he was also surprised by the criminal rather than common assault charge.

After hearing the basic evidence, with Brian Eli speaking up for me and my friend Fred Walchli testifying on my behalf, the judge decided that the case should be settled by a meeting in his office after lunch with the prosecutors and the defence attorney to discuss some kind of plea bargain. In the meantime, he said he ordered all of them not to discuss the case with their team or their witnesses. He then recessed the court for lunch.

The judge was a simple, honest man, who wore his cowboy hat on the street and he took his lunch, as always, at a busy little greasy spoon on Hastings Street. During the break, to his surprise, he found himself seated near the prosecutorial team and their witnesses who didn't recognize the guy in the cowboy hat at the next table. In direct defiance of his order, they were discussing the case and possible plea agreements they may or may not accept. The judge finished his soup and sandwich and slipped back onto the street, still unseen.

When he called the court to order, he looked at the Attorney General's star prosecutors and said, "It is time to get back to the criminal proceedings, but they are no longer going to be about Chief

Derrickson. I am dismissing that case. I was sitting beside you in the restaurant and I heard you discussing it in clear defiance of my order. And in dismissing the Derrickson case, I am ordering the state to pay triple Mr. Derrickson's full legal costs. And I want to see you both in my chambers tomorrow morning."

It was an indication to me that there were still decent people in the white world, and I walked out of there with all of my costs covered. But I would soon be spending exponential amounts on further legal representation.

On the reserve, the accusations against me were reaching a fever pitch. The Action Committee was having one of its final meetings at Lloyd Eli Sr.'s place to plot their final actions against me. Suddenly, they all came running out of the house with Dave's ex-wife, Barbara Derrickson, who was one of the leading forces in the opposition cabal, screaming to call the police because Ron Derrickson was trying to gas them. When authorities arrived, they discovered that the source of the "gas" was a backed-up sewer and the joke among my dramatically shrinking group of friends was that Derrickson's enemies were so full of shit they had lost their minds.

It was around this time that I was told by someone who was in a position to know that my phone was tapped by a couple of RCMP detectives at the Kelowna detachment. I was even given the names of the cops and I knew them both. I shared this information with Brian Eli and to amuse ourselves on our calls, we would talk about how one of the officers was having sex with the other one's wife. I am not sure what the effect was on the cops, but it did lighten up the mood a bit.

By this time, the mood definitely needed lightening. Events had gone far beyond Larry Derrickson's and Barbara Derrickson's nonsense. On August 12, 1986, the justice minister announced that the government was launching an inquiry. Order-in-Council PC-1986-1816 named Judge John E. Hall as head of the Royal Commission mandated "to inquire into certain matters associated with the Westbank Indian Band and certain matters relating to the Department of Indian Affairs and Northern Development." The hearings would take place in the Westbank school auditorium throughout 1987 and the report was published in 1988.

Judge Hall had been a prominent B.C. lawyer with the firm of DuMoulin Black. But he had little or no knowledge of Indigenous issues, communities or people. He had graduated from the University of Western Ontario Law School in 1963 and he was called to the B.C. Bar the following year. Hall spent two years as a Vancouver prosecutor and in 1978, he was president of the Vancouver Bar Association. He became a Queen's Counsel (QC) in 1982 and his most high-profile case was as a counsel to the Crown in the Clifford Olson case. Three years after the Royal Commission into Westbank was over, he was appointed to the Supreme Court of British Columbia, and then he went on the B.C. Criminal Court of Appeal.

But for me, the inquiry began with a squad of RCMP barging into my business office to cart off all of my files and my account books. It would be 10 months before I would get them back, and in the meantime we had to operate our business essentially blind.

This would be the most difficult two years of my life, and the stress came closer to killing me than Richard Cooper's bar ever had.

I did get one parting shot, however. In the immediate aftermath of the assassination attempt, the York family faded away and the other mobile home park operators who had some involvement in the plot were walking on eggshells. But during the hearings, the five-year leases that I had spiked with the time-bomb clause after the assassination attempt began to fall due and my would-be assassins got the shock of their lives when they saw that a rent increase, based on the value of not only the land but their buildings and their improvements, would skyrocket. I watched as one by one they went bankrupt. As we moved through the government hearings I at least had revenge for the wounds their agent, Mr. Cooper, had inflicted on me.

CHAPTER 12

A Royal Commission on Me

The final front that made up the perfect storm of forces heading my way was the local one. As the orchestrated campaign by local white businessmen and their Progressive Conservative mouthpieces was taking shape before my eyes in the spring of 1986, I decided that I could no longer stand for chief. If I were elected, I would be helpless with all my energy taken up defending myself and offering a standing target for my enemies. So I announced I would stand aside in the August 26 election. My decision was the only one I could take in the best interest of the band, but it allowed my opponents to slip into office. And it was at that point I became truly fearful. I knew that I had done nothing wrong, but with my opponents now making up the new chief and council, I was suddenly vulnerable to being set up by phoney evidence coming out — not only from the local Progressive Conservatives and their murderous white business clientele but also from a band council office that had, in important ways, already joined forces with them and, who I was suing for defamatory statements about me.

This included the new chief, Robert Louie, who had been one of Kayban's followers. In the future, Robert Louie would play an important role in Westbank politics, and given the role he played in Kayban's crazy Westbank Indian Action and Advisory Council, I was obviously not going to be a fan of his. But in office, Louie also turned out to be a classic establishment Indian, someone who was very adept at feeding off the public trough, accepting watered-down versions of our rights from the government and then being rewarded with high-paying posts on government advisory boards and committees, which added exponentially to what became a substantial chief's salary.

The way it worked was that in one year, Louie would pay himself $150,389 as Westbank chief, but he was also paid an $800-a-day per diem and a salary of $122,800 as the government-paid Land Advisory Board chair, with $35,456 in travel funding. This was in addition to the $25,599 in travel expenses he charged the band. I can only imagine what these payments amounted to when you took all of his boards and committees together, which included the National Aboriginal Economic Development Board, First Nations Finance Authority Inc., All Nations Trust Company, Kelowna Chamber of Commerce, United Native Friendship Society, the Premier's Advisory Council of Aboriginal Affairs, the First Nations Lands Advisory Board and Peace Hills Trust (Financial Institution).

With this new, politically pliable chief as one of my attackers, I was afraid I was not going to be the subject of an inquiry but of a set-up arranged between the band office and the Progressive Conservative Indian Affairs department.

But when I finally looked at the actual mandate of the committee, I was reminded that my accusers had to not only frame me but also the Indian Affairs department that I had worked in coordination with. This was evident in the mandate to investigate "certain matters associated with the Westbank Indian Band of Kelowna, British Columbia that have been the subject of public controversy" involving allegations of impropriety "on the part of officials of the Department of Indian Affairs and Northern Development (DIAND) and of Councillors of the Westbank Indian Band (Band) in connection with the affairs of the Band."

So my accusers had to actually prove that the Department of Indian Affairs was in on my "crimes" because I had been working in consultation with the Department every step of the way, and they had reviewed each action I had taken and determined that I was not only blameless but served as an example for other Indigenous leaders to follow.

Even knowing all that, it is almost impossible to describe the weight on my chest that the inquiry represented. As soon as the Royal Commission was announced, I learned quite brutally that people tend to equate accusations with proof and, as the Action Committee's accusations were aired in the media — among them, that I had stolen $15 million and socked it away in a secret Caribbean bank account — many of my acquaintances began crossing to the other side of the street when they saw me coming. Among these, I was startled to see, was a lawyer who had recently been disbarred, which greatly irritated me because I should have been crossing the street to avoid him. But he beat me to the punch.

Now I was *persona non grata* virtually everywhere, and the local newspapers and radio stations continued to blare the false accusations against me as the Royal Commission hearings began in the gymnasium of the Westbank Band school in late 1986. My worries increased when I heard from my former secretary, Barbara DeSchutter, that she was threatened with prosecution on trumped-up charges if she didn't corroborate some of the baseless accusations against me. She was even warned by investigators that she could go to jail and lose her children if she did not join the chorus of denunciations against me.

Finally, in the summer of 1987, I was called to the stand and testified under oath for 24 days, beginning on June 5. It was gruelling. Every day I faced government lawyers firing accusations at me and working hard to trip me up on any statement, as I tried to simply tell the truth and offer explanations for past actions they had already woven into a dark web to capture me. I was bitterly aware through all of this that the Conservative MPs who had spread so many lies about me — Lorne Greenaway, Fred King and Frank Oberle — were not even subpoenaed. This was one of the biggest travesties because these three MPs used the protection of parliamentary privilege to spread the harmful lies about me to create the monster, but were allowed to slink away without even being cross-examined.

After my 23rd day of testimony, I went out on a lake with my cousin Dave and a woman I was going out with at the time. I told Dave that I'd had it. I just couldn't go on with this bullshit. Dave reacted angrily. "Don't be a fucking loser, talking that way. You'll get through this. Don't let them get you down. Stand up and fight. Don't be a fucking loser!"

But really, I was at the end of my tether. Everywhere, there were accusations against me. I stopped reading the local papers, but even when I picked up a national newspaper like the *Globe and Mail*, I would turn a page and find articles like "Wrongdoer or Just Wily? Animosity for Rich Indian." Being on display while the press turns your name into mud and facing outrageous accusations in the commission hearings day in and day out — and feeling that this would never end — made me believe that these accusations would dog me for the rest of my life. I would never get free of them. My enemies, I felt, had already won.

It was late when I arrived back at the house from my day on the boat with Dave. I headed for my desk in the den, where I still had the revolver that I used against Richard Cooper. I was opening the drawer to take it out when I was startled by the presence of someone in the room. I swung around and saw what looked like three Native women in the shadows. Not all women — one was a girl of about nine, the other looked about 30 and the third was quite old. This was the strangest moment of my life. The older woman put her hand out. She was standing eight feet away, but I could

LEFT: A free-range Okanagan kid on the family land.

BELOW: With my mother and brother Noll (on the left) in front of our small, rough-hewn house.

Me with Noll and our
dog Sport.

Happy on the
hillside in the spring
sunshine.

ABOVE: Sitting on the wagon with Noll. (I'm on the right.)

LEFT: About the age of 12, standing beside my father's car.

As a young man in an Indian headdress.

My father playing the guitar with my son, Doug.

ABOVE: With my daughter, Kelly, in the late 1970s.

LEFT: Portrait of a young chief, around 1976.

Doug with his son, Matthew, my grandson.

Happy to hold my
grandson Matthew.

ABOVE: Back to business.

LEFT: Kelly with her second in a row Native American Music Award in 2018.

Recent portrait.

feel this powerful energy. She didn't say anything, she just smiled at me. I then knew I had to stay strong. I felt the strange warmth of her energy, a warmth that didn't leave after she disappeared. It stayed with me not only for the rest of the day but for many days — in fact, three months later I could still feel her energy. I do not know who they were or where they had come from — somewhere from the other side perhaps — but from that moment on, I no longer had thoughts about blowing my brains out. From that moment on, things began to change.

Fred Walchli took the stand after me at the inquiry and began to bat away the ridiculous accusations, giving detailed explanations of my activities in consultation with the Department and put forward the results of the Department's investigations of Westbank that found my work exemplary. Including providing detailed audits of the band's books every single year where every cent was accounted for. While it had been relatively easy for the racists like Kayban and the mobile home park operators to portray an Indian as a ruthless gangster, it was a little more difficult to paint Fred Walchli, the regional superintendent of Indian Affairs with a lifetime of public service, as part of the gang. It would also have to have included a dozen other Indian Affairs officials who supported Walchli's explanation, including Paul Tellier, then the highest bureaucrat in the land as clerk of the Privy Council, who had served as John Munro's deputy minister of Indian Affairs during the first half of the 1980s. As the hearings progressed to their conclusion, I could sense Justice Hall's growing impatience with the unsupported accusations against me and against the Department of Indian Affairs.

By the time the $10 million public inquiry was over, no one was surprised when I was absolved on every serious charge. I certainly do not agree with everything Hall said, and would object to some of his characterizations (though not his suggestion that I can be arrogant at times — I certainly can be). But he at least gave a sense of how far the accusations were from reality.

He began by quickly dismissing all the accusations around my handling of the Toussowasket issue. He pointed out that one feature of Indian land that made it desirable to developers was that there was relatively little by-law regulation of the land. "Chief Derrickson felt that this was an area that needed study and possible improvement. He believed regulation could generate income and ensure better quality developments. Chief Derrickson was not a man to hide his light under a bushel. He had been relatively aggressive in acquiring land for his own use and he was determined to pursue an aggressive policy in getting a better return on reserve lands from the lessees operating mobile home parks. Unbeknownst to these lessees, a very new broom indeed had arrived.

"As it happened, Mr. Derrickson became chief at a time when a different system of Departmental administration came into effect. Rapid change often causes discomfort. Additionally, periods of rapid change put stresses on people and systems that may cause both to malfunction at times. [Mr. Derrickson] was a man for all seasons but, like many men of action, he caused in some others quite strong reactions. Relations between him and certain mobile home park lessees became increasingly acrimonious — Mr. Crosby complained to Departmental officials and politicians about what he perceived as problems relative to lessees and band and Departmental administration.

"A mobile home park owners' association was formed in 1982 in response to a number of initiatives taken by the chief in 1981. Acrimonious relations existed between the band executive and a number of park operators. Some park operators questioned the ethics of the band executive, and in particular, Chief Derrickson. Complaints were conveyed to members of Parliament and the media carried stories about conflict at Westbank."

The report described the attempted murder against me in 1982 and even connected the Yorks to the aftermath of the attempted assassination by describing the meeting in the York household in Edmonton where they tried to get Larry York Jr. to take the blame for the attempted hit for a $30,000 to 50,000 payoff. It then chronicled the continuing campaign of the mobile park operators to have me removed from office, culminating in them working with the political opposition in the community.

"In 1986, dissident elements within the band, spurred into action in part by a non-Indian 'consultant' [Kayban], vented their frustrations in some strongly worded petitions to the minister, suggesting grave improprieties on the part of the chief and band administration. It was alleged that the local Department of Indian Affairs was either supine or corrupt and could not be trusted to give an accurate version of affairs at Westbank.

"Unfortunately, some of the highly charged allegations emanating from Mr. Crosby and those members of the Band who comprised an 'Action Committee' were viewed too credulously by certain parliamentarians. These individuals, believing their constituents, took an alarmist view of events at Westbank. There were problems at Westbank and in the Department of Indian Affairs, but not of a serious criminal nature."

As justices go, Hall was the usual white, upper-class lawyer, but he had come to the inescapable conclusion that none of the serious charges against me were legitimate. In his concluding comments, he suggested that I was probably guilty of acting in conflict of interest in a couple of my personal deals and with family members, but not seriously so. In this, the judge did not understand how impossible it is to operate on an Indian reserve without at times dipping into conflict of interest, because Indian bands were, and to a certain extent remain, kinship communities. While there was a strong focus on Noll being my brother, the kinship nature of our community was also reflected in the fact that the guy falsely accusing me of murder was also a relative — my cousin Larry. That is part of life in communities such as ours. Friends and enemies are all still family. And you can't function on an Indian reserve without dealing with family.

In the immediate aftermath of the hearings, I set about in earnest to clear my name. I proceeded with all of the lawsuits that I had begun in 1986, because I wanted to have all of the accusations against me properly addressed and adjudicated in a court of law so the accusations could finally be laid to rest. I set about to systematically sue every single person, including my internal opposition that had coalesced around Harold, for defaming me. Some of the people I sued were not wealthy, but I was not after the money. I wanted those false allegations examined and dismissed one by one and the defamers held accountable by the courts. In all, I sued 11 people and I won every case. And each court victory helped me recover a piece of my name, which had been trampled on for so many years while I was serving as chief. It was part of my liberation.

When the slander and libel judgement came down against Kayban and the 11 band members working with the Westbank Indian Action and Advisory Council, I was personally awarded $410,000 in damages plus costs, then the largest libel settlement in Canadian history. (The previous high had been a $125,000 judgment against the CBC for its attacks on Ricard Vogel, a former Attorney General.) The case had been taken not only in my name, but in the names of the band councillors at the time, Brian Eli and Harold Derrickson, and they were awarded $40,000 each. With court costs factored in, the case would cost the respondents more than $750,000.

Those held responsible by the court were: Robert Louie, Anne Marie Tomat, Mary Derrickson, Larry Derrickson, Lloyd Eli Sr., Clarence Clough, Barbara Derrickson, Gary Swite, Rose Derrickson, Barbara Coble, Bonnie Coble and Nicholas Kayban. The amount would eventually be reduced on technicalities to do with suing a group rather than an individual, but the precedent would stand in law, and in her 85-page decision, Justice Patricia Proudfoot did not mince her words in condemning their unfounded attacks on me.

The people found responsible by the courts and their relatives were furious about the judgement. After spending the mid-1980s trying to destroy my reputation, they began to mutter threats against me and my family for suing them. It was another bitter period for me. The anger of this group was so strong that the CBC show *The Fifth Estate* did an episode on me, where they described me as the most hated man in B.C.

I experienced this feeling when I went to the funeral of a Westbank Elder and I was seated beside my daughter and a woman Elder from Penticton. While we were waiting for the service to begin, I leaned over to Kelly and said, "Lots of people here. I bet when I die there will hardly be anyone."

The Penticton Elder overheard me and leaned over Kelly and whispered, "Oh yes, Ron, there will be many, many people at your funeral."

Then, with a smile, she added, "They will all be there to make sure you're really dead!"

I laughed at that, because it was quite a witty thing to say. But for the most part, my terrible reputation in the community was nothing to laugh about, with a stream of death threats immediately after the settlement was announced.

What worried me was that some of the threats were not only directed at me but against my children as well. I had a talk with both of them. Doug by this time was a young man of 22 and he seemed nonchalant about the whole thing. He assured me that he would be careful, but also that he could take care of himself. I was more worried about my daughter, Kelly. She was only 15 at the time — a very vulnerable age — and I sat her down and told her that she had to be very careful in the community because of the boiling anger against me by many of the most powerful people.

A couple of months later, when the anger against me by the community members I had sued was still hot, Kelly did have a moment of fear. She was walking to school and a dark-coloured station wagon drove by her twice and then disappeared up the hill. When she crested the hill, the car was parked and the driver was standing beside the passenger door. He lunged toward her and Kelly ran like hell to the nearest house and banged on the door until they opened it. The station wagon sped away, but it was enough to convince me that Westbank was not safe for her. I sent her to a boarding school in Victoria. When it came time for her to go to college, I sent her to Switzerland.

I was not going to run from the people on the reserve who were trying to run me off, but I was not going to risk putting my children in what I knew from experience could be a murderous atmosphere.

CHAPTER 13

Back to Business

Even after I left Indian politics and the commission and successive courts cleared my name, I was left with one unfinished piece of business. The final act during this period came when John Munro was targeted for the sort of persecution that I had just weathered. In 1989, Munro was charged with 37 counts of fraud, corruption and other offences and subjected to a Progressive Conservative show trial. Among the most serious accusations was that he had paid out $1.5 million to Indigenous groups who in return donated part of the money to his 1984 leadership campaign. I found my name being raised here, as well as one of his supporters and campaign donors. I was visited several times by investigators and I told them, and stated under oath in court, that it was rubbish. Money the band received from the Indian Affairs department went exclusively to the band and was closely audited by outside accountants every year. Any donation I gave to Munro came out of my own pocket and was made in complete transparency and in respect of the Election Act.

After I testified, Munro flew out to meet with me. I understood the gratitude he felt for one of the few people, like me, who had stood beside him when all others ran for cover. It was the type of gratitude I felt for Fred Walchli when he testified at the Royal Commission in unreserved support of me. The evening Munro arrived at my house was my mother's birthday, and he brought her a lovely gift. She cooked us one of the delicious Japanese dinners that she had learned from the camp inmates during the war, and to my mother's delight, Munro had two big helpings. My father played his fiddle after dinner and sang and it was a nice break for Munro. I could see — and well understand — the unrelenting stress he was under. All I could tell him was to hang in there and keep fighting. He would beat them in the end. And he did. In 1991, after my testimony in Ottawa, the judge threw out all 37 trumped-up charges against him, and Munro then successfully sued the government for $1.4 million for wrongful prosecution.

Finally, that chapter of my life ended and I was ready to get back to business. Although to the surprise of many, including myself, I would find myself back in the saddle as Westbank chief 10 years later, for what has been described as the War in the Woods.

But first it was time for business. The decade between 1986 and 1998 was among the most important in my business life. At the beginning of this period, I was in my mid-forties and the skills I had acquired in building the community businesses I could finally devote to building my own, which, contrary to my detractors' assertions, had been largely neglected in my years as band chief. My holdings were scattered and I was running my operation out of an amusement park that I had built called Old MacDonald's Farm. It had a petting zoo, pony rides, waterslide, minigolf and picnic and food concession area — and, most popular, a fishing pond that I stocked with trout. The business was good in the summer, but the real reason I kept it was because I loved watching the kids come to the pond and have the thrill of catching their first fish.

But as often happens in life, there was a big hurdle to overcome, in the sudden and unexpected collapse of the North American real estate market in 1989, which carried on through the early 1990s.

There was no single cause for the plunge in the business cycle in 1989, but it was partly a reaction to the overheated economy and rampant real estate speculation of the 1980s, coupled with dumb monetary policy that brought the North American economy down with a thud. When, in the summer of 1990, the U.S. launched its first war against Iraq in response to its invasion of Kuwait, oil prices were sent skyrocketing and business and consumer confidence plunged to new lows. It was a deep financial hole and it came at the worst time for me. This recession would take down real estate companies like Cadillac Fairview, the Campeau group and even the mighty Reichmanns, who were the biggest real estate company in the world at the time, and I had to find a way through it.

With my newfound freedom in 1986, I had invested everything I had in a major real estate development, putting my capital and a lot of borrowed money in a suburban housing development with 160 houses. With the initial plunge in real estate values, I suddenly found myself $10 million in debt with 159 houses in the middle of construction. In the poor market, 50 of the buyers pulled out and walked away and I had to go to the banks and ask them to stay with me while I weathered the storm. Again, I made the necessary deals to allow me to pay interest on the loans while I tried to wait out the market.

While I waited, I looked around for deals where I could make some quick profit with minimum outlay. I found one while I was driving by the Brenda Mine just south of Westbank. It was a copper mine that was in the process of shutting down, and I noticed that they had four large steel buildings that were housing their equipment. I pulled into the mine site and went to the manager.

"What are you going to do with the steel buildings?" I asked.

He shrugged. "No idea," he said.

So I offered to buy them on the spot for $10,000 each and said I would send a team to dismantle and move them. After some checking with the owners, he agreed and I moved them to my property on Louis Drive in Westbank and I was in the warehouse business. Over the next year, I picked up two more, and when they were painted up they rented quickly and I earned back the original outlay and the dismantling and re-erection costs. In fact, they looked so fine that I moved my own operation into one of them from the previous office I had at Old MacDonald's Farm, which I was forced to close when the insurance was raised from $17,000 to $80,000. The closure was not a financial problem, because the land that it was on was infinitely more valuable than the small business operation, and I was later able to develop it into a significant commercial property with a major grocery store tenant. But I did miss the family pleasure it gave and the kids at the fishing pond.

By the early 1990s, the real estate market was picking up again and I was back in business with the house sales starting again at a brisk pace. I quickly saturated the market in the Okanagan and I decided to extend my operation north into Kamloops.

I took over a small Century 21 office in a closet-sized room in downtown Kamloops, and as it turned out, my timing was good. I had sharpened my real estate skills in the much more competitive Kelowna-area market so I had an advantage in Kamloops. The office went through a constant expansion, to the point where I ditched the Century 21 affiliation and went on my own under the name Inland Realty. By the time I sold the company, I had 69 employees, including 25 secretaries, and we were controlling more than 70 percent of the Kamloops market. One young woman who had been working with us for a month or two while she got her licence closed several deals on her first day with a licence and made $86,000 in commissions, which she turned around and used to purchase one of our houses for cash. It was heady times with our best client, as it turned out, being Philip Gaglardi, the B.C. highways minister whose family had major real estate holdings across the province, including Sandman Inns, and gave us around a million dollars in business a year.

Closer to home, I purchased the Shelter Bay Marina property, which was located on lands I was renting out at the foot of the Kelowna bridge, making it easily accessible for the boat owners from Kelowna. The original property was built by Tim Bird, a local businessman who was co-owner of a big sports store in Kelowna. When the sports store got into trouble, he sold his interest in the marina to another businessman, who leased all of his rental equipment from me but then refused to pay me the $80,000 he owed me. So I went to the law firm that worked for me and I said, "Put one of your young lawyers on this full-time and I will pay his salary." My young lawyer had the guy in court 87 times in one year, often in Vancouver. The guy would get off the plane from a hearing in Vancouver and the bondsman would meet him at the airport with another notice to appear. Finally, instead of simply paying me what he owed me, he came to me and told me that he gave up. He wanted to sell the marina to me and move on. I said, sure, that would work. And from its modest beginnings, I developed the marina into a major undertaking with more the 250 berths with access to shore power and pump-outs, full services for boat and maintenance and repair, a marine store and gas dock. I managed to turn it into a lucrative business, bringing in $2.6 million a year from moorings alone and gas sales earned three-quarters of a million more a year, while the store and related services added to our growing revenues.

Almost everything I did during this period made money. But while most people are skeptical when I say it, money was nowhere near the prime motivator. I loved the challenge of business — accepting the risk and attacking problems head-on. As I mentioned earlier, money earned is only the way you keep score in the game and provides the chips you need to continue. For me, business was not only a substitute for a nine-to-five job, it gave me the same thrill as speedboat racing. In both, I played to win. The truth of this is reflected in the fact that I found it just as exhilarating to put together successful business ventures for the band as chief — when I had no financial interest whatsoever — as I did in putting together my own private deals.

One of my core businesses became operating mobile home parks, some of which I took over from my former leaseholders and tormentors. From the beginning I was determined to give people value, and my tenants seemed to appreciate this, because they stayed with me. I know this because I put in their individual leases that when they celebrated 20 years with me, I would give them a free month's rent, and over the years I have given out more than a 100 of these free months. The secret, of course, is upkeep — making sure the place was well-kept and the trailers always in top-notch repair. One way of ensuring the constant renewal of the place was to put in the lease a clause requiring them to upgrade their unit when they were going to sell. This kept the park first-rate and also made sure the tenants got top dollar for their unit when they left.

Turning marginal parks into profitable businesses is something that I came to excel at. I bought a mobile home park on the Indian reserve at Langley, B.C., just outside of Vancouver, at a fire-sale price because it had a big problem with a leaky sewage plant. The previous owner had built the plant under government order, but the thing didn't work and sewage was still leaking into the Fraser River. As soon as I bought the place I was given an order to vacate. I went to the environmental department and asked for 60 days to get the place cleaned up and they agreed.

I brought in the best engineer who had experience on the system, and within three days, he determined that a pressure valve wasn't working. We ordered the part and it arrived 13 days later. While he was reassembling it, he found that the chlorine dispenser was clogged and put together a maintenance schedule to solve that and the other performance issues with the system.

In 21 days, the system was working perfectly and the environmental department came down and tested the outtake water and gave us a clean bill of health.

In later years, the property became the subject of an important court case when the government tried to collect taxes from me, even though it was on Indian land. They took me to court, claiming that a Langley Band member would be exempt from the land tax. Even though I was a status Indian, I was not a member of the band, so I should pay local municipal taxes. I refused. I fought it as an Indigenous rights case arguing that as a status Indian I would still have the exemption on any Indigenous land. I won, setting what would be a Canada-wide precedent for on-reserve investments by status Indians who were not members of the band where the business was located.

It was, overall, a happy period for me. I had put together a strong staff and the office was a lighthearted place. We worked as a team and like when I was chief, the staff didn't hesitate to have fun at my expense. They teased me for my lack of modesty — I know I can be arrogant, and don't hide this part of my personality. I recall one day in particular, when my office manager, Cathy, said in exasperation during a meeting, after I questioned one of our activities, "It is not always about you, Ron." Rod Cook, who I was still using as my appraiser, said to her, "Cathy, didn't you know that the RMD motto is: 'Me! Me! Me?'" Which of course the staff immediately picked up as the unofficial, and endlessly repeated, motto of the company.

During this happy time time, I still had a nagging sense of unfinished business. You would think that my unhappy experiences at the end of my 10 years as chief would have turned me off Indian politics altogether, but throughout this period I was still closely watching what was happening in the national and regional spheres. And they were troubling times. The national scene was dominated by the fallout from the constitutional patriation debate of 1980. It was then that the great George Manuel led the Constitutional Express, a train filled with a thousand Indian protesters, to Parliament Hill in Ottawa to demand the recognition of Indigenous rights in the renewed British North America Act that was then being patriated from Britain.

The arrival of the B.C. Indians in Ottawa worried the new national chief, Del Riley, as much as the Liberals, because my friend Bobby Manuel — who was heading the delegation on the train — had come within one vote of beating him for national chief a couple of months before.

To the surprise of many, George and Bobby Manuel managed to force the government to include in the Constitution the new Section 35 (1): "The existing aboriginal and treaty rights of the aboriginal people in Canada are hereby recognized and affirmed." The content of those rights were to be set out in a series of federal-provincial constitutional meetings held with the representatives of the status Indians, Inuit and Métis peoples that were held between 1983 and 1987, and then collapsed when the government tried to withdraw on one hand what the Constitution had given on the other.

But Indigenous issues could not be so easily dismissed. Our people were able to take their revenge when the Manitoba MLA Elijah Harper sat in the Manitoba Legislature clutching an eagle feather as he refused to give the required unanimous consent to pass the Meech Lake Accord, which had been designed to satisfy Quebec's constitutional demands with nothing for Indigenous people. Because of Elijah, the accord failed and our people had been able to send a message that we would not be brushed aside.

That message was given with even greater force the following year, in the summer of 1990, when the dispute over a golf course expansion in Oka, Quebec, turned into a shooting war that pitted the Sûreté du Québec, and then the Canadian Army, against the Mohawks of Kanesatake and Kahnawake. Like every Indigenous person in the country, I followed these events very closely and made some significant, and very discreet, cash donations to the Mohawk Warriors to pay for food, medical supplies and legal representation in their confrontation with the Canadian Army.

Later in the decade, in 1995, the shooting war moved closer to home with the Gustafsen Lake standoff on ranchlands near 100 Mile House on the road to Prince George. It was then that 400 RCMP paramilitaries descended on a handful of Sun Dancers in a camp defended by tough Indigenous nationalists like the Secwépemc Elder known by the *nom de guerre* of Wolverine. The paramilitaries attacked with military helicopters, exploded land mines and fired more than 7,000 rounds at the camp and it was a miracle no one was killed. Once again, I gave cash donations. This must have been noticed when a hit list — that some said came from the RCMP — was leaked to the press with the names of people they wanted out of the picture permanently. My name, as well as that of my friend Grand Chief Stewart Phillip, was on the list.

In the end, Gustafsen Lake was a perfect example of Canadian government lawlessness and brutality in dealing with Indigenous peoples in B.C. This was recognized internationally when James Pitawanakwat, one of the Warriors who fought alongside Wolverine, fled the country and was given political asylum in the U.S. because of the illegal actions of the RCMP during the standoff.

The political unrest was sparking new efforts in Ottawa to finally pacify B.C. Indigenous peoples with a quick solution to the land question, which would involve giving us millions in cash and 1 or 2 percent of our original territories in exchange for extinguishment of our Aboriginal title. For many at the time, this seemed to be the best we could hope for, and many communities joined what became known as the B.C. Treaty Process to negotiate a deal for their community.

Westbank, under its current leadership, was one of the first to take a seat at the table. I was not sure about this. Surrendering Aboriginal title seemed like a mistake, from both a cultural and purely business point of view. The land was all we had and who we were. Surrendering the land was to surrender ourselves.

If I was skeptical about these land deals before, I was convinced that it was a crazy idea after December 1997, when the Supreme Court of Canada came out with the Delgamuukw decision on Aboriginal title. It had been brought by a Gitxsan hereditary chief, Delgamuukw (Christian name Earl Muldoe), who was suing on his own behalf and that of the members of the Houses of Delgamuukw and Haaxw, and with others suing on behalf of 38 Gitxsan Houses and 12 Wet'suwet'en Houses.

The decision was of course complex and in some areas it gave with one hand and took away with the other, but in one area it was clear: our Aboriginal title existed, it couldn't be extinguished without our consent and it had an unmistakeable economic element.

The implications of this were enormous. From here on in, extinguishing our title for a couple of hundred million in cash over 20 or more years was no longer simply dodgy — it was crazy. The math simply didn't add up. For a nation of 10,000 people, Canada might pay $200 million or so over 20 years to end up with the ownership of many hundreds of square kilometres of Aboriginal title land. Break that down and it works out to about $3 a day per person ($3 x 10,000 people x 365 days x 20 years) for land containing literally trillions of dollars of resources. And after the 20 years, you even lost the $3 a day.

The Delgamuukw decision was telling us that Aboriginal title was not an abstract holdover from history that we could cash in for money; it was a real economic ownership in our vast lands. It was still unclear how this would shake out. Even our national organizations seemed stunned by the decision. I was vaguely aware of George Manuel's son Arthur — Bobby's brother — launching an organization of the Interior tribes to defend our title, but I was not at the time connected to this. My own immediate concern about Indigenous lands was much more local than that.

While the Delgamuukw issue was swirling around, I was concerned about the land I had purchased as Westbank chief from the cut-off lands fund in Gallagher Canyon. Now, more than a decade later, they had still not been turned into reserve land. That was part of the deal and I had brought it to the final stages when I had stepped down in 1986. At the time, it seemed we were only months away from having Gallagher Canyon confirmed as part of the reserve. But since then, the band leadership had completely dropped the ball on the issue. That is why I told myself in August 1998 that I would put my name forward as chief again, to spend one term back to get the job done on Gallagher Canyon.

Looking back, I think it went deeper. I felt I had been railroaded out of the job in the tidal wave of lies and false accusations against me. I had in the intervening time been cleared of wrongdoing in the $10 million Royal Commission and in the series of civil actions against those who attempted to assassinate my body and character. So I decided that I would go back to finish one more two-year mandate and then leave on my own terms. In a way, getting re-elected as chief would be the final act of vindication. And that is what it felt like on September 5, 1998, when the election results came in and I once again won the support of my people.

It was a happy night. But of course I did not realize I was about to get involved in a war in the forest that would lead me into a new international struggle for Indigenous rights, alongside the great George Manuel's second son.

In Indian politics, more than any other area in life, you have to be very careful of what you wish for.

CHAPTER 14

War in the Woods

When I ran again for chief in September 1998, my plan was simple — first, get the Gallagher Canyon lands recognized as reserve lands, and then work to recapture the band's previous economic dynamism, which had been in decline over the previous dozen years. Nothing radical. Nothing dramatic.

But what was I thinking? This was an Indigenous community, where there was always something flying in out of nowhere that you could never have predicted.

The insanity that I had faced as chief in the 1980s had been largely cleared away by the Royal Commission and by my many lawsuits, and the ejection of the Crosbys and the Yorks and the whole angry nest of white trailer park owners. Still, there were left-over internal tensions.

For example, as soon as I was elected chief, the employees who had been hired by my opponents in the outgoing administration decided to form a union out of fear that I would come in and fire them all. I had no intention of doing that and the idea of a union didn't concern me in the least. As a welder, I had for a long time been a member of an industrial union, and was proud of that fact. The problem was that the members did not form a local union or a union of workers in our Okanagan Nation, but brought in the B.C. Federation of Labour to represent them. I knew from my own experience that a large, powerful, white institution like the B.C. Fed had no business in our band office. From my industrial union experience I knew the type of paralyzing power such an institution could wield in a way that could easily sweep aside the band membership and their right to choose the course for their community.

So when I met the B.C. Fed negotiators I told them this. That I was not at all against a union and would happily negotiate an agreement with a local union, but that I did not believe that a big international union should be installed in the middle of our tiny band office. The union negotiators, all white people from Vancouver, immediately got their backs up and warned me that they would come at me if I didn't back down. But if they thought I would be intimidated by that, they hadn't done their research on me. I smiled and thought, OK, let the games begin.

I called my team together and told them that the union wanted to negotiate with us and by law we have to negotiate with them. So let's give them something to negotiate. We sat for a couple of days and came up with a total of 2,800 issues we wanted to discuss with them.

In our first negotiating session, I put all of the 2,800 issues on the table for discussion. I saw the anger in their faces and then I watched their spirits sink when I began with the issue of priority hiring. I said as a self-governing Nation, we reserved the right to establish our own priority hiring system. First, the band would give priority to Westbank Band members in hiring for all jobs. Next would be the resident spouses of band members. Then other band members and then other natives living on the Westbank Reserve and then Natives on other Okanagan Indian band lands. Then Interior Salish members of the Interior bands tribal councils and then the

Coastal Salish peoples. Then other Natives of British Columbia. Then we covered the Natives of every other province and territory and I said at the end, that was it. A non-Native would never be allowed to work for the band other than as a consultant, who would not be covered by the union agreement. The Vancouver negotiators squirmed in their seats but said nothing. And we went on like that for several meetings until they simply stopped showing up.

During this time I was also working toward getting reserve status for Gallagher Canyon, and by the end of my first year in office, it was well on its way to becoming a reserve, although the final papers didn't arrive for signing until two days before my two-year term was up.

While that long, complex process was continuing, I was also drawn into what was becoming a highly charged debate surrounding the Delgamuukw decision, which was the backdrop to my visit to the B.C. Forestry office in Penticton and to ask for a permit to cut trees on our traditional lands — which the Supreme Court had recently acknowledged we still had an economic interest in. The forestry official looked at me like I was child and said that was impossible. Permits for all of the 7.6 million cubic metres of logs being taken out of our territory in the Okanagan Valley had already been given out to the big companies. Next year, he said, we could participate in the auction for the rights to the small undistributed areas. But that was it. We could make a bid, but there was no guarantee we would get anything.

"But this is our timber," I said.

The forestry official shrugged. "Maybe you can take some of the blowdown."

My final words were: "So, we get nothing?"

The forestry repeated, "You got nothing." And he laughed when he said it.

I felt like a fool. Woodpeckers and termites would get far more wood than he was offering my people, who were the original owners of the land. I headed home, dispirited. But when I was approaching Westbank, the words "all the provincial permits had been given out" stuck in my mind. If there are no provincial permits for us, I thought, the hell with it. I'll get an Indian permit.

By the time I was back at the office, I had a plan. I called my council together. At the time, it was made up of Chad Paul, Mike DeGuevara and Mickey Worstik, and I told them I wanted to lead the community out to log on our traditional land with an Indian instead of a provincial permit. Up until then I had not seen eye to eye with the council on all issues and I was worried that they might refuse to support such a radical initiative. But I was pleasantly surprised when the council said they would back me wholeheartedly on this. I was especially glad that Mickey Worstik was on side, because he was a logger himself and would be invaluable in overseeing the operation.

With my council behind me, I called the Okanagan Nation Alliance Office — in effect, our national government — and asked them if they would issue me an Indian logging permit for our traditional land. Up until that moment no such thing existed, so of course there was some confusion about what I was asking for. But when I finally convinced them that I was serious, they were more than happy to comply.

That is how the War in the Woods began.

It was the beginning of September in 1999. The land we selected was on our traditional territory near Hidden Creek, a section that was scheduled to come up for auction that year, but no permits had yet been issued. Mickey Worstick began pulling together a team of first-rate Okanagan loggers. I told him we wouldn't have heavy equipment, just chainsaws and fellers, but I wanted them to work fast. This was not to be a symbolic action, it was a real logging operation and we wanted to take the timber down safely and efficiently so the province would know we meant business.

Mickey was delighted by the idea of logging under an Okanagan permit and we made sure that it contained all of the province's safety codes so they would have no reason to shut us down. This was an important precaution because sure enough, workman's compensation and the labour code people came swarming to the site to see it they could use the work and safety code to shut us down without having to face our Aboriginal title claims in the courts.

Early on the morning of September 7, 1999, Mickey led his crew to Hidden Creek while we issued the press release announcing that Westbank was making history by logging with an Indigenous rather than a provincial permit on our traditional off-reserve lands. Instantly, our office phones lit up like a Christmas tree with press calls from throughout the region and then from Vancouver and beyond.

The next wave of calls came from local Indigenous organizations trying to figure out what the hell was going on. Most of them were as confused by our action as the white journalists.

I headed to the site the next day and by then press cars and some unmarked RCMP cars were lined up along the side of the logging road.

Mickey and his crew were doing their job with dozens of trees down and the timber neatly stacked.

While I was there, the local forestry official sauntered up. Politely, even a bit nervously, he told me that we were illegally logging on the SBFEDP Block (#101) of the Hidden Creek site, and he said he was giving us "a verbal order to cease operations."

Then he turned away without waiting for a response and hurried back to his car.

I told the gathered reporters that "the harvesting of our timber grew from frustration led on by the province ignoring Aboriginal title and rights under the Delgamuukw decision." I said that we had asked for a fair share of this billion-dollar industry that was built stealing our trees, and after attempting to obtain what the band felt would have been a reasonable amount of timber, we were informed they were eligible for a few hundred cubic metres of "blow-down." The remainder of the 7.6 million cubic metres harvested in the Okanagan Valley would remain under provincial control and awarded to non-Native commercial loggers.

"Delgamuukw says we are the owners of this land and that must be fully understood, respected and implemented in all future planning of resource extraction," I said.

A CBC radio reporter stuck a microphone in Mickey's face and asked what we were doing and he said simply, "If we're supposed to have rights and title to our traditional territories and stuff, how is that going to be put in place if we don't act on it?"

The news was splashed across the front page of every newspaper in B.C. and it was the top of every newscast. On the forestry department documents I obtained from B.C. Access to Information you can clearly see that the government bureaucrats were panicking because the first line in their collective email was urging everyone "not to panic."

That same afternoon I had a call from Arthur Manuel. Arthur was then the chief of the Neskonlith Indian Band near Chase and the head of the Shuswap Nation Tribal Council, as well as the head of an informal alliance of the Interior tribes. He was also a leading force in the national Delgamuukw Implementation Committee at the Assembly of First Nations. He told me he was backing our action 100 percent and the next morning he and his legal counsel, Wayne Haimila, were in my office. He had been lobbying hard inside the AFN for Indigenous peoples to take direct action to enforce our ownership of our off-reserve lands and resources, he said, and no one else was moving on it. "So I am here to help you in any way I can," he told me. And for the next 18 years, until his tragic death, we worked together in numerous ways — in B.C., across Canada and internationally, as well as co-authors of two books — to advance our peoples' interests.

In *Unsettling Canada*, our first book, Arthur wrote that he had been initially surprised to find me leading such a radical action because he had seen me as primarily an economic development chief. But he soon decided that I was "the perfect person to take the lead on this. [Chief Derrickson] had that legendary quality from his past successes that would make the government hesitate to try to slap him down, like they did so many other chiefs. Ron Derrickson was also a man that the government and the businesspeople in the region knew you could not take lightly or intimidate with a show of chest-beating. He had survived an assassination attempt and character assassination attempts and the federal judicial inquiry that cost of over 10 million dollars. Now he appeared willing to take on the government on the issue of Aboriginal title and rights. We were more than ready to follow him into the forest."

At that first meeting, Arthur and I looked at running both an international and national campaign for our timber rights. That summer, Arthur had been in Geneva visiting with the UN Human Rights Committee, and in Austria and Germany visiting with European solidarity organizations. We discussed trying to set up an international network to alert the world that we were only taking what was ours and that the white loggers had been for a century stealing our logs without compensating us.

In B.C., we decided that we would take out a full-page ad in the *Vancouver Province* identifying all timber taken off our Aboriginal title lands as "hot logs" and insist that the government negotiate with us for a share of provincial licences and pay us a royalty on all of the timber taken off our land. If not, we would threaten an international boycott of B.C. logs.

The local white press, after its initial surprise, started to holler for our heads. I told the *Kelowna Daily Courier* that our action was "in direct response to the provincial government's refusal to negotiate in good faith. We have been attempting to get a small slice of the 7.6 million cubic metres of wood that is harvested within our territory. To date, all we have been offered is a one-time harvest of 2,000 cubic metres of blown-down timber, which is a joke."

The paper and the local radio talk shows were immediately filled with citizens demanding that the government move in and arrest the lot of us, and along the fringes there were mutterings about local people taking the matter into their own hands, suggesting a violent attack against us. In light of this, Grand Chief Stewart Phillip's Penticton Band offered to provide "security" for our loggers and sent up some native security guys to guard the entrance to the site.

This support was crucial because Stewart Phillip was also the head of the Okanagan Nation Alliance and the newly elected chief of the Union of B.C. Indian Chiefs. With Stewart Phillip and Arthur Manuel in our corner, we had instant credibility in B.C., Canada and beyond.

We would need it in this fight. The local mill owners, no doubt at the governor's behest, announced they would not take our logs because they were illegal, and said that white mill owners from across the province would also refuse them. But we kept cutting. Within three days, we had cleared 500 logs.

From access to information requests, I learned that at the time, the government was laying out a four-step plan to deal with us. The first step had been to verbally notify us that we were in non-compliance of the code and demand that we cease our activity. If we continued to be non-compliant, they would follow up with a formal SWO (stop work order) demanding that we cease and desist the harvest activity. If we still refused to stop the harvest activity and ignored the SWO, then the minister would apply under Section 147 to the Supreme Court for a court order against us.

Once these preliminary steps were dispensed with, they could get to the heart of the matter: call in the RCMP and haul our asses off to jail.

On September 9, the B.C. Forestry minister, David Zirnhelt, announced that the government would be seeking a stop work order and he told the media he would talk to us only if we lay down the chainsaws first.

I replied in the media that I was willing to talk anytime, but we would continue logging. Zirnhelt then told the press that the situation was "escalating" and we prepared for an RCMP assault.

I believe that it did not come because of the support we were receiving across B.C. and in fact across the country. The national chief of the Assembly of First Nations, Phil Fontaine, said he supported me "because the title to this land has never been surrendered and for the government to refuse to recognize this is, in fact, an act of civil disobedience and disregard for the law." Under Arthur Manuel's leadership, all five of the Indigenous Nations in the Interior Alliance took a firm position in support of us and said that they were preparing to follow our example by going out to log on their off-reserve territories with Indigenous instead of provincial permits. And of course our first line of support were the young guys from the Penticton Band that Stewart sent up to defend us.

With that level of support, I was quoted in the media saying that "if the province or police try to stop us, this whole province is going to get shut down."

The minister then went on the radio to say that my statements didn't sound "very conciliatory" and he himself continued to stir the racial pot by saying he had to defend the legitimate white loggers versus the wildcatting Natives.

"Sure, the Natives didn't get their share of the resource, because when the timber licences were granted, they were tendered out to companies and First Nations weren't in the line-up, and certainly weren't granted rights . . . Is it fair to take it away from existing licencees who have investments and give it to someone else? So displace one set of loggers for another set of loggers?"

This was obviously a false equivalency, since we were not just one set of loggers — we had court-recognized Aboriginal title to the trees. They were our bloody trees. And it was clear that by "one set of loggers" against "another set of loggers," he was pitting the white loggers and their families against the Indigenous.

Local members of the Legislature wanted the government to act. One MLA said the government should "stop this nonsense immediately and the Natives should be punished for this."

Finally, Zirnhelt got in touch with me directly and asked for a meeting the next day, which I agreed to. But when he got back to me and said I would have to sign an agreement to cease logging before the meeting took place, I flatly refused. Instead, I went on the Rafe Mair radio show for a rollicking hour. Rafe, a former politician and determined muckraker, was one of the most colourful personalities on B.C. radio at the time, and unlike the dour mainstream media types, he played up the audacity of what we were doing and let me go on denouncing the injustice and hypocrisy of the government position.

The Rafe Mair hour helped increase the visibility of the conflict, and when our full-page ad warning of an international forestry boycott of B.C. timber was published, the issue exploded once again across the province. You could tell the government took it seriously because they first went silent. Then they issued a muted statement. "We are disappointed in this action considering the province has been working hard in the past few months to find specific opportunities to address the economic needs of the band." And they mentioned again their generous offer to let us have the blowdown trees.

In the same careful vein, NDP Aboriginal Affairs Minister Dale Lovick said, "We're going to try and have a meeting with Ron Derrickson and say, 'What happened?' We thought we had an arrangement. You can't overnight manufacture harvesting rights. You have to negotiate."

But along with the soft words, the big stick arrived in the stop work order that was delivered to my band office and to the Hidden Creek logging site.

This was the lead item in the Department's talking points that afternoon. "At 11:30 a.m. a stop work order was issued as is required under Section 123 of the Forestry Act to the band's office and the worksite. The Ministry is attempting to maintain communication with the Westbank First Nation."

By now they also tried to challenge our reference to the Delgamuukw decision. They said: "The Delgamuukw Decision did not remove the Crown's jurisdiction to manage land and resources in British Columbia. The Delgamuukw Decision only established principles around Aboriginal Title." On their good-cop side, they said, "We have provided 2,000 cubic metres of salvage wood to Westbank and provided the opportunity to another 13,000 cubic metres. All the timber in southern B.C. is already allocated with the exception of the small business enterprise program. But the whole program has only 600,000 cubic metres, which is what the band has asked for on an annual basis. We have a competitive process and encourage the band to take part on that basis."

The *Vancouver Sun*, which also saw me as an economic development chief, was scratching its head on this. "Mr. Derrickson is off-base . . . After he was elected chief a year ago, the Westbank's band interest in the treaty process lapsed. However as atypical and unlikely a rabble-rouser as Mr. Derrickson is (he is a wealthy business operator and the band has not been militant) his sabre-rattling has attracted wide admiration in the First Nations community."

This reference to wide admiration was partly due to Arthur working his magic. On September 10, the 68 Interior B.C. chiefs "passed a resolution that all wood taken from aboriginal land is hot." They also announced that they planned to take the resolution to the UN, asking that "B.C. timber be excluded from the world markets if it did not have the First Nations Stamp of approval on it."

When this announcement caused another increase in racist invective in the press and the same white-guy threats against us, the Penticton Band announced that it was upping its security for the site by sending 40 more men to Hidden Creek to protect the loggers. That was welcome news for us, but when I began to receive more death threats directed at me, I made sure that my gun was loaded and in reach. And of course I didn't answer the door to uninvited guests.

The tit-for-tat war of words continued. After we declared that all B.C. timber taken off our lands without our permission was hot, the minister reiterated that all the wood we cut on the site was hot, and he posted seizure notices forbidding anyone from removing it from the site without government permission. I then announced that all of the wood on the site would be used to build Elders' houses, and I underlined again that I would sit down at the negotiating table with the government if there were no prior conditions.

"The government is refusing to acknowledge the implications of the Delgamuukw decision of the highest court in the land so how can it expect us to sit down with it for serious talks. We are getting nowhere like this. Our people have been cutting trees for centuries for firewood, to build drying racks, homes and sweat lodges. Westbank members' rights to use trees is a birth right. They should not need permission from the province or anyone else. And our lawyer agrees we have the legal right based on the Delgamuukw decision. The province is trying to ignore the Supreme Court of Canada."

The next day, we upped the ante. Instead of Westbank standing alone, the Okanagan Nation announced it would step up and take shared responsibility for the Hidden Creek site. Any move against Westbank would be seen as an attack on the whole Okanagan Nation. Furthermore, the Okanagan were in the process of issuing their own stop work orders on all of the non-Indigenous logging operations throughout the hundreds of square kilometres of Okanagan territory.

This, I believe, broke the government's resolve. They saw that any escalation on their part would be met by an even greater escalation on ours. We were not going to back down or be frightened off. So I finally had a message from Forestry Minister David Zirnhelt. He would agree to meet me in Vancouver on September 15 without any preconditions.

I was not going to go alone. I contacted the National Chief Phil Fontaine and he offered to be part of the meeting. To further strengthen my hand, the AFN also organized a meeting of the B.C. chiefs for the same day, and we went to that meeting first and ran a kind of information session on what we were trying to accomplish.

When we met with the government, Fontaine began by urging the province to bargain in good faith. He criticized them for releasing media reports that said Westbank "was engaged in criminal legal activities as an attempt to create fear in the minds of British Columbians." Fontaine said clearly: "This is not about criminal activity, it is about the assertion of Aboriginal rights in their traditional territory."

Fontaine also told the minister that Native loggers have "rock-solid" support from the AFN, adding that a resolution had been passed by the Summit chiefs supporting the logging. "This is not an isolated incident," he said. "It is reflective of the deep frustration held by many First Nations communities across this nation."

Zirnhelt remained deaf to our words and insisted that the forest industry would continue to be regulated under the current guidelines.

"First Nations groups must go through appropriate channels to negotiate timber extraction rights," the minister said. "Those channels must be negotiated through the current treaty negotiation process. Two thousand cubic metres were offered to the Westbank First Nation under our direct award program and the Westbank First Nation has ignored our offer."

While we were meeting with the minister, one of my Westbank councillors, Chad Paul, made a fiery speech to the 80 chiefs who were still at the information session. It turned out to be one of the best speeches he ever made, because at the end of it, the chiefs were on their feet and marching over to the minister's office to show their support for us.

When we walked out of the meeting with the minister, we were met not only by the 80 chiefs but by hundreds of other supporters waiting outside. Phil Fontaine, always quick on his feet, said maybe he should thank the minister for "uniting the Aboriginal people in B.C. and across this nation" by not coming to the meeting with more to offer.

I then spoke to the crowd. "This isn't a joke anymore. I told the government that we would refuse to pay for trees that we already owned when they tried to force us to pay for a provincial permit, and we instead insisted that we receive a royalty for every tree cut from our Aboriginal title lands. The government has to recognize our ownership of our forests or face an international boycott."

Arthur Manuel was by my side. He said, "The stop work order

against Westbank shows that the province wants to bar us from our own land." And he said that he would soon follow us in logging his people's traditional lands.

Phil Fontaine echoed our words. We had had enough. "We're tired of being poor!"

Then Joe Mathias spoke eloquently, as he always did (although in Joe's case, his actions rarely lived up to his words). "Our resources are being depleted while we are at the treaty table," he said. Then he warned, "Maybe we'll just start exercising our traditional rights on our land, saying this is our land until you prove otherwise. Rather than the other way around."

The support for the Westbank Indigenous logging initiative was by now a rolling thunder. We had the backing of the Assembly of First Nations, the Union of British Columbia Indian Chiefs, the First Nations Summit and the Interior Alliance — all the province's major Native political groups — plus dozens of individual bands. Even the less adversarial coastal bands, which participate in the British Columbia Treaty Commission process as members of the First Nations Summit, were drawn into the fray. In fact, even my political enemies were forced to support me on this.

"First Nations groups have watched as the very lands being negotiated are stripped of resources, which are key to First Nations' future economic stability and self-sufficiency," Grand Chief Ed John, Chief Joe Mathias and Robert Louie, leaders of the First Nations Summit, said in a letter to the editor published in the *Vancouver Sun*. "First Nations groups have asked whether there will be any resources left by the time we finalize our treaties or are we negotiating for nothing more than barren pieces of land?"

Much stronger support came from the Union of B.C. Indian Chiefs, an organization that had a much more activist agenda. As the logging issue continued to a boil, the UBCIC held a three-day special assembly in Westbank. The political organization that represents First Nations opposed to the treaty process passed a resolution that supported the earlier resolution by Arthur's Interior tribes to take our grievances to the world stage by calling for an international boycott of B.C. wood products. As UBCIC Grand Chief Stewart Phillip put it, "The more Canada and B.C. try to use the courts, police and army to deny our Aboriginal title, laws and jurisdiction, the more evidence we will have to show the international community that Canada's wealth is based upon the theft of our lands and resources, which constitutes economic racism against our Aboriginal Nations."

Even media commentators like conservative Gordon Gibson were struggling with how to describe the Westbank logging. Gibson wrote in a *Globe and Mail* column published on September 21 that he isn't sure whether to call the logging "illegal" or simply "unauthorized." Aboriginal groups have no such trouble with their terminology. They are claiming the province is involved in illegal resource extraction on their traditional lands, an act of bad-faith bargaining.

Meanwhile, the logging continued. By September 17, Mickey and his crew had already cut 15 of the 50 acres at Hidden Creek. As an added protection against a police sweep to arrest all of the loggers, we set up a youth and Elders camp at Hidden Creek under the protection of Penticton Band security. This would at least discourage the RCMP from coming in with guns blazing.

"We don't want scraps," I told the people gathered there. "We want the reallocation of resources." I was proud of all of the people, the loggers, the security guys and the youth and Elders who had gathered there and were ready for whatever came at them. They were prepared to go to jail to defend our right to log on our own land.

By this time, the seriousness of our threats was starting to sink in and the press began to write about how our international boycott could devastate the provincial economy and they began to paint us as the wreckers of prosperity for all of B.C. residents. So I replied: "People of B.C., what do you say to the fact that Indian people have the highest unemployment rate, the highest suicide rate and zero opportunity? The Supreme Court of Canada has said we have rights. We want our share of the resources of British Columbia.

This is no longer a Westbank issue or even an Okanagan issue. This is an issue for the Indians of B.C., if not Canada."

Then the wildcat cutting operations began to spread. Nuxalk Nation Chief Archie Pootlass was one of the first to declare. "We are going out because 89 percent of our people are unemployed."

Arthur Manuel then announced that his Neskonlith community had received a logging permit from the Shuswap Nation Tribal Council, which he was conveniently the head of, and was beginning logging at Harper Lake, part of his people's traditional territory, which, like Hidden Creek, was up for auction that year. I began getting reports of bands across the province who were beginning or preparing to go out logging on their territory and I announced this to the press. At the same time, I was speaking with Arthur, who was working with his young international advisor and lawyer, Nicole Schabus, who would become his romantic partner, on a plan to get legal standing for Indigenous people in the Canada-U.S. timber dispute.

In a panic, Minister Zirnhelt travelled to Ottawa to discuss B.C. logging issues with Indian Affairs Minister Bob Nault and they decided they would finally have to use the old Indian Affairs standard, the court injunction, to criminalize our activities and move the RCMP in to haul us off to jail not for logging on our own land, but for defying a court order. Their new talking point was that "the individuals and bands engaged in illegal harvest are trying to use a legal decision to justify their illegal activities — the Supreme Court of Canada's decision in Delgamuukw does not give the Westbank or any other First Nation ownership of the timber that is being harvested."

After his meeting with the Indian Affairs minister, Zirnhelt said: "We are doing everything to enforce the law. We have never had anyone refuse to comply with a stop work order before. We are doing everything we can to make sure this doesn't get out of hand."

The government case for the injunction was put to the court on the week of September 21. But our lawyer, Louise Mandel, told the court that the provincial government may not have the power to interfere with Native logging. "The Supreme Court of Canada has ruled that the provincial Crown rights are encumbered by Aboriginal rights and only Ottawa has the power to alter that. The case boils down to who owns the trees."

The RCMP riot squad was no doubt preparing tear gas canisters for an assault on Hidden Creek when the government, as expected, received its court injunction against us. But we were all caught off guard when the judge refused them.

The judge said the government may be able to get an injunction in the future if Natives continued to log, but he said that instead of the usual case, where constitutional issues were set aside and Indigenous protesters were jailed simply for defying a court order, Aboriginal constitutional rights must be included in evidence before he would rule on whether or not we were defying the law. So the injunction was refused.

It was a major victory for our side. "I am in an extremely good mood," I told reporters. "You know, everyone has been talking about us logging illegally. Even the forestry department lawyer has said there was no offence committed here . . . B.C. is going to have to come to the table with a new attitude and sit down and resolve these issues."

The provincial government was now in disarray. We scheduled a meeting on September 30 with them in Kelowna, but the government failed to show up. Instead, we brought in 50 tribal council leaders for an October 1 meeting where the leaders reaffirmed their support for Westbank and approved the launching of an international campaign. And it was immediately after this meeting that Arthur headed down to Washington to begin the long road to have our international rights recognized, as we described in *Unsettling Canada*. What he and his partner, Nicole, accomplished was to have our economic interests in our own land recognized within NAFTA and the World Trade Organization and the failure to pay us for our trees recognized as an unfair subsidy to the Canadian logging companies. In subsequent trips to the Standard & Poor's Credit

Agency in New York, he also had the director of the Sovereign Ratings group recognize that Canada was, indeed, breaking international accounting principles by under-reporting the enormous accounts payable debt to Indigenous peoples.

I told the press that "this is getting more and more serious every day. There is a real rough element in the valley and they are not going to take any crap from anyone. I said in the beginning this was going to get bigger than Westbank. Now it is getting bigger than the province. The B.C. government could fall over this."

As if on cue, the opposition Liberal leader, Gordon Campbell, went crazy, calling for the government to say the hell with the courts and move in and start making mass arrests.

I accused Campbell of inflaming tensions and warned "if the government takes that approach, they would have an absolute war in the woods."

Finally, in mid-October we sat down with the government and they did what they had always said they would not do and awarded us a large section of cutting rights on our own land. As a stop-gap measure, it was enough, and meeting with our lawyers we decided to continue our case to the Supreme Court to have our logging rights on our traditional lands formally recognized, with the idea that this would also position us to charge a royalty on all of the timber that had been and was being removed from our land.

The government, too, seemed satisfied with that, to concede some of our own wood to us and to kick the substantive issues over to the courts. That, they said, is how this country is supposed to work. We use the courts when we have disputes to settle with one another.

But in fact, this is how the country does not work. Twenty years have passed and our case is still in the courts. The government has used every ploy possible to delay a ruling that they fear will go in our favour and break the monopoly of the B.C. Forestry Department on B.C.'s unsurrendered forests. Ours and the Neskonlith case that bears the name of Arthur Manuel are still in the docket even after his passing. This is the painfully slow and twisted course of justice Canada reserves for Indigenous peoples.

My final act in serving my people as chief for the additional term was to complete what I had come to do — getting reserve status for the Gallagher Canyon lands. It was with enormous pride that I saw a newspaper headline that the "Westbank reserve lands double in size" after more than a century in which our territory had been slashed, then whittled down, then slashed again until we were surviving on 2,500 patchwork acres scattered across three reserves. The final notice that reserve status for the new land had been attained came just days before my term expired.

The process involved in getting it for the new territory was, as mentioned, a complicated one, involving negotiation with both the federal and provincial governments, as well as two districts, the City of Kelowna and the Regional District of Central Okanagan. Our office lead on the file was Tim Raybould, our intergovernmental affairs consultant and the husband of Jody Wilson-Raybould, then a regional Indigenous leader who would later, for a time, be the justice minister in Justin Trudeau's government until she was forced out over the SNC-Lavalin affair.

Much of the work on this file was done with Jane Stewart, the Indian Affairs minister. She was a tall, elegant woman who came from an important political family that was very close to Jean Chrétien. She visited our band several times during the negotiations and was very helpful in spite of one of my council members, Mike DeGuevara, who joked about her height (*Indian Affairs always towers over us!*) and suggested she get down on her knees for a photo because she was so tall. He then asked for her phone number because, he said, "I'd like to take you out next time I am in Ottawa."

She responded to all of this with a polite smile and kept her promise to turn our new lands into reserve land. The Gallagher Canyon lands are now known as Medicine Creek Indian Reserve 12 and Medicine Hill Indian Reserve 11. After its initial purchase, the land was used only for cattle grazing, but now with reserve status, we left with a plan to build 100 community houses on the land. But this so far has not been done. I think I would have to return as chief a third time to move it forward, but that is a hill that I have already climbed enough times. I leave it to the next generation. My initial job, even if it was sidetracked by the logging issues, was to halt the shrinking land of our reserve and move it in the other direction — toward expansion. Today, the 2,500-acre Westbank Band area that I began with is now 5,306 acres. So I have done my bit to reverse the century of our land losses. This time I left the job of chief with my head held high, having accomplished more than I had set out to do and kept the faith of the people of the community who had once again put their faith in me.

CHAPTER 15

Ukrainian Beachhead

In 2000, I was 59 years old. I had been a farm worker, logger, welder, rancher, champion speedboat racer and, for many years, an entrepreneur, band chief, real estate developer and political activist. I had done all these things not because I was following a plan, but because I refused to follow one. Instead, I tried to stay open to opportunities as they presented themselves, and never hesitated to take a sharp detour when it seemed to lead toward an interesting path.

This was how I started a long relationship with Ukraine immediately after I finished my last term as band chief. It began with a phone call from Darrell Michaels, one of the white businessmen I knew in Kelowna. An investment banker who had been a Calgary stockbroker for many years, he was the guy who first approached me about investing in Northland Bank, which, as I described earlier, I joined as a director. Later I was to learn that the Northland Bank, even though it was ultimately a failure, was actually one of Darrell's more legitimate projects. He was a guy who was always on the make. He had almost as many wives as numbered companies, and he partied harder than anyone I knew. Some of his wives were insufferable, but they didn't last long, and most of his companies bordered on Ponzi schemes, so I learned to stay away from his "investment opportunities." But I did come to like him personally. He was a rebel in his own way and always an amusing guy to have a drink or lunch with. But I knew that after shaking hands with him, you better count your fingers to make sure they were all still there.

Although we were friends, we were not close friends, which is why I was surprised when I received a call from Darrell asking me to be the best man at his wedding — I believe it was the sixth of what would finally be seven wives. Even though the invitation came out of the blue, the request to be someone's best man was not something you refused. So I said, "OK, sure."

"One hitch," he said. "The wedding is in Kyiv."

"Where?" I asked.

"Ukraine," he said.

I wasn't even sure where that was, but I knew it was somewhere far away. And this idea did not bother me. The idea of getting far away for a break after the media battles I had been involved in during the forestry dispute and the heavier side of being band chief appealed to me. So I was ready in the fall of 2000 to explore the faraway world of Ukraine.

I decided I would stay for a couple of weeks after the wedding to explore the country. To save getting a hotel, Darrell arranged for me to rent an apartment that was a block from Bessarabska Square in downtown Kyiv, which to my surprise was a big and quite beautiful city.

The wedding was a very modest affair. The bride's name was Olga and apparently she came from a wealthy family, but the ceremony was in the "marriage house," i.e., the state marriage registration office, and lasted all of 15 minutes.

After the wedding they went for a honeymoon and I explored the city around the main square, the now-famous Maidan. I walked up the steep hill to Saint-Sophia, a Christian Orthodox church dating back a thousand years, with the original medieval paintings still visible on the walls. The city, I discovered, could be enchanting. My apartment was near the music conservatory and students would often play the violin on the sidewalk in the evening to busk a few *hryvnia* for supper, and it was hard to miss the fact that Ukrainian women were among the most beautiful in the world. As I discovered over the years, they can be the most charming as well.

I explored Kyiv as a tourist but with an entrepreneur's eye. My hired guide Elena showed me the nooks and crannies of the place and I discovered that behind the attractive surface, economic life had collapsed with the fall of the Soviet Union and the break from the Russian Federation. Ukraine was a place that was in need of almost everything.

That meant opportunity. And I was taken with the place. So when I left Kyiv after a couple of weeks, I was determined to come back.

And I did. Less than six months later, I returned for a part-vacation, part-business trip with Darrell, who was already single again and living there most of the year. We travelled down to Odessa on the Black Sea and I was introduced to the much more Russian part of the country, but with the same friendly and outgoing people. Travelling with Darrell meant that pretty well every day was party day, but through the haze I was able to confirm that this would, indeed, be a good place to do business. With the big caveat that you would have to avoid the shady characters that Darrell seemed to surround himself with.

Over the next 20 years, I would become deeply involved in a series of businesses — in real estate, agri-business and biofuels — in Kyiv and in what was then known as Dnipropetrovsk and now goes by Dnipro. I would indeed run into the local mafias as well as some of the nicest, kindest and most generous people I have ever met in my life. It also led to one of the most complex and convoluted business thefts I ever had the misfortune to be the victim of — in fact, it is so complicated that it would take a full book to explain. But what is clear is that Ukraine, and my dealings there, became an important part of my life. A business I formed there is now one of the leading biofuel firms in the world, which I have now, with my partners, brought into Canada — as I will describe later.

In the early 2000s, however, I was still very much involved in our Indigenous struggle by working with Arthur Manuel in his international campaign to have our Aboriginal title recognized as an economic right, and I funded many of his trips abroad. Arthur was one of the few Indigenous leaders who understood the importance of gaining international recognition for our struggle, and he was the only Indigenous leader I knew who applied macroeconomics to the life of Indigenous peoples. He sometimes made fun of our mainstream leaders, who went hat in hand to Ottawa to try to gain a few concessions from the lands that Canadians had stolen from us, and he urged his fellow leaders "to quit crying on the shoulder of the guy who stole the land" and instead build international support for our political and financial struggle for self-determination.

It was very early in our discussions about promoting an international boycott of all B.C. forest products that I suggested he launch his own organization, so he wouldn't be hindered by endless internal politicking in the other organizations he represented. That is how the Indigenous Network on Economies and Trade (INET) was born. Arthur began by contacting U.S. environmental groups and it was decided that the best way to bring Canada to the table was to intervene on the side of the U.S. in the Canada-U.S. lumber dispute. In 2000, he made submissions to the U.S. Department of Commerce arguing that Canada's policy of not recognizing Aboriginal and treaty rights was, in fact, an international trade subsidy to the Canadian forest industry. This brief and its main principles were accepted by the Americans and by the NAFTA panel, despite fierce opposition from Canada. When Canada appealed to the World Trade Organization in Geneva, Switzerland, Arthur and Nicole wrote a similar argument for them and they accepted it, which meant that, even though the Canadian government refused to recognize Aboriginal title in our territories, when Canadian forest companies harvested those trees and sold them in Los Angeles, for example, there was still a proprietary interest by Indigenous peoples that had never been paid.

What NAFTA and the WTO were saying was that Canada and the forest companies were cheating the original owners of those trees (some of which were older than Canada itself!), and because Canada was not paying us a fair share — or any share — it was able to sell the trees in the United States for below-market value. Not paying Indigenous peoples for their ownership interest was therefore a trade subsidy to the Canadian industry.

This would be an important victory in the move toward internationalizing our struggle, and of course Canada fought Arthur every step of the way.

As Arthur observed in *Unsettling Canada*, "Canada was furious with INET and the Interior Alliance when the WTO and NAFTA accepted our submissions, because they like having 100 percent control over the wealth created by our trees. Indigenous peoples from north of the Medicine Line need to partner with our tribes south of the Medicine Line to fight for a mutual benefit from the harvesting of trees from our territory. We should fight for decision-making on 'access and benefits' to our trees, and stop subsidizing the big timber companies that presently plunder our lands. Like all nations, we need to find a place for ourselves in the international marketplace."

Another expression of Arthur's unique vision that I was involved in during this period was his trip to New York to visit Standard & Poor's Credit Rating Agency to discuss how Canada was trying to hide its liabilities to Indigenous peoples from its balance sheets. This was something we discussed for months before he made the trip. As he later put it: "Canadian governments are used to lying to Indigenous peoples and the Canadian public about what they are doing in Indigenous policies, but it is a little more difficult to lie to the creditors." They were doing this by dramatically down-playing the cost of settling all of the extant land claims by largely ignoring the fact that virtually no treaties had been signed in British Columbia, as well as in tens of thousands of square kilometres of Indigenous territory in other provinces.

But the auditors general aren't so easily put off. They knew that B.C. Indigenous Nations can go to court to have their title recognized and this makes them, at the very least, a "contingent liability." And all contingent liabilities need to be reported on the province's books. Arthur pointed out that we could get a clear idea of the auditor general's point of view from the November 2006 Report of the Auditor General of Canada to the House of Commons, which looked at the federal government's participation in the British Columbia treaty process. The report described "differing views" between the Indigenous peoples and the settlers. These "differing views" are rather quickly dealt with in the report, but go to the very crux of the problem that is causing all negotiations between Indigenous peoples and the settler governments to fail: the auditor general of Canada clearly identifies that "participants must share a common vision of their relationship and of the future" for negotiations to be successful. They say that this does not exist under the existing British Columbia treaty process.

He went further by identifying government intransigence as the main obstacle to the negotiations, pointing out that the federal and provincial governments base their negotiations on "their own policies, and do not recognize the Aboriginal rights and title claimed by the First Nations."

The true size of this liability would have an enormous impact on B.C. and Canada's credit rating. When Arthur met with Standard & Poor's in New York, they admitted that Canada was hiding things on its books when it came to Aboriginal title lands. And until Canada settles with Indigenous peoples, this accounting debt and overall economic uncertainty will hang over them, scaring away investors. As Arthur saw it, Canada was founded on the balance sheet, and finally the balance sheet will be the force that will lead to fundamental changes.

These bold positions did not go unnoticed or unpunished in the wider Indigenous community. And Arthur ended up paying dearly for them.

In 1999, when our campaign in the forest began, Arthur was a political powerhouse. He was chief of his Neskonlith Indian Band, head of the Shuswap Nation Tribal Council, spokesperson for the Interior Alliance and co-chair of the Assembly of First Nations' Delgamuukw Implementation Committee. It seemed to many of us that he was heading to the office of national chief, which his father held and which Bobby had missed by only one vote in 1980. But as soon as Arthur began to challenge the real source of wealth in the country and demand that we be compensated for the vast wealth that was being confiscated from our territories, the powers-that-be — both Indigenous and non-Indigenous — began working to undercut him.

I will take a moment to describe how they went after Arthur here because it is yet another example — similar to mine — of how Canada removes any Indigenous leader who actually tries to stand up for his or her people.

Their first opportunity came with the Sun Peaks dispute. That was a massive ski resort development on his people's lands that members of his community, including members of his own family, most notably his twin daughters, began to protest. As the dispute escalated, B.C. Indigenous Affairs Minister Geoff Plant went directly after Arthur's political base on the tribal council by negotiating deals that undercut him with local chiefs and, to make their point even more dramatically, orchestrated a police raid on his house, complete with helicopters hovering above to make sure that everyone in the region knew he had been targeted. With the help of a certain prominent local Indigenous leader close to the Liberals

— who I will not name — they managed to have him ousted from the tribal council leadership.

Working with opposition within the community — and there is always opposition from within — they then went after Arthur's role as band chief and mercilessly attacked him and his family. They spread baseless rumours around the break-up of his marriage and jailed one of his daughters for protesting the Sun Peaks development. Bit by bit, they chipped away even at his local base until finally, the man who was on the road to national power even lost his band election in 2003. Without his band and tribal council positions, he also had to withdraw as spokesperson of the Interior Alliance, which he had been instrumental in setting up.

Within four years after he joined me in wildcat logging, Arthur had been reduced to zero politically. His radical approach had brought the Canadian state and their many Indigenous apologists — the-hang-around-the-fort Indians — down on him, and I have to say, I understood better than most the hellfire Canada can rain down on you if you stand up for your people's rights instead of begging for crumbs at their table, like so many of our leaders do.

The final irony, though, was that the destruction of Arthur's political career freed him as an activist and a strategist for the movement. He went on to build new alliances for Indigenous people, linking up with environmentalists and world-renowned activists like Naomi Klein, and he rebuilt a career on the international level to the point where he was the co-chair of the Indigenous Caucus at the UN Permanent Forum on Indigenous Issues.

His biggest continuing problem through all of this was income. He was only making $600 a month as chief, and without that he was broke. I became the main funder of his international work and supported the two books we would write together. I was happy to do this. Arthur was brilliant and principled, as well as one of the most honest and amusing people I had ever met. Before and after his major trips, he would drive down from Kamloops to Kelowna to meet with me and we would discuss the battle plan. Then, afterward, he would go through with me the results of his latest foray. Both of us were committed to the battle but equally, we enjoyed the camaraderie and the sheer audaciousness of things like his expedition to New York, where he stayed in a room at the 47th Street YMCA, then popped up out of the subway to visit Standard & Poor's on Wall Street to demand justice from the international guardians industry. Or Geneva, where he worked with Nicole Schabus to convince the World Trade Organization to chastize Canada for the theft of Indigenous lands and resources. Both Art and I had reputations as happy warriors and I always appreciated, along with his brilliant mind, his boundless sense of humour.

While I was working with Arthur on the economic issues for Indigenous peoples, it was also back to business for me.

I was working full-time developing my properties, negotiating for major commercial tenants and building up a considerable leasing cash stream into the business. One of the most important of these was the purchase of a local 18-hole golf course with a restaurant and very elaborate clubhouse. The guy who was running it had somehow managed to go bankrupt so I purchased it for just over $3 million. I rechristened it the Two Eagles Golf Course and installed a pair of $60,000 eagle totem poles at the entrance.

Soon after that, I got a surprise visit to my office from a local smartass lawyer with 15 homeowners bringing me a document to sign that would promise them the moon if there were any damage to their property from golf balls. He told me there were rules I had to obey and, oddly, asked me if I played chess. I responded, "Sure. Every day."

They hadn't played this game with the previous owner and I knew from my experience in real estate that having a golf course adjacent to your house is a pot of gold in terms of adding value to your property. At first I didn't know what to say to the lawyer, so to stall I asked them all to write their names and addresses on a sheet my secretary passed around. This instantly took them aback and gave me time to think.

When they finished signing my paper, I told them that I would definitely not sign any contract with them. If they insisted, I would close the golf course.

I could see the unease on the faces of the homeowners. But the lawyer responded with a "Ha! What would you do with the land?"

"I'll give it over to the community to build subsidized housing for the poor," I said.

I could see the alarm on their faces as they imagined poor reserve Indians installing shacks on the greens behind their house, and even the smartass lawyer had no response.

"Checkmate," I said as they hurriedly gathered their unsigned documents and left my office.

I was, in fact, proud of my golf course. Along with the 18 holes, it has a first-class restaurant, the Okanagan Grill, a golf academy and a $1.5 million maintenance shop so all of our equipment — from heavy machinery to golf carts to irrigation pumps — can be maintained and repaired on-site. I made arrangements for the Marriott chain to build a hotel on the golf course and this completed my development plan for Two Eagles: hotel, restaurant, golf academy and pro shop. Since I bought the golf course 11 years ago, it has been profitable every single year. I have yet to take any profits out of it, instead reinvesting everything to make it a world-class golf and tourist facility.

I also built my current office overlooking the fairway and I have filled it with one of my passions, Indigenous art. The collection grew piece by piece and even I didn't realize its full extent until an art dealer told me that over the past 25 years I had been the biggest purchaser of Indigenous art in Canada.

I had an even closer connection to the arts through my daughter, Kelly, who has made an important contribution both to Indigenous music and, through her music, to the Indigenous struggle. As I mentioned, I come from an extremely musical family with very talented musicians and while musical talent somehow skipped over me, it hit a new height with Kelly, and I have always been a bit in awe of her for that.

But I admit that for a long time I thought of music as an extra in life and not something you built a life around. As a young woman, she planned to be a lawyer and I wholeheartedly supported this dream of hers, because I knew it was a way she could take the fight for our people to a whole new level. So I was happy when she won a scholarship to a pre-law course at the University of British Columbia, and I was very proud to see her earning excellent grades that would make her eligible for law school.

Then I received the call. Kelly said she wasn't happy at UBC and she was quitting the university and enrolling in the Berklee College of Music in Boston. I could not fathom why she was doing this — throwing away a career as a lawyer to try to make money singing. In my mind, music was great around the kitchen table on a Saturday night, but certainly not a career, and a foolish thing to leave law school for.

My disappointment was so great that I kind of withdrew from her. Six months went by and we had almost no contact. Then she called me and said she felt terrible about the tension between us and she made me an offer. I should come to Boston in the spring to see the show that she was putting on as part of her course. If I didn't like it, all I had to do was say so and she would leave Berklee and return to law school.

The feeling of estrangement had been hard on me, too, and this seemed like a fair offer. So I agreed.

In the spring I went to see her show, expecting to be able to say at the end, "Kelly, your music is great, but it's a sideline — you belong in law school."

But I could not. I sat in the darkened theatre watching her on stage singing jazz — something I had never heard her sing before — with beauty and passion. After the show, I went backstage to meet her and I saw her looking at me expectantly. I told her I was sorry. This was her calling and I would help her any way that I could.

Since then, her talent and her many awards have been a source of pride for me. And I would soon see that through her music she would make her own important contribution to the struggle of our people.

CHAPTER 16

Active Energy

If there is a thread linking my business ventures it is probably finding ways to build an Indigenous economy on our traditional lands.

In Westbank, I fought for our right to maximize the value of our land to give us the financial means to advance our people. That was key. When I increased band revenues by 3,500 percent by starting new businesses and getting increases in our rental income, those revenues went into ensuring people had indoor plumbing, telephones and new housing. And when these things were taken care of, I set up the fund that gave cash payments to band members and a cash award to every child when they reached the age of 18. Similarly, when we went out on the land to log in 1999, the logs were supposed to be used to build Elder housing, and the precedent was used to extend our economic reach onto our traditional territory.

I have always championed our own economic development, free of the distortions of government handouts. It is the reason why the title of Arthur and my last book, *Reconciliation Manifesto*, had the subtitle *Recovering the Land, Rebuilding the Economy*. A healthy Indigenous economy underpins everything and it always has. Why were the coastal peoples able to produce such spectacularly beautiful totem poles and advanced decorative arts? Because they were resource-rich and they were excellent fishermen and woodsman and developed their crafts to the highest level. To do this, they needed a strong economy and they had one.

Our Interior Salish peoples did not have the resources of the sea, so they developed an economic model that used the resources of every part of our territory in its proper season. Winter on the lakeshore and moving through the grasslands to the mountain ranges to take advantage of every plant and animal that nature had to offer us. When the government stole our land and placed us on the bitter rations of welfare, they also stole from us our economic reality. Today, so many of our people cannot imagine any wealth except the dribble of earmarked dollars that come out of the government's programs and services tap. It is like the cocaine that comes out of the tap in the rat's cage. We constantly drink it because it is the only thing that makes our life bearable. But my fight is to say, enough, we have to get out of the damn cage. And for Indigenous people, that means reclaiming our heritage — our land.

After 2008, I was looking for a new project for Aboriginal title lands that could transform the economic reach of Indigenous people into the sustainable energy sector. And I finally found it in Active Energy, a company I co-founded in Ukraine with my friend Joseph (Giuseppe) Valoroso, who ran Valoroso Foods Ltd. in Kelowna, and Richard Spinks, a fellow entrepreneur who moved from his native Britain to Eastern Europe when he was still a young man, and who has become a good friend as well as a valued business partner. I had first become aware of Richard in Ukraine through his groundbreaking work with Landkom International, where he successfully created a co-operative agricultural business that transformed the lives of many thousands of private land owners.

From the beginning I saw the new company, Active Energy, as a kind of template that could help create economic independence throughout Canada's Indigenous communities through commercialization of renewable forestry assets. That was my hope. But instead of a model for building Indigenous economies across the land, it turned into a model of how Canada still refuses to set us free to advance our interests by our own means.

Richard Spinks, who spoke the language in Ukraine and married a charming Ukrainian woman, had been a real help to me during my troubles there (the ones that it will take another book to fully explain). I had helped him when the country's political battles had him and his family ejected from their home in Russian-occupied Donetsk at gunpoint. So he was someone I came to trust in a fundamental way.

We first went looking for a promising company to invest in and we found a British company that was experimenting in turning wood chips and other forestry by-products into biofuels. It was named Active Energy — which was a bit ironic because it was largely inactive at the time. But we arrived with a plan. What it involved was a reverse takeover, and Richard — who had enlisted and served in the Falklands War when he was still a kid — had the coolness under fire to pull it off by weathering a series of very hostile board meetings.

We brought Active Energy first to the forests in a remote corner of Ukraine. On a sociological chart, the profile of the surrounding villages would not have been so different from Aboriginal communities in Canada. There was high unemployment, no welfare to sustain the people and a very high rate of alcoholism. Instead of moving in and simply taking the resources out, with the community benefiting from only a few jobs, we went in and partnered with the communities and ensured that a significant portion of the revenues stayed with them. We made money and it was a boon for the local communities, too.

It seemed like a winning formula and Active Energy Group grew rapidly. From our London base, we began to develop business partnerships and subsidiaries in Italy, Switzerland and Cyprus, as well as in Ukraine. The revenues via wood chip sales started with zero in 2012, but we sold $8.4 million USD worth in 2013 and $21.5 million in 2014, mainly to processing plants in Italy and Turkey. We even attracted the notice of the *Wall Street Journal*, which praised the difference the Active Energy Group had made in rural Ukraine, particularly "from the social perspective and the re-construction of the economic situation in western Ukraine."

We found an opportunity to bring it to Canada when Richard was visiting me in Westbank. He had been in Vancouver talking to forestry industry investors and he stopped by to fill me in on his meetings. While he was there, my secretary knocked on the office door. A Mr. Iner Gauchier would like to speak to me.

I knew Iner as a leader from the Alberta Métis settlement of Peavine. He had mentioned that he wanted to meet at some point. We hadn't set anything up but I said, "Sure, show him in."

I introduced him to Richard and he nodded without saying a word. What he wanted to talk to me about, he said, was investing in his community. But he didn't want to talk with the white guy there. Richard offered to leave, but I told him to stay and plainly told Iner that Richard was my friend and business partner, and if he didn't want to say something in front of the "white guy," then he could leave and there would be no further discussion.

That was how it began. We sat down and talked. Iner said they were looking for investors in their forestry sector and we said, OK, let's look into that.

We did not know if there was anything for us in working with the Métis, but we agreed to take a look and a few weeks after meeting Iner in my office, I visited three Métis communities and met with their leaders — Iner Gauchier from Peavine, Greg Calliou from Paddle Prairie and Gerald Cunningham from East Prairie. They were part of the eight-community Métis Settlement General Council that had negotiated a significant land base for their people in the 1990s — the only Métis group in Canada with their own land base, with a total of

1.25 million acres of land, a piece of land roughly the size of Prince Edward Island.

The Métis Settlements General Council itself was very closely tied to the Alberta government, like our Assembly of First Nations is to the federal government. In 2013, the Alison Redford government in Alberta funded the Métis General Council with $85 million worth of infrastructure and governance-strengthening money to enhance "the productive relationship between the Government of Alberta and the Métis Settlements under what was known as the LTA, or Long Term Agreement." This sounded benign enough at the time, although with my own experience of measures designed to encourage the "productive relationship" with government, it should have set off warning bells. Indeed, by the end of this story, the LTA and indeed all government funding for the Métis Settlements was being used by the Alberta government to quash any ambitions they may have had for the economic development for their people.

But the guys at the community level, who I was dealing with, sounded solid and sincere enough. They were looking for new opportunities for their people and they said they held, collectively, the rights to 250,000 acres of merchantable timber — although it became clear once Richard began auditing their forestry that it was significantly greater, due to the fact that they had not cut the forests for over a decade and had no idea whatsoever of what was actually on their land. The work Richard and I did with AEG and outside forestry consultants identified more than 28 million cubic metres of sawlogs and another 30 million of "biomass." In the end, we and AEG reached a "bankable" independent valuation of over $300 million US that they were completely unaware that they had. Suddenly, the government's attitude towards the three settlements involved in our deal was understood. They didn't want the settlements to be able to escape from reliance on their handouts through the LTA by building a business around their own assets.

Much of it was thought to be of reduced value, because it was made up of non-commercially viable trees like aspen. But aspen and poplar are, in fact, an excellent source of biomass fuel. Especially after early 2014, when Active Energy made another breakthrough in converting even sawdust into biomass fuel granules that could be used in micro-CHP (combined heat and power) commercial and residential boilers and large-scale power plants. This meant that 50 percent of every tonne of raw timber that was processed at mills that was turned into waste was now a viable fuel source.

After I visited the Métis, I met with Richard and we discussed the parameters of a deal. First, I wanted the project to be Aboriginal-controlled. I would invest on my own for 10 percent and Active Energy and the Métis could split the rest evenly. So, 45 percent each. With my 10 percent, the project would be 55 percent Indigenous. This would be a new gold standard for Aboriginal partnerships, with the Métis share of 45 percent about 10 times what the province and their "business friends" were paying, if at all, in provincial stumpage fees and oil and gas royalties.

Then we sat down with the leaders from the three Métis communities and sketched out an agreement. What we came up with was the creation of a new joint venture company called Kaquo (Cree for "all together"), which would be jointly owned by the Métis, Active Energy and me under the 45-45-10 formula.

The potential revenues of Kaquo reached into the hundreds of millions of dollars a year, and to show good faith, Active Energy would kick in $350,000 in operating capital immediately and pay each of the communities $100,000 as an advance on royalties. To protect everyone involved, important decisions like choosing the chairman and any changes whatsoever to our initial agreement would have to be unanimous. You could not think of a fairer, more progressive agreement, and there was real excitement when we got together in Westbank on July 18, 2014, to officially sign the Joint Venture Agreement.

All of the partners saw this as a landmark deal in developing the Aboriginal economy in Canada, and we were careful to ensure in the agreement that any development had to adhere to internationally recognized environmental and sustainability standards, the highest international forestry stewardship criteria, the Métis Settlements Act and all associated legislation. I knew from bitter experience that we needed to belt and brace this or government would do their best to undermine us as Natives. In addition, all commercial transactions that we entered into would include an obligation to provide local employment for Métis citizens and a commitment to contribute to corporate social responsibility programs that benefit Métis communities, beyond anything seen before in Canada.

Phase 2 of the project, already in the planning stage, was to cut out all of the costs associated with getting the biomass to market by building our own power plants on-site to turn our product into 80 megawatts of electricity that we could then sell to the grid in Alberta. The effect of this would be to increase the potential earnings of all partners by several times more than we would earn with the biomass alone.

The media buzz around the deal was extensive and very positive, but behind the scenes in the Alberta government, the Aboriginal Relations ministry wheels began to spin, searching for ways to kill the deal.

Their point man in this was the minister, who had a familiar-sounding name: Frank Oberle Jr.

I recognized the name instantly, but at first, I couldn't quite remember where I knew it from. Then I remembered that Oberle had been one of my Progressive Conservative character assassins. But he had been a federal politician, and this was provincial politics. When I initially saw the photo of him, he did look familiar and it was only later that I realized that this was, indeed, a very unwelcome blast from the past. He was the son of Frank Oberle Sr., the nasty B.C. Conservative MP who had grilled me on the Indian Affairs Committee in 1983, then treated Leonard Crosby with kid gloves, even calling for Westbank to be put into receivership so Crosby could have "security of tenure" on our lands.

When I faced his son in Alberta, I did some research on Frank Sr. and found out he was a German immigrant who arrived in Canada in 1951, when he was 19 years old. He was too young for Hitler's army but had been in the Hitler Youth, and his family had followed the Nazis into Poland where they seized land from Polish Jews and gave it to master race Germans like him. So he came from a family who were themselves settlers in someone else's land, and when the Soviet Army swept in, the Oberles fled back to Germany. In 1951, the young Frank left Germany and joined the other racist white settlers in British Columbia on stolen Indian land. It is no wonder that he looked on Leonard Crosby as almost his brother. And now I had the misfortune of being confronted by his son in Alberta, who had his father's arrogant manner when we were trying to develop an Indigenous economy for the Métis people there.

It did seem that Frank Jr. was waiting for us, because his department claims it was a single letter protesting the agreement with the Métis that they received on July 28 — 10 days after the signing of the initial deal — that set off their "investigation."

The letter-writer, whose name has been blanked out in the government records, was a sitting councilor from Peavine Métis Settlement, and he referred to the local leader, Iner Gauchier, as someone who had previously claimed to be a "fierce protector of Métis rights."

"Why would anyone agree to provide 10% plus other fees to an Indian and 45% to a foreign-based company?" the letter-writer asked. "Mr. Gauchier has been in court since 1999 to remove selected Indians from our community and now he agrees to give 10%+ of our community to an Indian. Something does not add up."

So that was it. One Métis racist in Peavine confiding to a white racist in Edmonton and the battle was on. The government of Alberta would throw everything they had against us to try to block the deal.

It started out as a whisper campaign against us, but in the fall of 2014, we tried to counter it as we went along. We went ahead with creating the structure of the new company, Kaquo, which would be jointly owned by the Métis, Active Energy and me. While we were working through the business issues, the office of the Alberta Department of Aboriginal Relations, headed by Frank Oberle, was beginning to move into the picture. In response to the racist letter, which the government likely solicited in the first place, the minister announced he took "complaints from the Métis Settlement members very seriously and that protecting public interest is a statutory responsibility that I take seriously."

Then he began to throw spaghetti against the wall to see what would stick. The department began to criticize the deal because non-settlement members would get 55 percent of the value. They said community members had not been properly consulted and due diligence had not been carried out, and said that the agreement had not been posted in one of the community offices.

These were all phoney complaints. The complaint that the communities were only getting 45 percent of the benefits can be seen for the red herring that it was when you consider that the province itself only gets around 5 percent for the oil and gas resources that it owns and even less than that in forestry licences. For the holders of the resource to get a return of 45 percent of the revenues is unheard of anywhere in the world. And the communities' interests were protected by the fact that with a 45 percent stake in the company, they would be involved in the decision-making every step of the way. As further protection, the corporate constitution we had adopted required unanimity on all of the important issues.

Despite the government's hostility, we had our big coming-out party at the Oasis Centre in Edmonton on January 26, 2015, in an economic development summit we called Working Together to Better Our Communities. Of course we made an attempt to invite all of the government representatives so they would get to know us better and maybe it would give us a chance to allay some of their more irrational fears. But the government was not, apparently, interested in coming to an understanding. They were out to sink us.

Our event was hosted by the great Canadian actor Tom Jackson, and the 300 attendees included forestry industry people from across

Canada; members of the Alberta Métis communities; guests from other Métis, First Nations and Canadian Aboriginal groups; and senior international executives from Active Energy Group.

Because of the government's snub, there was a sense of defiance in the room. There were speeches by Iner Gauchier of Peavine Métis Settlement, Greg Calliou of Paddle Prairie Métis Settlement and Gerald Cunningham of East Prairie Métis Settlement, as well as by me and Richard Spinks. In one way or another, all of us referred to the ongoing battle to assert our rights in a world designed by others. I was also pleased, and I admit proudly, that my daughter, Kelly, was also invited to perform at a time when her music was attracting more and more attention in North America. (A CD sampling of Kelly's music is included in the inside back cover of the book.)

During a brief introduction, Iner Gauchier told the gathering that the work about to be undertaken had already achieved success in other parts of the world.

"What we are doing here to get on our feet isn't new," he assured the room. "It might be new here in our world in Canada, but it isn't new in European countries. They've done a lot. The template is already set and we're reliving what they have done."

Richard then told the gathering that the newly formed company was a business that will create opportunity and provide a platform that will eventually allow Aboriginal communities to achieve economic self-sufficiency.

Richard pointed out that the first acres of land and the first project of this kind that he was involved in was in Ukraine, and he described the operation in the remote area with huge unemployment and how he was able to give the people work, revenues and new hope for the future.

Iner Gauchier talked about his own business experience, which began at an early age with his dad as a logger. He said that when he won the election in 1999, he didn't expect to win, but when he did, "I was the saddest man in the settlement because I knew what the fights were to get on our feet." He went on to describe an early attempt by his community to get involved in the oil industry that was blocked by the government. "That's the government, that's what they do," he said. "The bottom line is we always have to band together to become stronger. We need to unite. Three of us settlements are now united and we'd like the rest to unite with us as well."

Paddle Prairie Chairman Greg Calliou echoed Gauchier's statements about working in unity, and he encouraged the other communities to adopt the Kaquo model and become directly involved in building their own economic future rather than leaving their future to outside interests.

Gerald Cunningham, chairman of the East Prairie Métis Settlement, described the background and history of the Métis settlements and the various acts and transfers that created them. He spoke about the intent and about the money that was paid out with an expectation a decade ago that the settlements would be self-sufficient by 2007.

"For the most part, the settlements still rely on government funding. In order for us to change that, we have to start doing things for ourselves. We have to take responsibility for our future and we have to be willing to do whatever it takes to make progress happen. It's time that Aboriginal people get together to establish partnerships and capitalize on opportunities, whether they are local, provincial or national.

"Life is short and opportunities are few, so we have to make the most of this opportunity presented to us. By working together, we can go far and bring strength and unity to all Aboriginal people in our region and across Canada."

I was billed as the keynote speaker and I spoke about my fight at the Hall Commission. "Ottawa spent $10 million with a Royal Commission of Inquiry to try and get the dirt on me because I was fighting them for our rights — not my rights, *our* rights." I told them that books were confiscated and that I was left to run the business for 10 months without them.

"Life has not been without trials for me, but one thing I never lost was my pride, my desire, to be an Okanagan Indian." My experiences with government are that they continually undermine Aboriginal people while eroding their rights and this has only furthered my resolve to "respect and help Native people all across Canada."

I told the crowd, "there is $200 million of investment agreed with New York financiers already and that there would be significantly greater revenue to the settlements to be made in the first year alone than the entire LTA would provide to all eight settlements." I explained that that's available for all eight Métis communities — and other Indigenous peoples. "We don't limit this to just the three Métis settlements; we want the eight settlements to be the catalyst, the example for every tribe, band, treaty, Nation in Canada and the United States. We want the Métis to say to their brothers, 'OK, this is what we've done. We can help you do it, too.'"

People left in an upbeat mood. We had set the table and invited the government and they had refused to attend. So the attitude was well, OK, we would go and serve the banquet without them. But the government was not going to let that happen. The following day, just as Richard was heading to the airport to catch his flight back to Kyiv, Alberta Premier Jim Prentice officially announced he was moving to block the Kaquo deal.

The tool his forestry minister, Frank Oberle Jr., would use would be the Métis Settlements General Council, which as I mentioned is the Métis version of the Assembly of First Nations. Like the AFN leadership, all of their salaries came directly or indirectly from the government. This is how power works in Canada: using government-funded Indigenous organizations as the new Indian agents to control our peoples. In this case, the government had permanently buried their power inside the constitution of the Métis Settlement General Council, which it had helped set up in 1990, by ensuring that the General Council, which they directly funded, had veto power over community initiatives.

Our Kaquo communities were only three of the eight settlements in the General Council, and the government-controlled body was moving to legally block us from proceeding. When our lawyers began to look at their legal basis for doing so, they found this in the organization's constitution: "The Métis Settlement General Council makes policies that are binding on the General Council members. *Policies which are developed in consultation with the Minister of Indigenous Relations have the same effect as Alberta law and are published in the Alberta Gazette* [emphasis mine]." In other words, the long arm of the Alberta government could still reach inside the General Council to steer the organization in any direction it wanted. On timber rights, it explicitly stated, "Under General Council's Timber Policy, General Council transferred ownership of the timber rights on the Settlements land to the Settlements but retained certain *supervisory rights*. Pursuant to s.227 of the MSA all actions taken by Settlements must comply with General Council Policies. If the Settlements make a decision or take an action that may not be compliant with a Settlement Council's authority and responsibility under the Timber Policy, the General Council may seek a review by the Appeals Tribunal."

So, in the end, Alberta succeeded in blocking Kaquo, an agreement that was about equal shareholding and equal say between Métis and a publicly traded energy company that truly set an example of what could be done. I personally and Active Energy as a company were ready to contribute the capital, expertise and business connections while the settlements brought their timber rights and their own forest management plans to the table. This deal was, and remains, unheard of in resource development on Indigenous lands, with 55 percent Indigenous control of the entire project.

When the Alberta government blocked us, they said the Métis didn't need us. They could do it without us and to counter the disappointment, they offered to put up $10 million so the Métis could purchase sawmill equipment. But that never went anywhere. They didn't have the capital — Richard already had pledges for $200 million in investments to get things moving — or the experience in the industry, the two things we were offering. So they failed and the sawmill equipment was left to rust.

Premier Prentice fared even worse. A year after blocking us, he was out of office, defeated by Rachel Notley's NDP in the May 2015 election. It ended not only his political career, but a 44-year unbroken run of Progressive Conservative rule in Alberta.

A year after that, Prentice was killed in an airplane crash — ironically enough, in Kelowna, a few kilometres from my home — when the pilot inexplicably flew the Cessna Citation into the ground shortly after takeoff. The two other passengers killed were Ken Gellatly, father-in-law of one of Prentice's daughters and descendent of the famous Gellatlys who stole Chief Tomat's irrigation water for their tomatoes; and Shelton Reid, a retired Calgary businessman from the energy sector. Transport Canada never fully explained the crash, deciding that the most likely cause was "pilot disorientation." Others have pointed to more suspicious causes. I have heard claims that Prentice had recently learned about a scam involving a Mustafa Oil deal in the province involving at least one of his former cabinet ministers and was about to report on it. Under this theory, the accident was not an accident. Perhaps one day new information will come to light to clear this up, or at least explain why the Cessna plunged to the ground shortly after takeoff on a clear October night.

As far as proof that our Alberta Métis deal was sound, this can be seen in the very friendly discussions we began with the new Alberta government in 2016. But by then, Alberta had largely slipped off our radar, with AEG losing over $2.5 million in the deal. The Métis, of course, lost exponentially more. Finally, much of the forest that could have generated hundreds of millions of dollars of profit for them was consumed in the Chuckegg Creek wildfire of July 2019.

At the time, we had moved on to negotiations with a U.S. power supplier, Birmingham-based Georgia Renewable Power, looking for a renewal product, with Newfoundland for a forestry partner.

One of the hallmarks of my business career has been persistence, and we continued to talk to Greg Calliou about resources partnerships. Today, more than a decade later, we are in the late planning stage to build an environmentally innovative, low-carbon-emitting plant in the Paddle Prairie Settlement that will use Métis forestry biomass in energy production. Unfortunately, Greg Calliou died in late 2019 before seeing his dream for his people realized. But there is a plan to name the groundbreaking plant after him.

CHAPTER 17

Idle No More

While we were trying to build a new model for sustainable economic development on Indigenous lands in Alberta, I was still working with Arthur Manuel on his international initiatives. My role was as a consultant and as his main supporter in funding his trips to present the Indigenous case to international human rights bodies, where Arthur denounced Canada's treatment of Indigenous peoples.

By 2012, Arthur had emerged as a leading voice of international Indigenous resistance — to the point of being elected co-chair of the Indigenous Caucus at the United Nations Permanent Forum on Indigenous Issues. The political prospects in Canada in this period were more frustrating, with the hang-around-the-fort Indians in the national organizations and in the B.C. Summit, engaging with the government in an endless series of pointless roundtable discussions, where the only thing on the table was the government proposals to finish off the seizure of our lands.

My own activism over the years apparently did not go unnoticed during this period, because I was contacted at the end of 2011 by the leader of the Union of B.C. Indian Chiefs, Grand Chief Stewart Phillip, who was someone I always respected as one of the few genuine fighters among us, and who told me that I had been nominated by UBCIC members to be given the status of Grand Chief. I was surprised, because I had thought they only awarded the Grand Chief title to the UBCIC leader, like Stewart, and to the founders of the organization. My brother Noll had been awarded the Grand Chief title as a UBCIC founding chief, but I hadn't heard of others outside of that select circle receiving the honour. Stewart told me that it was not something they usually did, but a couple of chiefs were going to put the resolution in front of the membership at the next general assembly, and he wanted to make sure it was OK with me.

Of course, I was flattered. This was not something anyone could turn down, because it was recognition from your own people.

I was invited to the general assembly in Richmond on February 24, 2012, where the proposition was being made to the chiefs from across British Columbia, and I was touched by the speeches in my honour. The resolution that was finally put forward to the assembly read in part:

> **WHEREAS** Ronald (Ron) M. Derrickson, is a member of the Okanagan (Syilx) Nation who was born into poverty in a tarpaper shack, and is now one of the most successful entrepreneurs in Canada and internationally;

> **WHEREAS** Ron Derrickson served as the chief of the Westbank Indian Band for six terms between 1976 and 2000. Under his leadership the Westbank Indian Band became one of the wealthiest reserves in Canada, with twelve profitable band businesses he helped to develop;

WHEREAS Ron Derrickson always supported the work of the Union of B.C. Indian Chiefs and considered Grand Chief George Manuel an inspiring man, who he began working with in the 1970s;

WHEREAS Ron Derrickson initiated logging action to assert Aboriginal Title and Rights in the late 1990s resulting in an agreement with significant logging concessions for his people;

WHEREAS Ron Derrickson recognizes the importance of asserting Aboriginal Title and Rights and pushing the federal and provincial governments back on their policies that violate constitutionally protected Aboriginal Title and Rights and international human rights and indigenous rights standards;

WHEREAS Ron Derrickson is committed to sharing his experiences as a leader, negotiator and businessman with his people, and using his standing and wealth to support Indigenous Peoples in British Columbia to build economic independence based on the recognition of their rights;

THEREFORE BE IT RESOLVED the UBCIC Chiefs Council wishes to formally acknowledge, honour and thank Ronald M. Derrickson for his inspiration and commitment to the Union of B.C. Indian Chiefs and to the causes of Indigenous Peoples in British Columbia;

THEREFORE BE IT FINALLY RESOLVED that Ronald M. Derrickson is hereby granted the title of Grand Chief of the Union of B.C. Indian Chiefs.

The resolution had been sponsored by the chief from the Splatsin Band of the Secwépemc Nation and the Xaxli'p Band of the Lillooet Nation — two of the Nations that had been strong supporters of the great Okanagan Chief N'kwala. It was formally brought to the floor by Stewart himself, who was a leading force in our Okanagan Nation. When he called on the assembly to make my appointment as grand chief unanimous, I watched as a couple of my sworn enemies — band members who had been part of the vicious attacks on me in the 1980s — bit their tongues and allowed the assembly to make it unanimous.

As I headed back to Westbank, I was surprised to find that I really did feel different. My past commitment to my people had always been unquestioned and I had been a band chief for more than a dozen years, but this honour did not seem so much like an acknowledgement of past activities but an inducement to do even more. That, I realized, was probably Stewart's reason for conferring it. It was an elbow in the ribs. To hold the title of grand chief meant that you could no longer contribute half measures. You had to be all-in. If I was thinking about passing my final years in tranquility on the sidelines, this honour would not allow it. A grand chief is a grand chief for life and that, finally, would be my term of service.

As it turned out, 2012 would be the year when the battle across the country would also be stepped up quite a few notches.

I was meeting with Arthur that November and we were doing a kind of year-end political assessment of where we were. On the positive side, we looked at his international work. As co-chair of the Indigenous Peoples Caucus at the UN that spring, he had succeeding in getting passed a resolution that called on the member states to "acknowledge that the doctrine of discovery, both in theory and in ongoing practice, constitutes the subjection of peoples to alien subjugation, domination and exploitation. It is the denial of fundamental inherent human rights, is contrary to the Charter of the

United Nations and is an impediment to the promotion of world peace and cooperation."

The Indigenous peoples of the world demanded that the Permanent Forum acknowledge and transmit to other UN agencies that "the doctrine of discovery is an expression of racism, xenophobia and discrimination — that it represents a regime of systematic oppression and domination by one racial or religious group over another, and it is committed to the intention of maintaining that regime. As such, the continuing operation of the doctrine of discovery should be recognized as a crime against humanity and should be condemned as such."

On the domestic front, however, things continued to look dismal. The Assembly of First Nations had begun another series of meaningless consultations with the government on the land issue that they were calling the Crown–First Nations Gathering. The first one was held in January 2012, but the whole thing had collapsed by April, when the Indian Affairs guy who was running the consultation admitted that he actually had no mandate to change the highly restrictive federal government claims policy, despite what had been suggested in January.

In early fall, the government put what it really wanted on the table — essentially the surrender of our lands under the terms it had always demanded — which included extinguishment of our title, legal release of the Crown for past violations, elimination of reserves, removing tax exemptions and assimilation into the existing federal and provincial order of government.

A month later, on October 18, the government introduced its omnibus Bill C-45 to Parliament, which included funding cuts to political organizations and gutted Canadian environmental legislation. Among other changes, it cut the Navigable Waters Protection Act and replaced it with the Navigation Protection Act, which excluded more than 98 percent of the country's lakes and rivers from federal environmental oversight, thus unlocking them for abuse by resource extraction companies and opening them up for the passage of oil and gas pipelines.

We looked around and we saw people throwing up their hands, not knowing what to do. Arthur, though, was full of ideas, and while he had a strong following among the more radical Indigenous youth and he had an international profile, the AFN had largely pushed him out of the national debate. During that meeting, I suggested that we write a book to give him a platform for his ideas. After all, he came from a great family of fighters and he had been an activist since his student days, when he was leader of the Native Youth Movement at the same time his father was the first National Chief. He had a great story to tell and he could trace his own political trajectory, and I could add my experience as a negotiator, along with my experience in the War in the Woods, and together we could make a forceful what-is-to-be-done statement.

Arthur was instantly interested in the possibility. He said his friend Naomi Klein had been telling him the same thing — get a book out to provide a platform for his ideas. Arthur told me he would contact a writer friend who we could call on to work as an editor and he would contact him first thing in the new year. At the time, Arthur was preparing to travel to Guatemala, where he was meeting with activists and where he would stay on to take part in the Mayan celebration of the end of the Long Calendar, which was to take place on December 21. This was much in the news that month, because according to the Maya, December 21 marked the ending of their full 5,125-year calendar and the beginning of a new one. So we joked about our fears for the end of time and our hopes for a new dawn beginning.

We didn't know that the new dawn was already beginning. As Arthur later pointed out in *Unsettling Canada*, the new dawn began "like all important events in the world, with the women."

Namely, four Prairie women — three Indigenous (Jessica Gordon, Sylvia McAdam and Nina Wilson) and one non-Indigenous (Sheelah McLean). While Arthur and I were chatting in my office that November, these four remarkable women launched the Idle No More movement, which would "call on all people to join in a revolution which honours and fulfills Indigenous sovereignty which protects the land and water."

That November, the women had organized a "teach-in" in Regina on the government offensive against our land and sovereignty and on what it would mean for grassroots people. They called the event Idle No More. The event attracted a certain amount of local interest, so more teach-ins were held in Prince Albert and North Battleford, then further afield in Winnipeg. The numbers of people attending increased dramatically, each time with everyone expressing frustration at the idleness of our leaders in the face of the unrelenting assault on our rights. So the women called for a mass demonstration on December 10. People who had been waiting for someone to do something while our leadership continued to dance to the government tune flooded onto the streets. There were mass rallies of thousands of Indigenous peoples in Vancouver, Whitehorse, Edmonton, Calgary, Saskatoon, North Battleford, Winnipeg, Thunder Bay, Toronto, Montreal and Goose Bay–Labrador.

The next day, Chief Theresa Spence of the Attawapiskat First Nation announced her support of the Idle No More movement, and began her hunger strike in Ottawa. I watched all this in amazement. It was as if a sleeping giant had awoken in front of us — Indigenous people across the country in the streets, and sometimes in the halls of shopping centres, drumming their songs and demanding their rights.

The Conservative government was certainly watching, because after this display they set to work on their infamous Bill C-51, which redefined "terrorism" in such a way as to include the activities of environmentalists and land defenders. Amnesty International even pointed this out, and that seemed to be the very purpose of the bill — to first intimidate and then incarcerate any Indigenous people who stepped out of line. This was one of Stephen Harper's last government bills, and it was telling that it was supported in the House of Commons by the Justin Trudeau Liberals.

But our people would not be deterred. When Arthur returned from Central America, we met and discussed the new developments and decided that the book was more important than ever. A new generation of activists needed to have a sense of the history of the struggle from someone who had been part of it for the past 50 years, and Arthur, with his unique family background, was the guy who could deliver it. I recognized the need and I reduced my part of the book to the final chapter. I wanted this new, young and energetic movement to have the benefit of Arthur's experience and intellectual brilliance.

I would not be without access to that Idle No More energy myself. While the events were unfolding on the TV screen, my daughter, Kelly, was home for Christmas and we talked at length about the Indigenous struggle in a way we never had before. The images on the TV screen had touched some of her bottled-up feelings about being Indigenous in a way that nothing had before.

In the following months, she Skyped often from her home in California, and we talked about the unfolding events and she told me that she was excited about a new song she was working on about Idle No More movement and its power. I was pleased to have a front-row seat to her creative efforts and I even worked on the lyrics with her. It would almost immediately become a popular song of the movement as well as one that would earn her several important awards. Here are the lyrics:

IDLE NO MORE

Can you look in the mirror
While our people live in squalor?
Raping Mother Earth
While we fight to protect her
In the name of our Father

These things we can't ignore
Can't turn a blind eye
It's time we dry the tears
All our children cry

If we expect to survive
We must stand heart in hand
With eyes open wide
To save our home and native land
The miracle of God
Has gone from light to dark
How long must we live
With a hole in our hearts?

We wait and wait and wait
And watch this silent war
Now we must stand idle no more

Waters turn from blue to brown
Desecrate our sacred ground
Skies have gone from blue to grey
Help us now oh God we pray

We wait and wait and wait
And watch this silent war
Now we must stand idle no more

Now we must stand idle no more
Now we must stand idle no more

The song came out in 2014, and along with its popularity it had a deeper impact. As soon as it was out, Kelly's social media lit up with testimonies and support from people who said her words touched and motivated them. The strength of the Idle No More movement was, and is, that everyone is called to make a contribution in their own way, and the contribution of artists like Kelly have been essential in motivating the people to take action. Kelly's artistic leadership on the Idle No More front has won her acclaim as both a singer and songwriter in a genre she now calls "country tribal rock." Over the last five years I have been happy to work with her on this project, as a producer on her album *Warriors of Love*, which included "Idle No More" as well as a series of new songs about her Indigenous roots.

Among the most important of these was a song I worked on with Kelly at the lyrics stage.

It was her song about Indigenous youth suicides, which seem to pass through our communities in deadly waves. This was an issue close to my heart and I was very glad that Kelly was able to give it voice in her music — especially that she saw the cure for the suicide epidemic in having the young turn their anger away from themselves and into the world that was causing their pain. The refrain was "Rise up, rise up, warrior children / Be the change, rise up, rise up." Here are a few of the key stanzas:

> *Rain falling down*
> *But there is a storm going on inside*
> *Just a young Native boy*
> *No one to turn to*
> *Nowhere to hide*
>
> *Whiskey on Dad's breath*
> *Momma's crying is the only sound*
> *As he kneels beside his bed*
> *He begs god just take me now*
>
> *Little child I will fight for you*
> *Don't give in to your pain and sorrow*
> *Rise up rise up warrior children*

Be the change
Rise up rise up

Rise up rise up warrior children
Be the change
Rise up rise up
Rise up rise up

The song was written with a special concern for young people. But an Indigenous guy, who is now a band chief, told her in confidence that he was driving to his cabin with his loaded shotgun to end it all when he heard the song on the radio — and it changed his mind. When he arrived at the cabin, he unloaded the gun and took a new inventory of his life, and what he needed to do to change the world instead of removing himself from it. It was not Indigenous people who were broken, it was Canada that was broken.

This was a tremendously busy time. Although I was now in my early seventies, my company, the RMD Group, was still running more than 30 businesses in the real estate and service industries in Canada, along with my real estate and resource companies in Ukraine. During this period, I was also working with Arthur on the book that would be *Unsettling Canada: A National Wake-up Call.*

In the run-up to the publication, I organized a symposium in September 2014 with Arthur that we called Aboriginal Title — Value It! It was designed to wake up Indigenous leaders from B.C. and across Canada to the disaster of signing away their title in the modern treaties. I hosted it at my Two Eagles Golf Club in Westbank and I prepared a speech about how we had to stand up and defend our rights to our land and our independence from government, the same themes I was pushing in Alberta at the time with the Métis deal.

Among those who joined us was the Tsilhqot'in Chief Roger Williams. In June, the Tsilhqot'in people had won a landmark ruling in the Supreme Court that recognized Tsilhqot'in Aboriginal title to 2,000 square kilometres of their traditional territory *on the ground* as opposed to in principle, as the Delgamuukw decision had done. As we were speaking, Premier Christy Clark was addressing many of the chiefs who had a history of putting their Aboriginal title up for sale, and in my speech I blasted them for even showing up to the premier's gabfest when she was working hand in glove with Ottawa to steal their land under the guise of the bogus modern treaties.

There was a real sense of momentum at the end of the conference. I called Arthur over and said to him, "You should start thinking of another book." *Unsettling Canada* was in its last editorial stage, and I liked the way it wove Arthur's life and struggle together to give a sense of our movement over the last half century. But I thought it should be followed up by a book that not only laid out his ideas in black and white but pulled them all together to give a road map for action. "Now we're all Idle No More," I told Arthur, "but no one is offering solutions. *Unsettling Canada* identifies the problems. Now you have to follow with a book that offers solutions." I agreed I would fund the new book the same way I had the first one, and Arthur was very pleased. He said he would start on it that winter, as soon as he sent in his final corrections to the current manuscript.

Unsettling Canada was published in the spring of 2015. It was an instant success. Arthur toured the country, with coverage in all the major papers and on the main TV networks, and I met him for a large book launch in Vancouver. The book quickly became an unofficial bible of the Idle No More movement for the way it showed how badly we had been served by our Indigenous leaders for the past 30 years, and young Indigenous people flocked to the book launches. It even won the Aboriginal History Prize from the Canadian History Association, and for a week or so, it hit the bestseller list. I was pleased to see how it added to his stature. His message of no surrender was of crucial importance and now people were starting at long last to listen.

Arthur and I started working on the second book in the winter of 2015. It was in the final editing process in the late fall of 2016 when he left for the Standing Rock protest camp.

The Standing Rock Reservation was the Lakota lands through which they were constructing the Dakota Access Pipeline, which ran from the North Dakota oilfields down into southern Illinois, crossing under the Missouri and Mississippi rivers, and made it a major threat to the vital U.S. waterways.

The protest camp had started on the reserve in the spring of 2016 and it had grown to an enormous size by December. The paramilitary police were surrounding it and they were often using brutal force to keep the protesters back from the pipeline construction. I remember I was worried about Arthur going there and I told him that. But he insisted that he had to be there because he wanted to develop links between the Standing Rock land and water protectors and the battle just beginning in his own territory over the Kinder Morgan pipeline. In fact, he had just sent an open letter to Prime Minister Trudeau saying the Secwépemc people had to be consulted before the pipeline passed through their territory.

He was planning to do his own consultation with his people in the spring with a mass meeting on the land to discuss whether to allow passage of the pipeline on their territory. The week he left for Standing Rock was a bitterly cold one. But his spirits were high. He sent me an optimistic appraisal of the battle there and the connections he was making for the upcoming Kinder Morgan fight. I remember that he sent photos of him and Naomi Klein, who was also there for the protest, and his daughter, Kanahus, who would later be among those arrested.

After Standing Rock, Arthur went to meet his partner, Nicole Schubus, who was at a meeting of the Institute for Sustainable Development (IISD) in Cancun, Mexico. He wrote me because he had heard from the publisher of *Unsettling Canada*, who had been approached by another publisher who wanted to do a French translation of the book and wanted our approvals as co-authors. He also said that he had finished the draft of his part of the new manuscript, which would be published as *Reconciliation Manifesto,* and he would bring it to me so I could add my chapters.

He had registered at the Cancun conference with INET, but it was more or less a holiday for him, because he didn't have to report to anyone. Of course, his idea of a holiday was different from that of most people. He described a meeting with the UN Special Rapporteur on Indigenous Peoples and the Special Rapporteur on Human Rights and the Environment and other meetings he had already had or was planning.

He ended this with a very true remark: "No rest for the Indigenous activist."

He was back on his collective email list again trying to organize a meeting with activists across the country, including Naomi Klein, for February 7 on the site of the proposed Kinder Morgan pipeline to get them ready for the fight ahead. And he contacted me directly just after Christmas when he returned from Mexico to ask when we could meet.

It was at that meeting that we were going to put the finishing touches on the new book and he said he also wanted to bring me up to date and to discuss my offer to fund a Canadian activist as part of the U.S.-based Seventh Generation Fund, of which he was a director. The Seventh Gen, as they were known, were an important funder of Indigenous activism in the U.S. and they were open to supporting activism here if they had someone who could run a small Canadian office. We checked for dates and finally settled on January 7, a Thursday, for our meeting.

Arthur never made it. That Thursday morning I received a call from Nicole, who told me Arthur would not be coming. He was in the hospital. He had been coughing for a couple of weeks and he was having trouble breathing. The doctor thought it was pneumonia.

Then darker news came from his sister Doreen:

Dear Family and close friends,

At this time the family is asking for privacy so please DO NOT post on social media such as Facebook or Twitter etc.

As most of you know our brother Arthur is in the Royal Inland Hospital. Art was admitted late Thursday night with what at that time was thought to be pneumonia. He was having trouble breathing. Art spent the night in the Emergency ward. He has since been transferred to the Intensive Care Unit (ICU). I drove up from Vancouver today and just met with the doctor in the ICU at approximately 2pm. Art has been diagnosed with Congestive Heart Failure (CHF) and is on a respirator. This condition is considered "life support" because he is not breathing for himself, he is heavily sedated and a tube is draining fluid buildup in his lungs (a result of the CHF).

For the time being only family is permitted to see him. Family is rotating visitation. We are in the ICU waiting room. We are praying and hoping for the best and remain positive that he is strong enough to fully recover.

Alarmed, I called Nicole. She said there had been an improvement that day — they had found he had a leaky heart valve and it seemed reparable. But I heard the fear in her voice. I said, "I want to go down to see him."

She would be glad to have me there, she said.

In an air of unreality, Kelly and I drove the two hours to Kamloops and saw Arthur in the intensive care unit. He was unconscious and surrounded by his loving family. But they had the same fear in their eyes as Nicole. Arthur was laying unconscious and hooked up to the breathing machine. Kelly was optimistic that Arthur would recover and prayed for him at his bedside, but I knew that I was there to say goodbye.

At 11 p.m. on the night of January 11, 2017, Arthur Manuel passed from this world.

When I heard the news, I sent an email to his sister Doreen. I told her how awful it was to lose "my best friend, co-writer and traditional brother, who came from a long line of champions of the people, defender of native rights and a good honest, extremely intelligent, loyal and humble man . . . I never cry, but last night I cried for my friend. It's a great loss to our people."

The wake was held on Friday and Saturday with an open casket at the Adams Lake Indian Band gymnasium, with the funeral there on Sunday. People came from not only around the country but internationally to pay tribute to this special man who had been so swiftly torn from us. Even non-Indigenous politicians, like John Horgan, then-leader of the opposition in B.C. and soon-to-be premier, showed up to pay his respects.

I was asked to provide a eulogy, which I am including in full in Appendix III. I began by saying that I felt that I had always known Arthur Manuel, in the way many of our people know each other — long before we even meet.

I told them that his father used to stay with us when he was travelling the Interior on his political tours and how I worked closely with Arthur's brother Bobby when we were both chiefs at the same time. I summed up our political fight together in the forests and on the international scene and I pointed out how his passing left a deep hole in the protection of our rights, but I knew that our children and grandchildren would continue to carry the torch we passed on.

In closing, I quoted from a song about Arthur that Kelly was working on:

Patient is the man
And strong are his words
To fight without fighting
Never yells to be heard
Teaching Our People, humble and grace
This is my friend, I could never replace

Arthur Manuel, my dear friend, was laid to rest in the icy sunshine of that January morning.

I worked on the final edit of our second book with his partner, Nicole, and Peter McFarlane, who had worked as an editor on *Unsettling Canada*, as well as with the publisher, Jim Lorimer. It took only one final edit and the publisher had it out by the fall with the title of *Reconciliation Manifesto: Recovering the Land, Rebuilding the Economy*. The book went on to win the B.C. Book Prize for non-fiction and was shortlisted for the George Ryga Award, as well as appearing on the best books of 2017 lists of the *Globe and Mail*, *Quill & Quire* and the Writer's Trust.

In my opening section, I underlined what was the heart of Arthur's message from his writings and so many of our face-to-face conversations. I pointed out that Arthur was especially critical of the big-L and small-L liberals who are trying to distract from the real issues — the land question and the right of Indigenous Nations to self-determination — to a debate about programs and services. That was his genius — his ability to keep his eye on the ball. Trudeau was confusing everyone by using relationship language in addressing Indigenous issues, like he was discussing a failed marriage, and offering mea culpas for Canada's past behaviour and calling for reconciliation.

Arthur saw through all this. The breakdown of Indigenous-Canadian relations was not simply a behaviour question where if

Canada is nice, everything will be fine. The issue is not behaviours but fundamental rights — our land rights and the inalienable right to self-determination. These could not be remedied by apologies and hugs, but required recognition and restitution. "Canada," Arthur wrote, "cannot solve its Indian problem with measures that are designed — as they always have been since the first missionaries arrived, through the whole residential school experience and in the fitful Liberal bursts into nothingness like the Kelowna Accord — to fix Indigenous peoples. This will never succeed because we are not broken. Canada is the sick one in the relationship, suffering from what sometimes seems like an incurable case of colonialism. It needs to change profoundly."

The importance of Arthur's intellectual contribution to our struggle could be seen in the obituaries that appeared in the *Globe and Mail* and *The Economist* as well as in Canadian and Indigenous media across the country, where he was celebrated as the main strategist of the modern Indigenous movement in Canada. Grand Chief Steward Phillip described Arthur as a leader who "never took one step back," and by many as "the Nelson Mandela of Indigenous peoples." That was the depth and breadth of the esteem he was held in by our people. When the weekly podcast *Media Indigena* devoted an entire program to the theme of who could replace Arthur Manuel in the Indigenous movement, they found no one who had the stature, the political experience, the profound understanding of the issues and the impeccable character that gave him such a unique place. For me, Arthur is missed as a political force and even more as a friend. We worked together for more than 15 years and I think we made a difference.

CHAPTER 18

New Era in Westbank

Like business, politics has its own ledger, its own accounts receivable and accounts owed. As a businessman, I always strive to keep the books balanced. I always pays my debts — even in the most difficult times — and I do what I must to collect those owed to me. The political ledger is more abstract, but it is no less real. And I always strove to keep that balanced as well.

In our local political scene, I still had considerable accounts receivable. But in recent years, I had karma working for me and I was happy to lend her a hand in collecting that final debt.

The First Karmic Principle in politics and in life is *What goes around comes around*, and it was very much in evidence in Westbank.

The same opposition that had caused me such grief in the 1980s, and who I came back to defeat again in 1998, was back in power in

Westbank in 2010 when they made a profoundly stupid deal to build a private for-profit hospital in the community.

The $120 million 100-bed facility was designed to operate outside Canada's medicare system, serving any patient willing and able to pay the enormous expense for private treatment. Chief Robert Louie was behind it and he insisted that there was a large market of people in Canada who were leaving the country for health care who would be willing to pay for the same services at home.

His facility was designed to perform various medical procedures, including elective heart surgery, but it would not provide emergency, obstetric or psychiatric services. Louie promised that the hospital would create 300 jobs, and he announced that they would begin construction in 2012.

Health experts panned the project from the beginning, saying it was too complex to be run by a small reserve and likely would run into regulation problems from Health Canada for contravening the Canada Health Act. This was the central problem. Virtually all of the services they would be offering were offered in Health Canada-supported institutions and it was illegal to charge patients for procedures that were already covered under the Canada Health Act. My brother Noll was at some point brought in to raise money for the project. When he found it was impossible to interest investors in sinking money into a deal that they had no assurances was actually legal, he pulled out.

But Louie and the council ploughed ahead, sinking millions of dollars of band funds into the Lake Okanagan Wellness Centre Limited. It was structured as a limited partnership with Toltech Healthcare Medical Services Corp., which was controlled by a couple of white guys from Alberta, Lyle Oberg and Mark McLoughlin, along with an entity called Ad Vitam Healthcare Ltd., which was also controlled by Oberg and McLoughlin. These two were key to the project and both had high profiles — Oberg was an Alberta Conservative MLA who had jumped to the right-wing populist Wild Rose Party in 2011, and McLoughlin was a former CFL place-kicker for the Calgary Stampeders and B.C. Lions. To partner with this colourful pair, the Westbank Band formed its own Coyote Health Ventures. But there were other murky partners, like the numbered company 1046356, which was held privately by Brian Connor, director of finance for the band. Originally, Westbank was only supposed to provide the land for the facility, but it somehow got suckered into funding the start-up operations of the health centre and, by extension, all of its hanger-on companies. Meanwhile, the community was full of rumours that some of the white partners were buying new homes, expensive cars and yachts on our dime.

According to the original deal, Oberg and McLoughlin had the task of finding the $150 million in venture capital needed to fund the project. The 2012 date for the beginning of construction came and went. Then, in the spring of 2013, Oberg and McLoughlin announced that they had a commitment letter for the $150 million capitalization costs from the Oxbridge Group of Companies, and in jubilation the band announced that construction of the hospital would begin in the fall. But then fall 2013 came and went. The start date was moved back to the spring and then the fall of 2014. People started to ask questions. The answers were vague. It turned out the promised $150 million was never advanced and no one could say why. The RCMP were called in for an investigation. Band members became alarmed and, after several acrimonious band meetings, used the Westbank constitution to successfully petition for an independent audit of the project.

The auditor's report came in the spring of 2015, only three months before the band election, and it was a tough one for Chief Louie. It showed that the band was already in debt on the deal for between $7.9 million and $10.3 million. After originally offering to only provide the land for the hospital, Chief Louie and his council were somehow convinced by the partners to secure a mortgage on those lands from Canadian Western Bank. When Ad Vitam stopped making payments toward the mortgage, the band was left holding the bag. Finally, if the band wanted its mortgaged lands back, they would have to pay $7.9 million to Oxbridge. The auditor's report also said $2.8 million was owed to Oxbridge for brokerage fees, despite the loss of funds and the criminal allegations.

When the auditor's report came out, people began to petition for the immediate removal of Chief Louie and his council from office. His most vocal band critic in this whole affair was Roxanne Lindley, the daughter of my friend and first chief Norman Lindley. Roxanne decided it was better to wait and run against Louie in September than remove him from office by petition, so she announced she would be a candidate for chief.

I watched all of this with fascination. It reminded me of the furor over the Northland Bank in the 1980s. The difference was that in the case of Northland, the charges that the band had lost millions of dollars were only rumours — the band ended up losing nothing. Here, the enormous loss was confirmed by the auditor and it was clearly based on stupidity.

Louie had been the chief for a long time by this point and his electoral machine was embedded in the community. In many cases, chiefs can secure their election by giving certain family members jobs as well as other benefits to key people. In this case, he and his team came out in full force against the auditor's report, denying the loss and promising that the hospital would, indeed, be built. It was only delayed, they said.

Chief Louie's guys were also starting a campaign against Roxanne by claiming that as someone whose background was in the cultural field, she didn't have the qualifications to run the business side of the Westbank Band, which was itself a fairly big business. It was then that I decided to offer Roxanne a little help, by joining the race. I filed my papers as a candidate in August, and in a letter to community members I wrote:

> Some of you might be surprised that I am running
> for chief again. In a way, so am I. But many people
> asked me to run because it is obvious that we are

going backwards as a community. People have asked me to step up to try to get us moving forward again.

I have done this before. When I was first elected chief in the 1970s, this was one of the poorest bands in B.C. I was elected six times to change that. And we set this community on a new track toward prosperity.

We created many new businesses for the band and set the stage for the future. We were also able to give directly to the people. During my term, we gave substantial yearly Christmas benefits to all registered members, but this has dropped to $100 a year.

What we see today is a careless and wasteful use of band money. The greatest symbol of this is the financial disaster of the Okanagan private hospital that has cost community members more than $8 million dollars — that's a debt of more than $12,000 a person or $50,000 for every family in Westbank. This is scandalous — and we are still under the threat of more multi-million-dollar lawsuits.

The sad fact is that this lack of oversight and careless behaviour by the chief and council is not an isolated incident. We saw the same pattern in the chopstick factory project with the same result — bankruptcy and financial losses for the community.

I then promised that if I was elected, I would stay for only one term but would mentor the council on business management and set up some kind of financial advisory committee for the band so it could avoid getting into these sorts of messes in the future.

Of course, this was like waving a red flag in front of a wounded bull. Louie and his minions forgot all about Roxanne and went after me, trying to dredge up old accusations that had long ago been disproven — but more carefully this time, because I had successfully sued them all the last time. So they finally set up a phoney Facebook page to sling mud at me.

That was to be expected. But I was genuinely surprised by how many people flocked to me to tell me they were thrilled that I was running and would be so happy to have me back. I was also surprised to find the old political rush was still there. I was having fun.

I went to the all-candidates meeting on September 9, 2015, and the place was packed. The whole community was there to see the faceoff between me and Louie, and I replied by setting out a detailed "Westbank First Nation Renewal Plan":

> We have seen in the administration of the Westbank First Nation a slippage in all areas to the point where our future prosperity is at stake. This has led to serious financial losses for the community and as a result, a loss of confidence by community members in our chief and council. The incoming administration will have to urgently address these issues.

I repeated the charge that the private hospital debt had already reached more than $12,000 a person, or almost $50,000 for every family, and set out a plan for cleaning it up. I also attacked the current council for continuing along the dead end of the B.C. Treaty process, where they borrowed the money to negotiate with the government in an endless process that our people had already rejected. In the end we risked leaving ourselves with an enormous debt and absolutely nothing to show for it.

> Similarly, we must review how we have been dealing with federal and provincial governments. Under Self Government, we have to ensure that our peoples' interest and not outside interests are taken care of first.
>
> In fact, putting the people first has to be at the centre of everything we do. During my six terms as

chief we always worked to make sure that there were significant annual payments to the band members — generally several thousand dollars. If our business interests are properly managed and expanded, we can begin to increase our payments to band members to those historic levels.

With a politician's sense, I could feel the strong support in the room when I entered and felt it grow throughout the evening. It was by then 40 years since I had first stood up as a 34-year-old rancher and budding entrepreneur to run as Westbank Band chief, and I was delighted to see that after all the water under the bridge, I still had the support of my people.

Then I had to check myself. That was not the plan. I had entered the race because I knew Roxanne would have had difficulty denouncing the business failures of Louie, because she had no experience in the area. It would have been possible to bully her into silence on the issue — not something they could do with me. And with me in the race, they had forgotten about her and had focused their attack on me. As I later learned, Louie was also deprived of votes because many of his previous supporters had already voted for me in the advanced polls.

So at the end of my speech I announced, according to plan, that "I am withdrawing my name for the position of chief. I will not reveal who I support as chief except to say that I really hope *she* wins."

This left the meeting in complete disarray and confusion. But Roxanne's supporters were delighted by the move.

Chad Paul, who was running for councillor, smiled at me as I headed out of the room. "You fucked them again," he said.

In the letter to the community two days later I wrote:

First I would like to thank all of the community members for the support they have shown me. I have been truly honoured by it.

But as many of you already know, I decided to withdraw from the race. This was made easier for me because we already have an excellent candidate for chief on the ballot. I am speaking of course of Roxanne Lindley, who has been a loyal friend for many years. In fact, her father, who was the first chief of the Westbank First Nation, was a good friend of my father. Roxanne comes from the same stock — she is bright, well-educated and well-travelled. She has shown her commitment to the community in her work in promoting health and education through the John Norman Lindley Foundation.

If she is elected, I will gladly offer her and the community whatever service I can.

Because I withdrew later in the process, my name may still be on the ballot. But I am urging all of you, for the good of our community, to join me in voting for Roxanne Lindley as the first woman Westbank chief.

With my support, Roxanne easily beat Louie in the September 15 vote. I was happy to see a new Lindley chief, and very happy that this time it was Westbank's first woman in the job.

Immediately after the election, the Wellness Centre was declared brain-dead and was quietly removed from the life-support system that Louie and his gang had sustained it with during the campaign. Today it has dissolved into a festival of lawsuits, with all of the principals suing and counter-suing one another for the losses, while the principal actors have moved on to other schemes. Mark McLoughlin, one of the Alberta investors, has returned to his football roots with a job coaching place-kickers at the University of Regina. Both Louie and Lyle Oberg have gone into the cannabis business in the Kelowna area.

Oberg is chief policy and medical officer at a company called Flowr (sic), which has plans to launch across the country. Their publicity says they cultivate premium cannabis products and from "our cultivators to our executives, we work passionately to provide our customers with quality products that improve their lifestyles."

Louie has launched the Indigenous Bloom cannabis business, which operates from his home in Westbank. His operation was busted on a couple of B.C. reserves before the legalization law came into effect. This is now a legal product, but to me, selling something in our communities that makes our young people stupid and listless is not a route I would ever take.

You can understand from my own history with Robert Louie — who was part of that crazy Nicholas Kayban gang that spread the lies about me — that I never had much faith in him. Along with our political and personal differences, too many strange deals swirled around him. There's the hospital deal, where many still say there is a lot of material for the RCMP to dig up. And other side deals, like when his wife purchased Carter Abel's land, which was adjacent to land that had recently been sold for $500,000 an acre, for only $100,000 an acre, which angered many who thought Carter was being taken advantage of. At times, I even feel that I was being falsely accused of things that Louie and his gang were actually doing to the community.

But the Robert Louie era now seems to be over. Just like the Ron Derrickson era is over. And we now have a woman chief. We are moving forward. It is taking time, but we are moving forward.

CHAPTER 19

The Struggle Continues

Canada is also taking a long time to get its act together. The Trudeau government's sham reconciliation is collapsing under the weight of its own falsehoods. They even kicked Jody Wilson-Raybould, their prize Indigenous woman supporter, out of her justice portfolio and then out of cabinet and even out of the party, and in the past two years they have arrested more Indigenous land defenders than Harper ever did.

I am encouraged by the dedication of many of our young people, but I must admit, I am impatient at the rate of change.

I was reminded of how far we have to go in this country when I recently boarded an Air Canada plane with my daughter in Vancouver for a flight to Ottawa. I was going there as the winner of the 2018 Indspire Award for a lifetime achievement in business, even though I had been reluctant about making the journey.

The Indspire organization is impressive, with a great Indigenous pedigree. It was founded by John Kim Bell, a Kahnawake Mohawk who became a symphony orchestra conductor. It was originally called the National Aboriginal Achievement Foundation, but under the leadership of the equally impressive Roberta Jamieson, a Mohawk woman from Six Nations of the Grand River Territory, it changed its name to the much catchier Indspire.

Awarding Indigenous excellence in all pursuits, from the arts to sports to politics to science to business, has been its mission since the beginning, and the annual highlight is the televised gala where the awards are handed out. In Ottawa, I would meet with the other award winners for 2018, we would be feted by the House of Commons and the Senate and would sit for a video interview that would be played during the televised gala in the spring.

The fact is, I usually avoid these sort of things. As someone who has no trouble standing up to any sort of attack, I am actually a bit shy about being publicly praised. But due to Kelly's urging and the charm of Roberta Jamieson — who I learned actually started off in the movement as a young woman working for George Manuel at the National Indian Brotherhood office in Ottawa — I agreed to take part.

I will confess that I couldn't help feeling some degree of satisfaction about the impending honour when I got up that morning to head to Ottawa for the award. Fortunately, Canada's continuing racism was there to bring me down to earth. The incident began when we boarded the Vancouver to Ottawa flight. We were already tired from the early flight from Kelowna to Vancouver when we boarded and Kelly, who has serious back problems, moved the seat back to relieve the pain of standing and shuffling through the long lineup to board. Within seconds, a massive shove pushed against the chair with such force that she was flung forward. It was the guy sitting behind her. After throwing his body against the chair-back he stood up in the aisle and began verbally attacking her for impinging on his space. I saw Kelly frozen in fear and stood up and told the guy to stop speaking in such a threatening way.

The flight attendant intervened and the man sat back down. Then they asked us what we wanted for lunch.

My daughter was still shaken. She said she was worried that the guy would strike out at her again and asked them what they were going to do to make sure he didn't repeat the assault. The male flight attendant stared at my daughter. He told her that the guy was not a problem, but if my daughter was going to be a problem, they would have us deplaned.

She ignored the rudeness of his tone and told him again that she was nervous about the guy lashing out at her again.

The flight attendant said, "OK, that's it. I'm telling the captain to go back to the gate."

I had right away suspected there was more than a little racism behind their blame-the-victim approach — we have all seen the dangerous and even deadly contempt Native women have been treated with in this country. If there was any doubt, it was expelled in the next few minutes, when passengers called out for us to "sit down and have another drink" and "go back to the reservation."

It was a humiliation for both of us as we sat waiting for the captain's response.

Then he came on over the loudspeaker to inform the plane that because some passengers were not able to get over an argument they would be deplaning us. It wasn't an argument. It was an unprovoked assault. And my daughter was clearly the victim. But that is what they threatened and that is what they did. My daughter and I were escorted off the plane past all of the smirking white passengers. That is Canada today. An Indigenous person may be honoured in the nation's capital and at home, he may have a Rolls-Royce Phantom in the garage. But if there is trouble, you will be blamed. Even if you are the victim.

I noted later that Air Canada was actually one of the Indspire sponsors, but I was very happy to be able to switch airlines, and we flew to Ottawa that same day on WestJet. Unfortunately, I arrived for the reception in the House of Commons and the Senate, and the taping of my video interview the next day for the later televised ceremony, without my luggage.

The incident coloured my stay in Ottawa. I enjoyed meeting the other Indigenous award winners and I appreciated the work of Roberta and her crew, but the phoney smiles of the MPs and senators at the reception left me cold. The only white guy who I appreciated was the young man who stopped by my table at breakfast in the hotel and introduced himself as a UBC professor. He said he had been on the plane when me and Kelly were unceremoniously dumped off and he apologized for not standing up and saying something at the time. "There was no excuse for the way you were treated," he said. "You should sue them."

The next day, I was scheduled to leave for Kyiv directly from Ottawa. But the episode stayed with me for days and pulled me back to my youth. How bloody frustrating it was to grow up in this country, working in the fields, in the woods on the backbreaking jobs in the lumber camps and the winter on the streets of Vancouver, then ranching and building a business and becoming a leader of my people, and then find myself in my mid-seventies being thrown off an airplane like some kind of bum. No wonder so many of our people simply give up. Despite all of the progress, we were far from out of the woods, as I saw when we tried to build Kaquo, an Indigenous-controlled business, in Alberta. We can go so far and then we hit the wall of frowning white faces who tell us, *That's it, no further, get back.*

With Arthur gone, I have tried to support the other fighters who are left. The most important of these is Russell Diabo, a friend and ally who made a quixotic run for national chief of the AFN in the spring and summer of 2018. I will briefly describe his position here, because it is one that I can fully share.

Diabo is a Kahnawake Mohawk whose father was an ironworker in New York City, so he spent much of his youth in Brooklyn. But the family always kept their roots in Kahnawake, and Diabo was always a fighter. As a kid, he hitchedhiked out west to be part of the American Indian Movement standoff at Wounded Knee, and after going to university on the West Coast, he joined the fight as a policy analyst with many community chiefs, Tribal Council chairs, provincial-territorial leaders and with two former AFN national chiefs. He also worked with Arthur Manuel to set up the Defenders of the Land and has become one of the leading figures in the Idle No More movement. The young people call him "Truth Bomb," and he showed this in his campaign, which had the theme of *Truth Before Reconciliation*.

When Russ asked for my support, I was glad to give it to him. He said he wanted to see First Nations develop and implement their own self-determination plans for community development and nationhood based on restoration of stolen lands, territories and resources, or restitution where lands and resources aren't returned.

During the campaign, he said that as national chief he would make sure the AFN played a role in assisting all Indigenous Nations in building the foundation of their nationhood before they sit down with the government to begin true nation-to-nation negotiations.

"We are told by governments," he said, "and too often by our own leadership, that there is no alternative to the cookie-cutter surrender of lands and resources provided at the existing government negotiation tables. The fact is, we do have another course of action, one that is supported by the international laws that recognize all peoples rights to self-determination.

"We have seen rhetorical flourishes from this government in support of Indigenous rights and protecting the environment, but when it comes to action, it has done completely the opposite. The AFN has lost control of the agenda by allowing the Trudeau government to define our national rights through its land claims and fiscal policies, which reduce us to the status of municipalities and endanger our future as Indigenous peoples."

From the beginning, Russ's purpose was not to win, but to gather grassroots people to the cause and to expose the AFN leadership for what they are — hang-around-the-fort Indians out of touch with the people they are supposed to represent. I helped fund Russell's cross-country tour by car, which he called the *Beans and Bologna Tour* because it hearkened back to the days of George Manuel, when our leadership really did come from the people and fought for their rights.

In his speech at the AFN convention, Russell compared the AFN leadership to docile cattle leading the people into the chute that led to the slaughterhouse for Indigenous rights. You could feel the restless anger in the crowd of chiefs who were supporting the existing leadership. When Russell, as expected, lost the vote, he used his concession speech to denounce the Indian Affairs minister who had been caught during the voting secretly meeting with the Alberta chiefs to get pipeline support. It is telling that when he criticized the minister, Russell was actually booed by some of the AFN chiefs.

Imagine, booing an Indigenous leader for criticizing the government! But Russell was unfazed. He asked if those were "moos" coming from the crowd and alluded to the AFN cattle leading our people into the slaughterhouse, as he had put it in his earlier speech. Russell Diabo would not give an inch. He said he would continue the fight outside of the AFN and because the AFN was unwilling to make the change from within, they would be forced to make it from the people outside the organization.

Recounting how Russ waved away the boos to again accuse the chiefs of being cattle led to the slaughter, Grand Chief Stewart Phillip said, with a smile, that it was "the best concession speech I ever heard."

So it was a relief when I was leaving Ottawa, and the plane took off on the Great Circle arc to Amsterdam and then on to Kyiv. In the end, what I like most about Kyiv is that it is not Canada. It is my alternate reality, like a control group that allows me to see that special kind of Canadian racism against Indigenous peoples. The challenges in Ukraine are, of course, great. There are many crooks and my real estate and resource company holdings there mean that I often spend much of my visits working with lawyers. But the men and women who work for me in Ukraine, like my driver, Volodya, who is a walking font of knowledge of Ukrainian history, culture and politics; my executive assistant, Vika, who has a law degree and is completely loyal and extremely competent; my trusted accountant, Yulia; and my talented young researcher Katya Spinks, who helped me with this book — they are all extraordinarily smart and accomplished people. They all have that Ukrainian charm that is expressed in a lively sense of humour that tends to deflate pretentiousness of any kind. But what I like best about them is that they have big spirits — they are people who embrace life fully and do not have that ugly anti-Indigenous racism that underlies so much of life in Canada.

In Ukraine, I am welcomed for who I am. I saw this first-hand when I went to Yulia's wedding near Dnipropetrovsk. She was happy I came, she said, and delighted by the way I joined in the celebration. Most North Americans, she said, would have hung back, and their distance would have felt like disapproval to the people there. But she said I wasn't like most North Americans, that I seemed to feel things more deeply, like Ukrainians.

It was a great party. It lasted three days and everyone consumed litres of vodka, and I remember chatting and joking with dozens of people, all who insisted that we exchange contact information. In North America, that would have been the end of it. When the party's over the party's over. But in Ukraine, that was not the end. Countless people called me afterward, with greater or lesser ability in English, to see how I was doing and to suggest we meet again. It is this genuine human warmth that counteracts the other Ukraine — the one characterized by corruption, which I also experience in a profound way.

But with all of that, Kyiv has become my refuge. When I arrive at Boryspil International Airport outside of Kyiv, I am leaving the heavy part of Canada behind. The Canada that oppresses my people and puts roadblocks in front of any of our attempts to improve our lot. In Kyiv, I am not met by insulting words and marched off the plane because a white man is violently upset by my daughter trying to rest her aching back. Instead, I am met by Volodya, who is waiting for me with a smile and a handshake. Ukraine, for all of its troubles and upheavals, even its corruption and violence, is my escape from Canada.

CHAPTER 20

A Fund for the Future

I have given to many people and many causes over the years, but I will soon be in my 80th year. More than ever, I have been looking at what I will leave behind. Something that will outlast me and contribute to the betterment of Indigenous peoples.

One project I like is in Westbank where I am providing nine and a half acres of land and helping to build housing for the homeless, a women's shelter and a treatment centre. This project came from a Westbank councillor, Fernanda Alexander, who approached me to see if I would make a contribution to help our people with special needs. It is the type of thing I like to do because it takes care of people who need help the most and ensures they can live in dignity in our community. The project is still awaiting final approval by council, and this is another example of how our governance structures come up short. We often have too much trouble taking things from the planning stage to action.

In general, I do not give to institutions. I am not interested in building monuments to myself — like those who give an institution money in exchange for having a wing of a building named after them. Truth be told, I have not had that smooth of a relationship with most institutions, certainly not that I would want to subsidize them or even to become associated with them. To the contrary, my life has been more about trying to change them, sometimes even trying to tear them down, to build a bigger space for Indigenous people in business, politics and culture. And at every stage I have been fighting against the powers that be. For our land and for our rights.

So it wasn't immediately obvious to me what I should leave behind. A few ideas percolated in my mind for many years before I realized what I wanted. I wanted to leave to those who follow me the means to carry on the fight. Over the past several years I have been arranging my affairs to set up a large legal trust, of up to $20 million, to fight for Indigenous land and self-governing rights.

Setting up the trust can be a tricky undertaking, because it is important that it does not become a feeding trough for on-the-make lawyers or Indigenous-industry careerist bureaucrats. One rule I have is that no one on the legal team of advisors, or their firms, can access the funds. And the cases they will support have to be ones that first, advance our struggle in a meaningful way, and second, have a reasonable chance of succeeding.

Originally, Arthur and his partner, Nicole, were involved as people who could oversee the setting up of the trust. (Although I sometimes had the feeling that even Arthur was a little frightened by the idea.) Now, with Arthur gone, I am putting together the new team that will administer the trust and determine which cases get support. I should be able to make the formal announcement soon. It will be a gift to myself — knowing that I have left a tool that future fighters for our rights can use to continue the struggle for the land that I have been involved in all my adult life.

So that is to be my legacy — to continue the fight. Since my first day in the white school, I have known I would have to fight or submit, and battling for justice has been an important part of my life. It has made me a few very close friends — brothers-in-arms like Arthur Manuel and Grand Chief Stewart Phillip — and I am proud of the fact that so many of the good people who work with me today have been with me, literally, for decades. But as you have seen from my story, it has also made me my share of enemies. Most of those were battles on principle, but as I have also mentioned, I have never been accused of false modesty and I know I have rubbed some people the wrong way — for not, as Justice Hall put it, "hiding my light under a bushel." And whenever others attacked me, I always tried to give better than I got. So yes, I know I have made enemies. And among these, I wear my battles against the racist system in Canada as a badge of honour. That system is still there and I have fought against it all my life, using all my political and legal means and at times even my fists.

It is why I am frustrated when I see the leadership of our national organization today in the Assembly of First Nations twist their own souls to fit within the twisted universe of the Indian Act. They have become not representatives of Indigenous peoples but cogs in the machinery of the government that fuels their high living and greases their palms with per diems and four-star hotels. I can feel contempt for some of these people, but there are others, at the community level, who parrot the government lines and in their deepest souls believe that, indeed, the white man is better than us. For these I feel not contempt but sorrow. They have what has been called Stockholm Syndrome, where the captives, as a form of survival, absorb the ideas and opinions of their tormentors as a way to try to escape victimization. There are always many in our communities who try to jettison their Indian-ness to escape the punishment that it brings and embrace the god of whiteness.

It is these folks who adopt the completely stupid idea of reconciliation without giving us our land back or recognizing our right to self-determination. Me and Arthur tried to expose this fraud in *Reconciliation Manifesto*, but there are many who still haven't woken up to it.

Those who have, struggle to speak our truth. Many have found their voice through Idle No More and related movements. And I tip my hat to the four women who founded it, and to forceful spokespeople like Russell Diabo.

But most of our people at the community level are still searching. And they find themselves following the false paths laid out by government toadies that lead us not to our liberation but down the path into pointless feuding fed by jealousy and envy and the underlying despair that come from centuries of poverty and oppression.

When you come from a people that has been beaten back and routinely humiliated and whose only lifeline is a tiny government handout that is just enough to sustain life, even at a miserable level, you have been reduced to a level of complete dependence. You come to see that meagre monthly handout as the only thing between you and starvation, because in those circumstances, that is what it is: your only hope. So you are afraid of anything or anybody who might threaten that. When someone, somehow, breaks free, the response is not to celebrate and look for ways you, too, can break free, but to envy them. Because you yourself are still frozen with fear.

This is something, sadly, I have seen within my community and even my own family. When I have done well, I have not hesitated to help others, but because I had some success, many in my family and community would keep their distance, sending me only their resentment because they do not have what I have, and at the same time too paralyzed in their own lives to do anything to help themselves. We have to find a way as a community to overcome these negative feelings, which end up only harming us, and join together for the betterment of all.

But I suspect that it will still take more time to overcome these divisions and reach the stage where we truly understand the words of the great Chief Seattle, who said, "Take up one stick and you easily break it. But if you take all the sticks and put them together, no one can break it." When we reach that stage, we win.

Royal Commission of
Inquiry Documents

Officially, the inquiry into my work as Westbank Band chief was called *The Commission of Inquiry Concerning Certain Matters Associated with the Westbank Indian Band.*

It was presided over by John E. Hall, who was a prominent B.C. lawyer and it cost $10 million, then the most expensive Royal Commission in Canadian history. It had 14 staffers, sat for 84 days of hearings, examined 225 exhibits and heard from 67 witnesses. They included 16 Westbank Indian Band members, 15 Department of Indian Affairs officials, 10 Home Park operators, 12 business and professional people, seven auditors and accounting experts and nine others, including RCMP officers, B.C. bureaucrats and several former Westbank employees. Twelve lawyers worked on the inquiry.

In the following pages I have attached the mandate for the Commission and the details of its function. In Appendix II, I have attached Commissioner Hall's summary of his 500-page report. In his summary, the commissioner exonerates me of any and all criminal wrongdoing, but when he addresses Indigenous issues, his lack of experience and exaggerated sense of self meant his general observations are either erroneous, worthless or simply pompous nonsense. But it does give a good sense of Canada's approach to Indigenous peoples in the mid-1980s.

Conduct of the Inquiry

PRIVY COUNCIL

Certified to be a true copy of a Minute of a Meeting of the Committee of the Privy Council, approved by Her Excellency the Governor General on the 12th day of August, 1986.

WHEREAS certain matters associated with the Westbank Indian Band of Kelowna, British Columbia have been the subject of public controversy;

WHEREAS there have been allegations of impropriety on the part of officials of the Department of Indian Affairs and Northern Development (DIAND) and of Councillors of the Westbank Indian Band (Band) in connection with the affairs of the Band;

AND WHEREAS three reviews of these matters have been conducted and the resulting reports have been submitted to Ministers of Indian Affairs and Northern Development without resolving the concerns relating to these matters.

THEREFORE, the Committee of the Privy Council, on the recommendation of the Prime Minister, advise that a Commission do issue under Part I of the Inquiries Act and under the Great Seal of Canada appointing fir. John E. Hall of Vancouver, British Columbia to be Commissioner to inquire into and report on the circumstances of, and factors contributing to, the above mentioned controversy, allegations and concerns and, without limiting the generality of the foregoing, to inquire into and report upon

1. the manner in which DIA 11D, in headquarters and in the regional and district offices, has carried out its responsibilities and functions in relation to the

Band and to lessees and residents on reserves of the Band from 1975 to the present, particularly in relation to: the financial arrangements and transactions including Indian moneys, with the Band, the use of Band lands by Band members, lessees and other residents, the review by the Department of all by-laws made by the Band, to determine whether these responsibilities and functions were carried out in accordance with law, established policy and generally accepted standards of competence and fairness;

2. the exercise of Band government from 1975 to the present, and in particular: whether there has been abuse of office by chiefs or councillors of the Band, whether there have been conflicts of interest on the part of chiefs or councillors of the Band and whether any conflict should or could have been avoided, consider the impacts of these practices, if any, on the members of the Band and on lessees and other residents of the Westbank Indian Band reserves;

3. the activities of lessees and residents of Westbank Indian Band reserves in relation to

4. the Band, the Band Council and Band members, and in particular: whether these lessees and residents met their obligations to the Crown and to the Band, whether the activities of these lessees and residents contributed to tensions and conflicts with the Band; and

5. to recommend any changes to the Indian Act relating to the management of lands, Indian moneys and by-laws, or to the policies or the procedures of DIAND in relation to the said matters, or any remedies to specific problems, that may seem appropriate having regard to the Government's established policy of supporting and strengthening Indian self-

government on Indian lands. The Committee further advises that

(a) the Commissioner be authorized

    (i) to adopt such procedures and methods as he may consider expedient for the proper conduct of the inquiry and to sit at such times and at such places within Canada as he may decide;

    (ii) to engage the services of such staff and counsel as he may consider necessary or advisable, at such rates of remuneration and reimbursement as may be approved by the Treasury Board;

    (iii) to engage the services of such experts and other persons as are referred to in section 11 of the Inquiries Act who shall receive such remuneration and reimbursement as may be approved by the Treasury Board;

    (iv) to rent office space and facilities for the Commission's purposes in accordance with Treasury Board policy; and

(b) The Commissioner be directed to submit a report to the Governor in Council embodying his findings, and recommendations on or before June 30, 1987, and to file with the Clerk of the Privy Council his papers and records as soon as reasonably may be after the conclusion of the inquiry.

Table 1	
November 17-20	Westbank, B.C.
December 8-12	Vancouver, B.C.
1987	
February 2-6	Westbank, B.C.
February 9-13	Westbank, B.C.
February 16-19	Westbank, B.C.
March 4-6	Vancouver, B.C.
March 9-13	Vancouver, B.C.
March 24-27	Vancouver, B.C.
March 30-April 2	Westbank, B.C.
April 6-10	Westbank, B.C.
May 11-15	Vancouver, B.C.
May 19-22	Westbank, B.C.
May 25-29	Westbank, B.C.
June 1-5	Westbank, B.C.
June 8-10	Westbank, B.C.
June 22, 24, 25, 30	Vancouver, B.C.
July 2	Vancouver, B.C.
August 11-12	Westbank, B.C.
August 18-21	Vancouver, B.C.
August 24, 26-28	Vancouver, B.C.

CERTIFIED TO BE A TRUE COPY
CLERK OF THE PRIVY COUNCIL 53 3

Hearings Schedule

Total number of hearing days: 84
Total number of exhibits: 225
Total number of witnesses: 67

Witnesses and Individuals Appearing
Before the Inquiry

Westbank Indian Band Members
Barbara Coble
Harold J. Derickson
Richard N. Derickson
David Derrickson
Larry A. Derrickson
Ronald M. Derrickson
Rose Derrickson
Brian D. Eli
Mary A. Eli
Millie Jack
Chief Robert Louie
Roxanne Lindley
Thomas Lindley
George Michele
Bruce Swite
Lucy W.E. Swite

Department of Indian Affairs Officials
(Past and present)
Dr. Owen A.J. Anderson
Peter J.F. Clark
Frederic R. Drummie
Donald K. Goodwin
Ernest E. Hobbs

H. Alexander McDougal
Donna Moroz
Denis Novak
L. Myler Savill
Arthur S. Silverman
David G. Sparks
Gabor Szalay
Gordon C. Van der Sar
Frederick J. Walchli

Mobile Home Park Operators
Jack E. Alexander
Leonard R. Crosby
Nicholas Dachyshyn
Donald A. Lauriault
James B. Lidster
T. Darcy O'Keefe
John K. Ross
Val Spring
Henriette York
Ted Zelmer

Business and Professional People
Andrew T. Archondous
Victor N. Davies
Gordon F. Dixon
Mervin G. Fiessel
Nicholas Kayban
Ward A. Kiehlbauch
Beverly P. Kingsbury
H. Grant Maddock
Dudley A. Pritchard
Edward C. Ross
Robert M. Turik

Derril T. Warren

Auditors, Accounting Experts and Northland Bank Officials
Kevin E. Berry, CA
Martin G. Fortier
Danier T. Hopkins
William D. Kinsey, CA
Patrick J. Lett, CA
Harold B. McBain
Donald A. Pettman, CA

Others
Claire B. Eraut, First Citizens Fund (B.C.)
Linda Grover, employee, Westbank Indian Band
Sgt. Leonard H. Nyland, RCMP
Donald I.F. MacSween, B.C. Department of Highways
Senator Leonard S. Marchand
Robert Sam, First Citizens Fund (B.C.)
Norman Schwartz, administrator, Westbank Indian Band
Barbara Shmigelsky, former employee, Westbank Indian Band
Sgt. Brian H. Vance, RCMP

Part IV Submissions
Chief Clarence "Manny" Jules
William D. Kinsey, CA
Chief Robert Louie
Chief Joe Mathias
Chief Sophie Pierre
Chief Paul Sam

Final Submissions
Cecil O.D. Branson, QC
Leonard R. Crosby
P. John Landry

John A. McAfee
John S. Maguire
John F. Rowan, QC
Duncan W. Shaw, QC

Counsel Appearing at the Inquiry
F.J. Walchli, former regional director general, Department of Indian Affairs
Touche Ross Ltd., liquidators of the Northland Bank
John F. Rowan, QC
Donald M. Smith
D. Geoffrey Cowper
Duncan W. Shaw, QC
P. John Landry
Cecil O.D. Branson, QC
John S. Maguire
John A. McAfee
Frederick H. Herbert, QC
Sharon L. Fugman

Inquiry Staff
Commissioner John E. Hall, QC
Counsel, experts, administration
John F. Rowan, QC
Donald M. Smith
D. Geoffrey Cowper
William D. Kinsey, CA, investigative accountant
John R.D. Iwanson, investigator
Maureen E. Cowin, executive secretary
John T. Laurillard, hearings officer
Lise M.M. Carriere, secretary
Report production: Mary Ann Allen, Marguerite Cote, Marie Dionne, Paul Ollivier, Jean Wilson

Justice John E. Hall Report Summary

This Commission of Inquiry was assigned two particular tasks. Its first task was to investigate certain matters of controversy surrounding the management of the Westbank Indian Band and the relationship of the Department of Indian Affairs and Northern Development to the Band between the years 1975 and 1986. Additionally, under this heading, the Commission was requested to look into the activities of lessees and residents of the reserve lands of the Westbank Indian Band during the same period.

The second task assigned to the Commission was to consider the Indian Act, R.S., c.1-6, the existing primary legislation governing Indian Affairs, and to recommend any changes to that Act, to the management of Indian lands and monies, or to policies and procedures of the Department of Indian Affairs and Northern Development that were deemed to be appropriate. I was also asked to consider and recommend remedies for any specific problems that might be disclosed during the course of the Inquiry, having regard to the government's policy of supporting and strengthening Indian self-government on Indian lands.

The Order-in-Council establishing this Commission of Inquiry is included in Appendix E of the Report. Therein the terms of reference are fully set out.

The Westbank Indian Band is located just outside of Kelowna, British Columbia. The Department of Indian Affairs and Northern Development (hereinafter referred to as "the Department") is a federal department under the direction of the Minister of Indian Affairs and Northern Development. The Headquarters of this Department is located in Ottawa/Hull and the regional office is located in Vancouver, British Columbia. The district office of the Department which deals with the Westbank Indian Band is located in Vancouver as well.

At the outset of the Inquiry, I decided that it would be desirable to hold hearings in the Westbank area to give those interested the best opportunity to be heard. In addition, I held some hearings in Vancouver. All persons who sought standing before the Inquiry were granted standing, and funding was made available to allow for the legal representation of former executives of the Westbank Indian Band as well as the current executive and members of the Band. The Department of Indian Affairs and Northern Development was represented by counsel throughout the course of the Inquiry. Mr. Fred J. Walchli, formerly the Departmental Regional Director General in British Columbia, was also represented by counsel. The Westbank Indian Band and its development company had considerable dealings with the failed Northland Bank; accordingly, the liquidator for the Bank sought and was granted standing at the Inquiry.

This Inquiry was not an examination of one specific event, but rather concerned several issues that occurred over a lengthy period. It considered some 11 years in the history of the Westbank Indian Band and the Department of Indian Affairs and Northern Development. Over this 11-year period, the Westbank Indian Band made substantial economic progress. Because of their location, the

Reserves of the Westbank Indian Band were well situated for residential development.

Between 1975 and 1986, there was a very substantial growth in the number of mobile home parks located in the Okanagan Valley (particularly in the Kelowna area), due to its generally pleasant climate and its location halfway between Vancouver and Calgary. The Westbank Band shared in this growth, with population increases in both B.C. and Alberta and transportation improvements greatly enhancing the value of the Band's lands in recent years. The pictures at the beginning of this Report give an overview of the geography of the inhabited Reserves of the Westbank Band. The Band's economic progress was aided in 1983 when it received several million dollars from a reserve lands cut-off claim. In the period 1982 to 1984, large sums of money accrued to the Band and more particularly to some Band members, as a result of a project to upgrade the provincial highway which traverses Reserves 9 and 10. Because of the Band's improved economic situation, it was able to be more aggressive in obtaining better banking treatment. It is not always easy for Indian bands or individuals to obtain good financial services. In late 1982, the Band took a substantial share position in the Northland Bank, and began to become an increasingly large depositor. At the same time, the Band and its development company were granted substantial lines of credit and began entering into sizeable loans.

Chief Ronald Derrickson was also dealing with the Bank in his personal capacity and became a substantial borrower. In the spring of 1984, Chief Derrickson became a director of the Bank, resigning in August 1985, just prior to the demise of the Bank. The failure of the Bank resulted in the deposits in the Bank (standing to the credit of the Band or the Band company) being put in jeopardy. The Bank ceased paying interest on deposits. The Band thereafter refused to pay interest on loans owed to the Bank. As it turned out, the amount of money on deposit was not vastly different from the amount owing in loans, and that matter is apparently being worked through at the present time, although at the conclusion of the evidence in the Inquiry it had not yet been finally resolved.

The Chief of the Westbank Indian Band between 1976 and 1986 was Ronald M. Derrickson. By accident or design, Mr. Derrickson had become something of a "media figure" over the years. He was viewed by some as a capable administrator and skilled businessman. Others, both within and outside of the Band, viewed him as a petty tyrant who could bend the Department to his will to the advantage of himself and his family.

When Chief Derrickson came to power in the summer of 1976, he discovered a number of problems. A major development initiative, Lakeridge Park, located on Reserve 10 near Okanagan Lake, was in serious financial trouble. This ambitious residential subdivision had been commenced under the administration of his brother, former Chief Noll Derrikson. It had not progressed nearly as well as had been hoped.

When Ronald Derrickson became Chief, the project was heavily in debt and sales of lots were weak. At the same time, his brother Noll's mobile home park (Toussowasket) had just been completed and was having serious financial woes. Built with the assistance of government funds, it was overloaded with debt and had a high vacancy rate. Various other mobile home parks were being operated or contemplated by non-Band members. Some were not well managed and many were returning what seemed to Chief Derrickson to be grossly inadequate rents.

One feature of Indian land that made it desirable to developers was that there was relatively little by-law regulation of the land. Chief Derrickson felt that this was an area that needed study and possible improvement. He believed regulation could generate income and ensure better quality developments. Chief Derrickson was not a man to hide his light under a bushel. He had been relatively aggressive in acquiring land for his own use and he was determined to pursue an aggressive policy in getting a better return on Reserve lands from the lessees operating mobile home parks. Unbeknownst to these lessees, a very new broom indeed had arrived.

As it happened, Mr. Derrickson became Chief at a time when a different system of Departmental administration came into effect. This change was necessitated by the closure of district offices of the Department of Indian Affairs. This was also the time when Mr. Fred J. Walchli took over as Regional Director General in B.C. Mr. Walchli had a background in land management and was keenly interested in improving the economic return on Indian lands.

Chief Derrickson was not viewed with universal acclaim in his own house (the Band). Some members of the Band considered him to be power-hungry and intent on the too rapid development of Band lands.

Undoubtedly there was an element of jealousy present for he has been financially successful in the conduct of his own business affairs, but there also appears to have been a feeling of unease by some Band members that the Band was being hurried forward at an unreasonable pace. Some saw opportunity, others foresaw a looming train wreck.

Geographically, Indian reserves are islands that are located in provincial seas. Some provincial laws of general application may apply, but many do not. Under the Canadian constitution, the federal government has responsibility for Indians and Indian lands. The tenure of Indian land is different from that of non-Indian land. Essentially, Indian land may not be sold by individuals but can only be leased. This can make it desirable for lower cost developments (a developer is not forced to lay out a large sum of purchase money), but it also ensures a continuing relationship of lessor and lessee that can and did lead to friction between Indian locatees and mobile home park operators at Westbank.

One subject that troubled the Westbank Band was the asserted jurisdiction of the B.C. Rentalsman, a functionary who had authority to control rents for residential tenancies in British Columbia in the late 1970s and early 1980s. Chief Derrickson wanted the Rentalsman and all his works banished from the Reserves without delay. Only then, in his view, could Reserve lands return a proper economic rent. Tenants at the mobile home parks fiercely resisted this. A comprehensive rentalsman by-law under which the Band could appoint its own rentalsman was purportedly enacted, but was apparently disallowed by the Department. The jurisdiction of the B.C. Rentalsman was sustained by the courts. This Rentalsman controversy played a large role in the Toussowasket mobile home park story told in Chapter 2 of this Report.

By-laws were enacted to raise revenue and to better control development on the Westbank Reserves. These by-laws predictably brought howls of outrage from some mobile home park operators. Chief Derrickson became the lead negotiator for rents on the Reserve and in many cases also had a personal interest in the land involved. He undertook to raise rents significantly. This too provoked complaints from several lessees. Allegations were made that the Chief wished to bankrupt the park operators so that he could have the improvements in place accrue to himself or the other parties for whom he was negotiating.

A mobile home park owners' association was formed in 1982 in response to a number of initiatives taken by the Chief in 1981.

Acrimonious relations existed between the Band executive and a number of park operators. Some park operators questioned the ethics of the Band executive, and in particular, Chief Derrickson. Complaints were conveyed to Members of Parliament and the media carried stories about conflict at Westbank.

In the summer of 1982, an individual assaulted Chief Derrickson at his home in Westbank. The individual was arrested and later sentenced to a substantial term of imprisonment. Shortly after his arrest, the police established that he had acted on the instructions of some third party or parties. Chief Derrickson was certain in his own mind that this "hitman" had been directed by certain of the mobile home park operators. This incident and the resultant charges created an outburst of media attention in British Columbia and nationally. Attitudes hardened. Chief Derrickson viewed himself as surrounded by a host of enemies. Mobile home park operators who had entered into agreements with the federal government to lease Indian land viewed transfers of authority over such leases to the Band executive as a failure to live up to the terms of the agreements. There were suspicions that the Department of Indian Affairs was corrupt or negligent. Many park operators came to feel that the Chief was power-hungry and determined to oust them from the Reserve lands and reap the benefits of their improvements.

At the same time that the mobile home park controversies were outstanding, the failure of the Northland Bank in September 1985 occasioned acute anxiety to many Band members who had never really understood or been kept properly apprised of financial transactions. They feared financial ruin from the machinations of the Chief. Many of these machinations existed largely in the minds of certain Band members, but because information on financial matters had been jealously hoarded, a considerable amount of misinformation and rumour was circulating.

In 1986, dissident elements within the Band, spurred into action in part by a non-Indian "consultant," vented their frustrations in some strongly worded petitions to the Minister, suggesting grave improprieties on the part of the Chief and Band administration. It was alleged that the local Department of Indian Affairs was either supine or corrupt and could not be trusted to give an accurate version of affairs at Westbank.

The Department was beset by growing demands from various Indian groups throughout Canada. It was operating under an Indian Act that had not been substantially updated since it was enacted in 1951. This governing statute does not reflect the major changes in Indian society in the past 35 years. The Department was going through a difficult transition period of devolution of power to Indian government.

During the first 70 years of the twentieth century, Indian issues tended not to be a high-profile area, but Indian people became much more vocal and politically active in the 1970s. This was particularly true in British Columbia, where there were various controversies and internal quarrels between different groups and factions. The Department came to be viewed by many Indians as a dismal relic of the nineteenth century standing in the way of progress. In 1975, a number of district offices throughout British Columbia were occupied by Indians dissatisfied with the present state of affairs. The Department acted on their demands to close some district offices. Thereafter, matters of local administration were increasingly managed from Vancouver. Modern transportation and communication facilitated this process of more central administration, but clearly some local "on the ground" awareness of conditions at individual reserves would be lost. On balance, these changes were positive, but at times the Department tended to lose touch with local concerns.

With regard to the Westbank situation, the Department felt it was being pilloried unfairly. It wished to have the air cleared and to have some consideration of new directions in policy, as well as possible statutory change. It had gone through a period of quite dramatic policy change with very little statutory alteration. I comment further on these matters in Section 11 of this Report.

Previous studies and reports had been commissioned concerning affairs at Westbank, but it was felt that previous investigations had lacked sufficient powers of compelling document discovery and testimony to achieve the best results. It was felt that a full inquiry was needed to resolve the issues at Westbank, as well as to examine certain broader issues of Departmental policy and possible statutory change.

This Inquiry was constituted in August 1986 to consider Westbank specifically and the Departmental concerns generally. I found at Westbank an exemplification of much that causes tension between Indian and non-Indian people in Canada. Indian people were more or less invisible in Canada for much of the twentieth century. Living on reserves, they were a people set apart and were often treated as second-class citizens. Given the economics of earlier times, their lands usually were not economically desirable. By and large, they were not a factor in the economic life of Canada.

After World War II, Canadian society underwent a number of changes. Affluence increased, as did social consciousness. Indian lands became more valuable, sometimes as a result of underlying oil or gas deposits, but more usually because of proximity to expanding urban areas. Westbank was in the latter category. Land that had marginal utility became and is becoming more capable of enhanced utilization.

There is a progression of leasing from agricultural uses and sign leases, through mobile home parks and recreational uses, to full-scale residential and industrial uses.

The process of growth and change is one that always generates a certain amount of controversy and tension. At Westbank, there has been economic tension between Indian lessors and non-Indian lessees. There were jealousies and controversies between different factions in the Band. The Department was in a state of transition from the older "Indian agent" style of management to a new approach of granting greater autonomy to local Indian governments. Westbank had the fortune or misfortune to be rapidly escalating its economic activity at a time when the Department was moving away from active involvement in the management of individual bands. With regard to leases and leasing activity at Westbank, there was a very real vacuum of authority. One witness said Westbank was on the "cutting edge of change." At times, largely because of the personalities involved, it resembled a battle zone.

I heard from most of the Westbank mobile home park operators. Some could get along with Chief Derrickson, some could not. Getting along with the Chief involved what appeared to some to be capitulation. The Department was placed in a difficult position, but by failing to grapple more decisively with troublesome issues, it allowed the situation at Westbank to become increasingly explosive. The increasing wealth and political power of certain members of the Derrickson family caused resentment among some Band members. The Band administration elected to become involved in a major way with the Northland Bank. The collapse of that bank was a catalyst that caused a great amount of controversy to erupt at Westbank. There had been the earlier violent assault on Chief Derrickson that received wide publicity. There were increased calls for an inquiry to discover the real facts at Westbank concerning lessee issues and financial matters of concern to the Band and Band companies.

I found that the mobile home park operators did have some legitimate complaints. The Department was not always adhering to the terms of their leases in the setting of rents. The Band introduced a by-law regime in a chaotic fashion and there appeared to have been an absolute failure by the Band to undertake prior consultation with those affected. The Department failed to make clear to either the park operators or the Band executive what were the spheres of authority of the Department and the Band — confusion persisted and controversy grew.

While Mr. Leonard Crosby, the head of the Mobile Home Park Owners' Association, was far too extravagant in his attribution of evil deeds and motives to Chief Derrickson, there was a core of fact to his allegation of failure by the Band administration and the Department to adhere to lease terms concerning rent revision and to his allegation that the Band rentalsman by-law was misrepresented as being in force when it was not. Unfortunately, some of the highly charged allegations emanating from Mr. Crosby and those members of the Band who comprised an "Action Committee" were viewed too credulously by certain parliamentarians. These individuals, believing their constituents, took an alarmist view of events at Westbank. There were problems at Westbank and in the Department of Indian Affairs, but not of a serious criminal nature.

The most pervasive problem I found was that of conflict of interest. It seemed to be a concept virtually unknown (or wholly ignored) at Westbank. The Department, while professing to have standards in this area, could on occasion demonstrate remarkable lapses in enforcing these standards in the field. The problem is and always will be a source of continuing difficulty in human affairs. It will come to the fore in developing economic societies. The familial nature of many Indian bands makes the conflict situation even more delicate and difficult in Indian government. The problem will be increasingly seen in bands as they become more active economically. I think the recommendations I make to address this problem in Section II of the Report can contain the problem. The publicity of this Report concerning the obvious lapses at Westbank can also be a powerful force for the application of correctives at the Department and band levels throughout Canada. As I note elsewhere in my Report, Ronald Derrickson failed during his tenure as Chief to be sensitive to conflict-of-interest issues.

Indian band government must be run in an orderly and businesslike fashion. That is what self-government demands. This will create a climate of confidence among band members and it will ensure better relations between the band and outsiders dealing with the band. Open government that is free from conflict of interest concerns is the ideal to be sought. At Westbank, there was a strong and wilful Chief who failed to act always in a procedurally correct manner. It was the old problem of a government of men and not a government of laws.

I found no corruption in the Department of Indian Affairs, but I did find failures to come to grips with problems and bureaucratic fumblings. The Department was not vigilant in seeing that conflicts of interest were avoided. It failed to answer the concerns of lessees about rent-setting difficulties.

It should always be remembered that the dramatic changes in Indian Affairs in the period 1975–85 made it an intensely difficult period for Department personnel. I heard faint suggestions from some quarters that the lives of Indians would be improved only if the Department were abolished. It is quite unrealistic to demand that the Department be abolished. It performs and will continue to perform very valuable functions. Bands that have the ability should be encouraged to accept the fullest measure feasible of self-government, but many bands are going to continue to need wide-ranging support from the Department. The key factor to keep in mind is that various groups in Indian society are at very different stages of progress due to accidents of geography and history. Different regions have different needs, and I have made recommendations for some statutory and policy changes to accommodate the differing needs and aspirations of the various groups served by the Department.

There will be inevitable tensions between Indian and non-Indian groups. In practical terms, this means conflict between Indians and governments. Some issues will be susceptible of a political solution, others may become the subject of litigation in the courts. These tensions are and will continue to be painful to all concerned, but they are doubtless a necessary concomitant to the passage of Indian people from a lesser to a greater status in Canadian society. In the second section of my Report, I have made specific recommendations for statutory and policy changes that seem to me appropriate at this time.

A Commission of Inquiry has many functions. I think that most of the participants in this Inquiry have now a greater knowledge of themselves and of the relevant facts. That knowledge will be invaluable to them in their future conduct so that certain errors and excesses of the past may be avoided. Persons in political life will be more conscious of the fact that caution and circumspection are called for when allegations of wrongdoing are made to them. The Department of Indian Affairs is subject to many diverse pressures. Sometimes the noise level exceeds the substance level. I have made suggestions for dispute resolution methods that can hopefully winnow out matters of controversy that should not become high-profile political issues.

Indian affairs in Canada were long neglected. In more recent times, they have received a great deal of attention, perhaps in some areas a surfeit of attention. Issues such as self-government cannot be worked through too hastily. There is a necessary process of searching for solutions. This Inquiry, coupled with the current reviews under the aegis of the Office of the Comptroller General, can provide insights and highlight needed changes. The legislative base is rudimentary and not entirely suited to the more complex modern conditions we live in; changes would be very helpful in some areas. Hopefully, the Inquiry has cleared the air at Westbank and can, by its recommendations, indicate some changes and initiatives that will allow better administration in the future.

Report Summary of the Attempted Assassination Plot Against Me

In the summer of 1982 occurred a truly shocking incident. Ronald M. Derrickson was set upon in his home at Westbank by an assailant and was severely injured. This matter and its resultant charges has already been dealt with by the Criminal Courts and I do not wish to trench on conclusions reached in earlier proceedings where evidence was led and conclusions were arrived at based on evidence heard by other tribunals.

However, it is abundantly clear that the assailant of Chief Derrickson did not drop from the sky by chance. The individual who was found to have actually committed this brutal assault was a person known to relatives or associates of relatives of Mr. Bruce York. The assailant came from Edmonton and relatives of Bruce York were located in that city. A Mr. Tsu of Kelowna pleaded guilty to a charge in connection with the attack, but Bruce York and his relatives were acquitted of conspiracy charges laid arising out of the assault. I heard evidence from a Ms. W. that after the assault (and after conspiracy charges had been laid), Bruce York was heard to offer compensation to someone if they would agree to plead guilty to the crime. This conversation occurred in Edmonton, she said, at the residence of relatives of Bruce York. That, in and of itself, obviously proves nothing against Bruce York. Such evidence could be admissible at law to support an inference that a person possessed a guilty mind concerning the crime, but it could be equally consistent with a legitimate wish to avoid any entanglement in criminal charges. Ms. W. said in her evidence before the Commission in answer to questions from counsel for the former Band executive:

Q: What did they indicate had gone wrong in reference to this hit?

A: Well, at first they didn't know, they just announced that something had gone wrong and somebody had gotten shot.

Q: Were there any discussions at that initial meeting, if I could just take you back for a moment, in reference to the nature of the business transaction, or what type of relationship they were involved in with Mr. Derrickson?

A: Yes. There was some reference made to a lease on a trailer home, and that Ron had reneged on the lease and that they were out to get him, or something along those lines. It's been a long time ago.

Q: What do you recall the next incident involving this matter as being, after that?

A: When the charges were laid.

Q: All right. Can you tell me what happened then?

A: Yes. They were sitting in the basement, discussing that—

Q: Now, if I could just stop you there, when you say "sitting in the basement," was this, again, at Larry York Senior's residence?

A: Yes.

Q: In the city of Edmonton?

A: Yes.

Q: All right.

A: St. Albert, actually.

Q: St. Albert?

A: Mm-hmm.

Q: And you were present?

A: Yes, I was.

Q: And who else was present at that particular discussion?

A: Bruce York, he came in from Kelowna. Flew in from Kelowna. There was also Larry York Junior, Larry York Senior, Murray [and] me.

Q: And all these people were present at this conversation that took place?

A: Yes.

Q: All right. Would you tell me what was discussed then?

A: What was discussed was that Larry York Junior should take the—

THE COMMISSIONER: When you speak of charges, Miss W., as I understand matters, there was a chap called Cooper, who had been arrested shortly after this incident in Kelowna. I think he was charged with attempted homicide. Is that the charges you are talking about, or are you talking about charges that were laid against Mr. Bruce York, and I think maybe Larry York, and others?

THE WITNESS: No. There was charges apparently laid against Cooper, fairly subsequent, like almost right away after the incident happened. But, it was some time before, if I remember correctly, it was sometime before charges were laid against Larry York Junior, Larry York Senior, and Bruce York.

THE COMMISSIONER: Fine. Now, when you speak of "charges" that you were present at a conversation, is that the second series of charges you are talking about?

THE WITNESS: That's the ones against the York family, yes.

THE COMMISSIONER: OK. Yes, all right. All right, now I understand. Yes, carry on.

Q: And there were discussions about those particular charges?

A: Yes, there were.

Q: And you were present?

A: Yes, I was.

Q: Could you tell me what was discussed?

A: What was discussed was Bruce York offered Larry York Junior an amount of money, I can't quite remember whether it was $30,000 or $50,000, but it was a large sum of money for him pleading guilty to the charge, and letting the other two go.

Q: Was Larry York Junior prepared to accept this money and plead guilty?

A: No, he wasn't. He said that he would do that if there was a larger amount of money. I remember distinctly that he said that he was looking at perhaps three to five years, and for him to take a charge like that, he'd have to get paid more than that.

Q: And was that the first time that you had met Bruce York?

A: Yes.

(Transcripts: Volume LXIX, pp. 10,331-10,335)

Eulogy at the Funeral of Arthur Manuel

Sunday, January 14, 2017

I feel I have always known Arthur Manuel in the way many of our people know each other. We knew of each other before we even met, because my father was a friend of his father. George Manuel would stop off to visit our house when he was passing through Westbank. We would gather money for gas for George, and a lot of our band members would contribute what few coins they had. My dad even shot a deer and sold it to our Chinese friends to get that money for gas and hotel. That link between our families has continued throughout my entire life.

In many ways, we also lived parallel lives. Like most Interior people, our families travelled south to work as day labourers and fruit pickers. I believe the Indian fruit pickers were physically damaged by the poisons and chemicals that were sprayed on the fields and orchards.

During my first 10 years as chief at Westbank, Bobby Manuel was Neskonlith chief and we worked closely together on all of the important issues our people faced. We became friends and through my friendship with Bobby I also became friends with Arthur. He came to see me for advice when he was starting up his gas station, and in later years I followed his progress as he, too, went on to become band chief and then head of the Shuswap Nation Tribal Council.

When I ran and was re-elected Westbank chief in the late 1990s, Arthur was still active in the Interior and had set up the Interior Alliance to fight on land issues. When I decided to lead my people out to log on our Aboriginal title land with an Okanagan and not a provincial logging permit, Arthur was the first one to back me up — he brought the whole Interior Alliance to support me while I was in a battle with the government.

That was 20 years ago. Since then, we have worked closely together in all of our political work but he has become to me my traditional brother. We wrote *Unsettling Canada* together and we have just completed our second book. I have funded Arthur in his travels when needed in all of his activist activities throughout the last five or six years, including trips to Geneva, the United Nations and the softwood lumber dispute. I have also agreed to fund the Seventh Generation Fund, which Arthur convinced to move into Canada, in which he is a director. I did all this because Arthur is one of the most intelligent, dedicated, humble and knowledgeable leaders that I have ever known and he truly believes in all Aboriginal rights like no other man. Arthur Manuel was not only my most valued political confidant but also my best friend.

Arthur Manuel comes from three generations of Native activists that span over 70 years. Arthur's passing has left a deep hole in the protection of our rights, but it's comforting to know that his children and our children will continue to carry the torch for freedom and justice for all of our people. In closing, my daughter and I have started writing a song for Arthur and I would like to share a bit of it with you now:

Patient is the man
And strong are his words
To fight without fighting
Never yells to be heard
Teaching our people, humble and grace
This is my friend, I could never replace

KELLY DERRICKSON is a First Nation artist from Westbank, British Columbia. She studied music and earned her degree at the prestigious Berklee College of Music for Music Business and Performing Arts. She won the 2015 Coachella Valley Music Award for Best Country Artist and won Best New Artist at the 2015 and 2016 Indigenous Music Awards.

With over 350,000 views on YouTube, her single "We Are Love" was awarded Best Video at the 2019 Native American Music Awards. And Kelly has recently won Best Female Artist at the Native American Music Awards for two consecutive years.

Kelly is on in rotation on SiriusXM on channel 165, and her music is played on over 1200 radio stations in North America. She is daughter of Grand Chief **Ronald Derrickson**. What her father has worked to accomplish through leadership and politics, Kelly has worked to accomplish through music. They have both spent their lives working to improve conditions for Canada's Indigenous people.

Over time, she has developed a style called "Country Tribal Rock," unique to her and never done before. She is versatile, even releasing a version of "Amazing Grace," one of the best-known Christian Gospel classics.

She is the voice of her Nation.

www.kellyderrickson.com